STARGATE 2012

Recovering the power for
Earth's Imminent Ascension

By

Paco Alarcon-Kahan

authorHOUSE®

AuthorHouse™
1663 Liberty Drive, Suite 200
Bloomington, IN 47403
www.authorhouse.com
Phone: 1-800-839-8640

First published by AuthorHouse 7/16/2008

ISBN: 978-1-4343-8253-5 (sc)

Library of Congress Control Number: 2008903380

Printed in the United States of America
Bloomington, Indiana

This book is printed on acid-free paper.

A Course in Miracles quote:
A Course in Miracles, exercise book.
Foundation for Inner Peace.

*"The great Mayan prophecy says
2012 is the end of Earth time"*

*Dedicated to Archangel Michael and
Jesus, the masters of power and love.*

*Specially dedicated to the individual battle
against darkness every being must undertake
with himself for his liberation, so that his light
is awakened inside and shines without limits.
Also dedicated to the power of God in each one.*

"Where there is no light, the only thing to do is to turn on the light… All else is secondary."

"Without power it is not possible to ascend spiritually."

Don't Fear Your Own Evil

Only when you have faced your dark
side are you capable of exercising love,
strength, passion and true compassion.
Before that, the evil in you, your own
dark side and your inner ghosts condition
you to a very subjective and idealized
expression of love, and therefore a very
self-centered one. It is those forces hidden
in the personal psyche the ones that create
misfortune and attract disharmony to
your life. It is not bad luck or external
mysterious forces.

"Nothing touches he who has purified himself.
Jesus descended to hell. On the third day he
resurrected."

Thus we all have to descend to the hell of
our own darkness to resurrect to the highest
and truest love. The need to recognize, face,
transmute, illumine, love and liberate our
own evil is urgent. It is the integrated union
of yourself that saves you. Not separation or
denying your dark side. That only keeps you
in vicious cycles that don't let you advance.
It is the deceit of a false enlightenment
which, without you realizing it, takes you to
judgments and to the belief that the "evil ones"
are out there. If you don't illumine your shadows

*and dark areas, how can you pretend to be in
The Light?*

Only from the light your creations are of light.

Kahan

Gratitude

All possible gratitude to Archangel Michael
who gave me the vision of this whole work at
a crucial moment. He has sustained with
me the consciousness of Divine Power through
many battles of light, and has given me true jewels
for the liberation of my power and that of others.

Immense gratitude to Jesus, who engaged with me
all the way from the beginning in this mission, and
who explained in all detail what was going on in
the most difficult moments of the intense work of
the illumination of the dark, in the planet and
humanity over the last few years.

These teachings and consciousness are the product
of their enlightening presence and constant work
through this source. This work of light shines thanks
to them both. They supported me through everything
in the mighty task that has produced this creation
of light.

Thanks to all the people who have been there at the
crucial times to support the light and the teachings
making them more available to humanity and the Earth.

Words cannot express the infinite gratitude and love
I feel for the power of God and its Blue Light and its
mighty manifestations in me in so many ways. And also
for support of the Violet Light that has made all this
possible. To all beings of light here and in the worlds of
light, that have helped me know and understand what
true power is. Deep thanks to Universal Compassion for
all her gifts of grace in the form of this work, which has
and will continue to bless so many.

Contents

STARGATE: THE FACTS
The New Planetary Reality

THE DARK

THE LIGHT

ELEMENTS OF POWER
Seeing Through the Eyes of Ascension

FINAL REVELATIONS
The Consciousness of a New Humanity

SUPPORT SECTION
Support for Ascension and Power

Foreword

*Power is the greatest joy there is; God lives in it. Power is life —
faith, love. Light is a manifestation of God's power, and because
of the light, everything is. You have light, hence me and all. Light
sustains creation and life. Divine power is luminous and light reveals
Truth. What immense power that of beloved God. That is why light
is the creator of all; it defeats obscurity. In obscurity there, is no
vibration; in light there is. In vibrating, it creates and gives life, it
animates everything. Thus power is life.*

*The more power, the more vibration, the more life, the more love.
When you lose power your life fades away and your shine, your
love, fades with it. Obscurity enters, it makes itself present and the
divine moves away from you in its manifestation. An awakened
consciousness vibrates intensely because there is so much power
there that it emanates power; its activity of light is very intense and
it moves everything when entering in contact with it.*

*Power is evolutional. It makes everything evolve because there is a
great deal of vibrational activity in its field, and it makes everything
vibrate. Recover your power and you will all be happy — you will
lack nothing and you will feel in plenitude. I am with you and help
you with it.*

*It is very simple: if you don't have power, then you become weak
and shadows take over you; if you have power, you are invincible
— light emanates from you in total and absolute perfection. The
vibration of power must be taken to your body, mind, heart, to your
chakras — they all must be filled with power – must be taken to
your aura. Where there isn't light, it is a place that gets infested with
the negativity of the low vibrations and they suck power from other
more luminous areas in you. This weakens them. You mustn't give
low vibrations a chance — they freeze you. If you fall asleep they
take over you. An awakened, alert and diligent attitude must be kept
to stop at once the gelid airs of the lack of power: they solidify you;*

they lower your vibration in your bodies — energy fields. Hence the way is always to recover power. Believe me brother, sister reading these lines, power heals everything. If you knew how to apply it well you would be so young and fresh that the whole Universe would ask you for your secret. Ascend —enter into power and love — we are waiting for you.

Enough power generates the energy of love and total freedom. This you should understand, previous meditated reflection on the truth here contained. Find your source of power within. The accumulation of true power is spiritual development, because, as we have said, it increases the vibration and the person emanates more light. The greater the light, the greater the consciousness. Power is a rise in vibration — ascension — the greater the power, the more vibration. Therefore, without power it is not possible to ascend; without power there is nowhere to go. Vibrating high triggers power in the inert and the negative and obscure zones, and the chains of limitation and slavery jump, breaking into pieces.

Faith makes everything vibrate, hence it manifests; it is a mystery of God: it makes the particles of the Universe vibrate and takes them to organize themselves in that which faith sees. Thus, with faith everything is possible. Jesus said it: "Only with faith the size of a sesame seed." That is why faith is creative power, and nothing can stop he who has enough faith. Believe, have faith in divine power and you will be invincible.

I Am Archangel Michael.

Inside Foreword

Planetary Change

In 2012, it is expected an event that will transform the life on this planet completely. This event is called *ascension*. It means the elevation of human consciousness to Spirit. For this, the vibration of human beings has to increase dramatically. The present vibration of humanity and the manifestation of this world are considered a third-dimension manifestation. The ascension will take us to the so-called *fifth dimension*. The third dimensional world is a world of separation, duality, conflicts and absence of peace. The fifth dimension is a place of unity, light, love — peace. The difference is immense. The jump is big. For that, it is necessary to have a great amount of energy that will propel this world and human consciousness, as it is, to that level of light. Therefore, high vibrational energies are necessary. This is an impulse of huge magnitude that couldn't be achieved with the present energies on the planet. Therefore, the energies for the jump have to come from somewhere. That is what this book is about. The energy and facts, the dynamics and mechanisms for that higher dimensional jump, and the energies that make it possible with all the implications. All that is contained here.

When we ascend we will have a life beyond all the wonders and beauty we might have known in this world, and certainly without separation, suffering and death. A life without lack; a bountiful life full of love and joy. But to get there you must work to get ready and elevate your vibration and consciousness — in a word, your light — to the level of the fifth dimension. This is done by opening the heart and forgiving all: by knowing, experiencing true love and true compassion. Otherwise there is no access to the fifth dimension, at least not for now. This is why there is no time to waste. The event as we saw earlier is forecast for 2012 and that is just around the corner. So opening the heart and entering into love and compassion is crucial now.

All the events happening in this world now are a preparation for this event: climate change, consciousness revolution, political adjustments, religious changes, financial developments, healing methods. There are many people working for this event for the Earth. Some are here; many are in the invisible worlds, but the amount of activity and preparation for it is almost frenetic. It all started in 1999 when an energy door — a cosmic gate — opened for the Earth to bring new energies of consciousness into the planet. That door was called Stargate.

Stargate: Cosmic Opening for Earth

On August 11, 1999, a cosmic door opened for the Earth. A specific planetary configuration of extreme transcendence for the destiny of humanity took place in the heavens which produced an opening of the Earth to cosmic consciousness. It was called the *Stargate*. Something opened and for the first time in thousands of years new energies entered into Earth. They are changing everything. All aspects of planetary life are being challenged and changed through the benevolent and powerful influence of these energies. The order of things, systems, structures, consciousness are all changing. The aim is to establish a new consciousness on the Earth, a consciousness based on truth, freedom and love from the consciousness of true spiritual power. Since most human and world structures are based on fear, slavery and falsehood they all need to be dismantled and be recreated based on the truth and light of the new consciousness, which will create an impeccable world for an enlightened humanity. The period of time and consciousness that the Stargate opening initiates is what has been known as the Age of Aquarius.

We are talking about the cosmic opening of the planet. An opening of consciousness, from individual to divine; and as a planet, to a galactic consciousness. An opening to the reality of the galaxy and to the fact that there is a Universe out there that we are supposed to be part of. The Universe is not a huge empty space and we are meant to live in a small planet in it, and we have nothing to do with the rest of it. That is false. The Universe is our cosmic home. It is the cosmic home of cosmic beings, and that is what we are. We need to recover our cosmic consciousness which has been contracted on this planet into a physical body; we do exist on other levels of existence. But we are not as such "aware" because that consciousness cannot fit into our contracted existence on this plane of manifestation and into this physical body. We are huge beings. Our greatness has nothing to do with the perception of ourselves we have on this level. It is far beyond imagination. We are divine, and that is huge. We only know ourselves as humans, and that is very, very small. When we recover our higher dimensional consciousness – cosmic consciousness — we will realize there are many levels of awareness, let's call them dimensions of existence, and we are part of them all. We can manifest in many, if not all of them and that is something we are not aware of now. But in the process of recovering our power, our true divine dimension and therefore our cosmic consciousness, we will see all that is the normal thing to be and do. It is something we have lost, not something we will acquire. In that sense, it is a return to a state that is ours by divine right, and we have just fallen from it. In that fall we have experienced a great contraction and have ended up thinking, believing that we are this body and personality and that is it. We are huge beings with immense consciousness. In fact, we are the whole Universe, and I want to tell you that this is what all religions talk about and the direction they point out, whether clear or not. But this is not obvious many times, often due to human distortion.

As cosmic beings we embody our light body, a body of light that allows us to access the realms of the Universe and its different dimensions. It is the ascended body of Jesus, the resurrection body. And we too have it, and will be in it as we enter into the process of ascension. This is fundamental and necessary as divine beings we are – not human. Human is just a manifestation we are experiencing at this time upon this planet, but it is not the truth of what we are. We are expressing much less of what we are. We are limitless and divine. Many years ago, I had a spiritual revelation in which I experienced myself as being everything. Well, isn't that what the spiritual paths and religions talk about? It happened to me. I experienced that I was everywhere. It was powerful. It breaks all your concepts and it is very real. It has happened to many. It is also your essential reality. Being everything means there are no limits to your consciousness which exists in all things. We are one with God in truth; we should experience what He experiences when we touch that unity. That is the purpose of spiritual paths: to take us to the experience of Spirit.

For all this to happen there is a key element: the recovery of power. The recovering of power is essential for this to take place on the planet; otherwise it cannot happen. And this project is big. There are obstacles for this. It is a mighty task taking place on the entire planet, at an individual level and as a whole.

How It All Started

"Summer 1999... We are in a magical place on the peninsula of Yucatan in Mexico. The cosmic moment, key for the change in the planet closes in. We have had almost a week of passionate traveling; a reduced group of people with whom we are fulfilling the mission with which we parted from Merida, around all the area of Mayan archaeological enclaves: Uxmal, Sayil, Labna, Kaba. We are now in Chichen Itza, the greatest and most spectacular of the Mayan archaeological sites of the route. It is a mystical trip, an initiating trip. We are anchoring the violet light in all the main Mayan sites of the area, to activate their frequencies and prepare them energetically to receive the new energies that arrive on Earth now, with the great conjunction.

It is 5 a.m. of August 18; in an hour, it will be the conjunction. We must hurry. In the mysterious silence of the lush gardens of the hacienda which welcomes us under the disguise of hotel, we arrange ourselves in a meditation circle to connect with the cosmic conjunction announced by the ancient civilizations as the moment of the opening of the Stargate for the Earth and the beginning of the great change.

We know of the transcendence of this moment... for us, for humanity. We enter into the connection. We perform the anchoring of light and of the ascensional energies for the Earth. The energy is strong, the feeling deep. An all-pervading peace takes over the place and ourselves. For a while we enter into a deep spiritual experience... We know it has happened... the Stargate has been opened. Chichen Itza's great mystical pyramid has been connected and activated with the great cosmic energy... and with it, so has all the Earth."

This is how I lived the cosmic moment that gave origin to the wisdom and consciousness that has produced this book. From that moment on without expecting it, a number of inner changes start happening in me, subtle but powerful, and through my inner work the main consciousness of that change continued to manifest: the recovery of my power. All this goes hand in hand with the course that is created in me by the energies of the Stargate, that I start to impart with a great result of increasing self-awareness of power and change in paradigm for a great number of people.

Before Stargate Opening

I found myself before loads of information, all very interesting, and with so much alert about this event. I decided to know what had to be known on this subject. So I put aside all the papers, sat down in meditation and asked my higher self to transmit the information to me: what the situation was and what I had to know about this cosmic event so I clearly knew what was to happen, how and what it meant. What I received came from the spheres of my higher self, the ascended masters, especially Jesus and Archangel Michael. All of that has also gone into developing this teaching and the making of this book.

Through the years after this magical trip, I went on acquiring consciousness and understanding of what true power is, how it works, where it comes from and the fantastic life it brings. I have been experiencing the great effects of power recovery: the liberation of any chains of limitation, bringing freedom and joy through the retrieval of the part of my power that I had given away. I developed writings and course materials that arrived intuitively, and developed a second course on the recovery of personal power through the liberation of the inner dark side as the only means to arrive at true compassion. All that new knowledge material, the acquired expanded consciousness and the soul of those courses are the essential elements that make up the book.

The objective of this work is to become aligned with the energies that have been entering the field of the planet since the Stargate opening, and to reach the vibration level necessary to enter the fifth dimension in 2012; thus taking the definite step on the way to global and individual ascension.

Introduction

This book is about taking power and ascending spiritually. One cannot happen without the other. There is no spiritual ascension without integrating power. One can advance to a point in life and also spiritually without taking power, but just to a point. Beyond that, it is not possible to advance without it. That is why most of humanity got to a point of no evolution a while ago. Things were stuck for most people, and processes on the planet were the same over and over. People had not understood at large that they had to regain their power and that without it, things were going to stay pretty much as they were. So relationships, partnerships, working interactions, politics, spirituality and the general ways of living had reached a still point.

Love as the essence of all life was being considered from a dependent perspective, from a dependent consciousness, and therefore could not reach the beauty, shine and power of true independent love imbued with Divine Power. So, nothing was really happening on the planet... until August 1999 came, and the star alignment in the heavens brought a unique opportunity for an energy shift. This was the event known as the *Planetary Alignment* or *Stargate,* a cosmic circumstance capable of opening a huge door for consciousness and energy to come into Earth and change all that. Since then, things have been different. Whether people know it or not, they have been in a process of awakening and recovering their personal spiritual power. The energies entering into the Earth were not just any energies that happened to pass by at the time; they had a purpose. They were very specific in what they had to do: accelerate the vibration of everything and everyone on the planet towards the state of freedom. And that has two main stations: recovering power and exercising freedom. All this started a process in which all that stuck consciousness would be shaken by the new energy frequencies, high vibrational energy, and would liberate the inertia in which humanity was immersed, producing an awakening of consciousness. As stuck energies are accelerated, they become increasingly active and start moving, like a car that had no gasoline and suddenly gets an injection of fuel.

While stuck energies increase their vibration, they increase their movement and consciousness, so they seek the resolution of any unbalances or conflicts inherent in them. This happens to all energies: physical, mental, emotional, spiritual. Energy is consciousness, and it can be very conscious or unconscious. The higher it vibrates the more consciousness it has, and therefore the greater its light. So by the effect of the higher energies that entered in the Stargate opening, the slow energies of people and humanity have been accelerated, and therefore have increased their consciousness and light. All situations and people have been susceptible to being affected in this way. Pending issues of any nature within the mental or emotional fields, emotional problems due to unresolved emotional issues, mental obsolete attitudes that generate no love and therefore painful or disharmonious realities, and anything in those terms have been pushed forward towards their resolution and liberation. As they become accelerated, they move within the aura and consciousness of the person and are brought to consciousness from the unconscious levels, and come before the face of the person who is forced, so to speak, to look at them. Bringing consciousness to them gives them the chance to be resolved. As this happens, the levels of consciousness — mental, emotional, physical and spiritual — of the person are cleared and more light can enter and manifest in him: more spirituality. And therefore greater consciousness; which is the same as saying more divinity. As this happens, the person gets rid of his karma and manifests that greater divinity. A higher consciousness manifests greater love in each one and therefore the world becomes a place of light, harmony and peace.

This is a process of recovering power: the karmas hold power and consciousness away from the person. Anybody can understand that if something is unconscious there is no power in that area because we cannot use it: it is away from our conscious reach. It is like having useful tools locked in a cabinet and we don't have the key; they are useless. Thus we cannot use the power and function they provide us with. As blockages, like the ones mentioned before, are cleared, the blocked energy and consciousness they held become available to us. This is an act of power recovery. We see clearly that recovering power is linked intimately to spiritual activation and therefore to spiritual realization.

**There is a global initiation taking place on Earth,
a global opening of consciousness.**

Mankind has been stuck in a belief system that keeps its power away from it. Mankind accepted those terms and as long as that was the situation, the status quo of humanity wouldn't change. The "big powers" would hold the power of people, and humanity would remain slaves to them. As the awakening of the individual and mass consciousness takes place, due to the high vibration energies of the Stargate, the general belief system is being shaken and man looks to find greater truth within himself, and in the life around him. So he starts questioning within and without, and the belief system enters into a phase of being challenged. That is the beginning of a person's liberation and the start of a planetary revolution. In confronting that belief system the person stops assuming false truths and starts to decide what is going to be valid for him, setting new truths inside. Eventually, the global system has to adapt to the new consciousness of humanity as enough individuals awaken to a particular section of the global belief system and thus go on recovering their power, which was dormant inside.

We are in the middle of this process. You and just about everyone upon the planet are going through this situation to some degree. Here I present the keys to this situation and the secrets of this process so that this power awakening process can be realized fully and with mastery. In this way we truly move to the realization of our potential and the exercise of our own spiritual sovereignty, which for so long has been lost to humanity. Because as power awakens in us, we become spiritually advanced and eventually spiritually independent. This is a level of mastery.

Furthermore, as the Earth awakens its vibration and elevates its consciousness as a result, it moves towards that level of the fifth dimension. This is a level of manifestation of consciousness where there is enough light and high vibration so as to manifest unity, unconditional love and Christ Consciousness: a high level of realization of Spirit. This book focuses on that crucial necessity for humanity and the Earth to reach an awakening of inner power, which can take everyone to the manifestation of the fifth dimension, inside and outside. This is where we are going, and the urgency of this teaching comes from the fact that this is the unique opportunity to do it — there is no other — and also that this ascension is non-negotiable: the Earth is going to the fifth dimension. And it will take with it whoever is ready and vibrating at the right level of light and consciousness. You can go with it in 2012 or else be left behind in this present level of consciousness. So you'd better get ready for the quantum leap of love and consciousness awaiting humanity and obtain the passport that will take you there: recovering your inner power.

I am sure all the treasures contained here will take you a long way in the recovery and liberation of your power towards your spiritual sovereignty and freedom; in a word towards your spiritual ascension.

Paco Alarcon - Kahan
Spain
May 2007

Need Power to Ascend

Power is needed to ascend to a cosmic reality free from the third dimension which means limits, separation, death, and to access the fifth dimension, which means unity, power, wisdom, freedom and liberation from a system of slavery through limits and lack, to go to a dimension that has unlimited prosperity, no suffering, love, peace.

Towards a New Paradigm

The world is structured in the wrong way.
Structures are based on absence of God;
absence of light. So the human mind has
developed to compensate for that lack by
clinging to things and a material way of
life, a way of fear. Thus creating attachment,
control, manipulation, dependency, suffering;
producing fear and anger when what is, is
being challenged. Humanity needs to dismantle
itself and this world to become structured
again with light – love and faith. Then we
will have a new world.

This world is a mirage compared to what exists beyond.
There where we go, with the power of the Stargate.

This is the time in which people have to put
their spiritual evolution at the top of their
list of priorities.

Time is Over

There is no time, only time
to pack our cases and go.

Time is for letting everything go
and packing the essentials: love,
truth, wisdom, forgiveness,
luminous intentions.

There is only time to open the heart.
Only time for love, for service.
We are going to another dimension,
another world.

Stargate Awakening

Compassion is the highest state in the Universe. To be in it we must recover our power. Power is in the dark side inside. To reach compassion, we need to go to the dark side within. Recover power from it, illuminating the darkness. Then the door will open for compassion and we can sit on the throne of compassion. Then we can ascend to the dimension of light. This is the Stargate to love and compassion.

- One of the key aspects of the New Age, which is the man of Aquarius, is the new relationship he has with God as his partner for everything. This is the symbol of Aquarius: man with bounty from his God connection… true partners.

This is the aim of Stargate's awakening.

The Next Step

"Power is the essence of all things.
Without power nothing can exist."

Our next evolutional step is in our ascension: the movement to a higher consciousness. To do that, we need to recover our power. In it is our lost consciousness. But there is an enemy: the dark side. So a battle is waiting for all, as the will to ascend will take everyone to face their dark side and recover the lost power held prisoner by the dark. Then freedom is possible.

Ascension is about people processing their pending issues and working at their own illumination People will have to qualify for ascension and will have to vibrate in a state of unconditional love and compassion sufficient to hit the high vibrational levels necessary to go beyond this world… to the fifth dimension.

- The less ego the lighter you are and
  the more you can ascend. Then the
  high energies available will lift you
  like a feather to the higher dimensions.

True Power

The power we are dealing with here is true power, power that comes from Spirit — from spiritually awakened consciousness. This power is based on love and wisdom and respects others. The new power is a power that comes from within, different from worldly power that comes from outside, which depends on acquiring, not on being. The power we talk about here is independent: spiritually awakened power.

Earth's Unbalance: A Cosmic Concern

Earth is a planet in a system of planets and galaxies. As all systems, the Universe is interrelated: all parts of it are related to all others. All parts affect all others. All things must work properly for it to function well. An unbalanced planet affects the harmony of the whole system. Something wrong is happening on Earth. It has been going on for a long time. This is not a normal or sane way of living, people acting in detrimental ways against others in so many ways constantly. We are brothers and sisters… we are a family. Earth needs to change radically, soon.

As a piece in the cosmic system, it is known that the Earth is not well. And as part of it, it needs to be fixed. That is why there is a sustained effort by the higher spheres in the Universe to revert the situation of the Earth urgently. And this is why Stargate has opened to produce the new energies on the planet. Eventually the new energies will change everything and everyone on the planet, and Stargate will have fulfilled its mission.

*It is my wish that the awakening of the inner power
in each sentient being frees all hearts from shadows.
That compassion reigns as victor of the battle of power
against darkness, as the sovereign in each man's heart.*

Kahan

Ascension is a journey towards the light.
This book is about that.

STARGATE: THE FACTS

The New Planetary Reality

Stargate: Opening to the Stars
Human Time is Over

Something opens that has been closed for a long time. We open up to the stars — this is the message of Stargate. And we unite with them, with galactic consciousness for universal and cosmic unity. This is the awareness that shows us that we are not beings bound to a limited planetary consciousness, but we go beyond: our origins are cosmic. The time in which we have been humans shut away from our stellar origins, is over. We have been secluded from knowing and experiencing this greater reality of ourselves, that we have stellar connections and origins. And that through our spiritual powers being awakened and recovered, we return to the truth of the immensity and limitlessness of our being, with all the wonderful implications this has for us. Do not be afraid of this. From my point of view in embodying this awareness, it is far more frightening to stay in limited consciousness without Spiritual or Christ's powers, and having to die because you feel and believe that you are limited and have not awakened to the consciousness of eternal life. Therefore experiencing all sort of limits, illness and suffering... What do you say?

Isn't it time for something else? Haven't we all gotten tired of this game? Having to earn money to survive in a planet full of bounty. Having to live in the slavery of a system that lets you be cast away and die if you don't serve it, consuming what it feeds you. Are you not tired of illnesses, separation, conflicts, wars, hatred, violence, poverty, loneliness, sin, lack of love… uncertainty? Who doesn't want a different reality, one full of peace, love, unity, blessings, light, togetherness, prosperity, abundance? One free of illness and death and full of eternal bliss and joy. Let's all be honest inside. What do we really want? How do we want to live? Ask yourself these questions.

*Feel the power that comes from seeing what
you want and knowing that it is possible…*

We are talking about cosmic consciousness. The Universe is a big place. It is full of life, beings and wonderful places that are far superior in light and joy than the earth we know now. Do you grasp the words? It is not any more a consciousness that this is my country, city, planet… We are moving beyond planetary consciousness. The planet is not going to be the same. It is going to be a cosmic place. Earth is going to be opening to cosmic consciousness. We are part of a galaxy which is part of a galactic system of galaxies, where there are stars and planets where many intelligent beings live in harmony. The Earth is opening to that now. The new energies bring this opening. It might not be obvious right now, but the configurations of energies that make it possible are developing at this moment and it will be obvious soon.

This opening comes from heavens, and therefore it is divine intervention: grace that comes to dismantle the planet as it is. This is to free people because this system has them in slavery. It is the Matrix of the Dark. And therefore this change is returning to every being his freedom and rights, his power. But we must do our part to graduate to that reality, to earn that change. It is the moment to retake power, in which God says:

"The tyranny of the external power and control that has been exercised on the planet and on you is over. Now, through my grace, power is returned to you, and you will finish with the external tyranny."

What is ours is returned to us. We are recovering the consciousness of who we are, recovering the consciousness from limited to total: Universal. We are developing the wisdom that is inside us: healing, solutions, answers, resources. They are all there in the reality that God and I are one. In the manifestation that I have the power, the power of being free, and nothing and no one outside can condition me, and acquiring the clarity to see that it is so in the total expression of myself — of my being — without limitations.

New Energies: Dismantling the System

The external system of the Earth has been kept separated from the light, from the divine energies of high consciousness; it has been kept in an energy density we call matter, the third dimension, the physical plane, due to a way of living that has closed itself to the higher realities. Likewise, it has been the internal reality of man. In this way, the superior energies have not had access to this plane except through realized spiritual masters and through true meditation coming from spiritual initiations. Through these, individuals and people have had access to higher planes of consciousness and have been able to bring the energies of those planes to this one. This has kept a level of higher divine energies available in this lower plane for spiritual evolution, so those who wanted to know higher realities had access to them. Also, this presence of energies has helped balance the great disharmony present in the planet and humanity for thousands of years. Nevertheless those who have accessed them have been very few. This is changing now.

Now, with the opening of the Stargate, and since the shell that has maintained the separation of energies and planes of consciousness opens up, there is a halt in the influence that has kept those superior energies of consciousness and light largely outside of the system. Thus, higher dimensional energies of light have been entering the plane of the Earth since the opening of the Stargate in 1999. They are changing everything, especially the consciousness of people. Thus, now everyone on the planet can have access to higher energies – spiritual grace – for the liberation of their karma, their spiritual evolution and to access the spiritual power necessary to create a life of blessings. How much they access those energies will depend on the openness and readiness of people, but they are there.

The Ice is Melting

The new energies are increasing the vibrational rate of all energies in the earth system, producing an expansion in people's consciousness. The rising up of energies, frequencies and vibrations is going to be like the process of introducing heat to a huge ice block: it liquefies. It frees; it turns agile. The water becomes liberated; it flows, it moves; you cannot contain it. So this is what has been happening to Earth and humanity: they liquefy. This is happening at the physical level, as well as the emotional and mental one. This will allow the spirit trapped in the density of matter to come out, to manifest, in all and everything.

We have been living in a world of ice – a false world – and it is melting. It is going to show us reality. In becoming de-crystallised that ice ruling the planet for eons of time, is going to bring an adjustment period. That is where we are now. It is the intermediate period of transition, of moving between one reality and another. We move from the old one to the new one, and in the middle there is a process of dismantling, a falling of structures — political, social, economical, religious, personal, planetary — until the consolidation of the new frequencies and a new, conscious planetary order.

So if you have something that is not based on truth — work, relationships, your own identity, anything — be prepared for the dance. Everything that is not based in total honesty, sincerity, impeccability has been falling and it will continue to fall. For many, this is a liberation. For others who resist: confusion, desperation – in holding on to what is leaving them until they die to the inevitable – is the way until the surrendering to the light – to the divine reality – reaches them and then that liberation arrives.

This process also presupposes an acceleration of karmas and pending issues. If everything liquefies, karmas also do, hence the present acceleration of processes upon the planet at an individual and global level. Everybody is trying to keep up with their own unprocessed stuff — karma — which is finally catching up with everyone. Until now, the vibration and processes have been quite slow. But since the opening of the cosmic gate a few years ago, things have accelerated exponentially, year in and year out. All these processes suppose an integration with our light body, our divine nature of light, the Christ or Buddha nature.

This process of elevation and manifestation of the divine in all is what we call *ascension.* This ascension is a planetary one since it involves everyone. The ascension is individual, but the opportunity is for all. As a main feature of this order of events, we are going to connect more directly with God, without intermediaries. Nonetheless, there are spiritual guides who will help with a solid and timely connection with the mentioned higher realities; and from then on, it is you and God.

Stargate: Energy Boost

*"The energy of the Stargate is boosting
all other energies on the planet. It is
the power of God. It takes us to the
recovery of our divine power."*

With the energies of the Stargate you can become light because the energies that come into the planet are very strong. This means that your light can increase dramatically. Your light can be expanded far beyond where you are at now, and all your structures, physical, energy and aura can be impregnated thoroughly with light. And therefore your experience of being alive will be one of greater consciousness, lightness and luminosity. It will take you to a powerful experience of bliss and joy. In this way you will be filled with peace, love and higher awareness in all your vehicles of manifestation and personal structures. You will realize your unconditional unity with the Creator and experience love as it should be, giving you an experience of oneness with all.

In practical terms this means healthier, clearer, more influential, happier and more prosperous, not just a little but a lot. How many of those desirable states you experience will nonetheless depend on your present state of being. If you are open and not crystallized, you will be one with the energy and the consciousness coming in, and you will be taken straight to the Self – your higher divine experience. The energy will not find resistance in you. It will take you up with it and you will experience your own divine being – the ecstasy of your Self and all the treasures it brings. If you are crystallized, not open, or were so when the energy first came in, you might feel you are being shaken in some of many possible ways, and if the condition is very extreme you can feel you are being broken inside, shattered in thousand pieces like when a glass hits the ground and disintegrates. Believe it or not, this brings evolution.

The first option, in which you can be taken straight to the light of your soul, is quite unlikely unless you have been working seriously at your spiritual development for great part of your life, or at least intensely over the last few years. Otherwise, a version of the second option will apply. That is or has been the reality for most human beings since the opening of the Stargate. This is the reason why most of humanity has been in an existential crisis for the last few years and continues this way, to a great extent. This crisis manifests in all areas of the human being. The essence of this change is restructuring. At the physical level, the physical body has been experiencing a breaking down of blockages to free the energy; at the mental and emotional levels too, the blockages and crystallized energies will be breaking down so you can experience your true self. This is necessary in order for the light to enter into you the way it is supposed to, to activate your own light and Christ consciousness — the consciousness of your divine being.

Whatever remains after this process is your essence. But it might take a while, as it is probably happening already, in the process of making the light from the shadows inside you, and also in being rooted in the more fluid states of awareness that inevitably and thankfully come with this process; a process that essentially is going from the crystallized to the non-crystallized states, from the rigid to the fluid, from the dense to the subtle. What remains is your divine identity; everything else was a lie. That is the way you can rise as a warrior in the light, a spiritual warrior.

"I am the power of God in me."

Is a mantra for these times: it embodies the truth of what is happening and of where we are moving. The Ascended Masters said in a message at some point since the opening of the cosmic gate:

"Assume your power as a warrior in the light."

This energy boost of the Stargate which has this many implications, is going to radically change the expression on Earth at all levels. The energies are there acting on everything and everyone, but the level of accessing the new energies will depend on the state of being of each one. Important things like how purified they are physically and energetically, how developed their consciousness is, the readiness of their energy structure, how open the chakras are, the level of light of their aura and other relevant factors are crucial in how each is experiencing the event. Energy is there and available, but if these factors are not fine, the access to the energies will be limited. What will happen — and this is what is really happening on most of the planet — is that the energies will be doing their work in purifying, working karmas and moving the unresolved things in everyone making these issues conscious for people so they work on them, so they are ready for a new state of consciousness.

Since your power is given away, the new energy first hits you in the areas in which you have given your power and therefore are dependent: fears. The energy hits you there, showing you that it is there where you have given your power away and you are not fully assuming responsibility for yourself, for what you have in you, for what you are. And there is panic, anxiety, loss of control, because it tears apart the false ties that stop you being *you* and returns you to yourself, to your center. This is what is coming into the planet. The first thing that happens when you are returned to your center is that you are confronted with all that is not resolved in you and with your pain. This power gain presupposes that you are freed from parasites and vampires that live on your behalf, on behalf of you giving your power to them. You give power outside, but because you have renounce it from within. The parasites and vampires are also within. You need to wake up.

All power comes to you and if you haven't assumed it until now, the first thing that comes to you is to scream and run away. But in the measure in which you recognize it and assume it comes serenity, maturity wisdom and love. And you shine as the superior being of light that you are.

The Final Battle for Freedom

This is about the fight with your ghosts, who don't let you be *you*. It is like switching on a light in a dark room: fears and doubts are gone. This fight shows up outside in our relationships with the world and other people, and it is a symbol of our inner fight. It is a fight against our inner ghosts, against guilt, fear, doubt in order to free ourselves, in order to hold all our power.

The final battle is taking place. Get ready, this is the battle of the will of God in its mission to free the planet and humanity from the tyranny of the army of the dark. A team of forces and beings that have kept humanity in ignorance of what it truly is: a divine family of light. It is a battle that has to be fought with the sword of light, a sword of truth — the sword of freedom. With this sword, everyone can join the army of light of God. In this battle the tyrants outside fall; but if the tyrants inside don't fall we are in the same dilemma, because then those tyrants become external and create, again, a system of tyranny outside. Do you see what this means?

As my book *Return to the Sacred* says:

> ***"The inner tyrants are the most dangerous;***
> ***they are disguised as yourself."***

Needless to explain the realities of that danger since those tyrants are the most difficult to spot. Now you are the sovereignty, the power, the authority from your divine order. to be responsible for everything in you. It is important that you listen well and understand what this means: to take decisions from freedom.

This implies a number of things:

- Self-confidence
- Faith
- There is no God outside you that decides for you. You are the authority.
- Freedom from your awakened consciousness
- Freedom to create and being very clear on what it is you want to create.
- Maturity in consciousness: you cannot keep saying "It is the government" or "my boss." It is you.
- In being given the total responsibility for your power, you have to be very alert to know what it is you want.

That divine sword of truth is to give you the divine power to cut through ignorance – ignorance and darkness – in you, where you are and with whom you are. In this way you can cut, at the subtle level and at the energy level, the ignorance and darkness sown in you, in the planet and in other people by the "lords of the dark" — those people and energies that kept things without light in their desire for control of power. What we can call: the *Matrix of the Dark*. We have to cut the "matrix" a web of ignorance, control and dependency that has kept humanity and every individual in a state of weakness and slavery as it has taken, knowingly, power away from them and has been operating, not only in the external world but inside the individual as well, in the form of his belief system.

> **"As you increase your consciousness you acquire a discerning power which acts as a sword of Truth."**

The Fall of the Masks

The impressive momentum of this new planetary energy is producing changes in the entire status quo of the planet. This includes the status quo of humanity and the way it has lived for thousands of years. The Stargate energy is revealing all that which was hidden. As it enters into the human being it awakens his dormant consciousness and shakes his structures and lies, thus producing a change in the heart, a heart that has generally been closed, full of unresolved issues and lack of love. With this action the new energy aims at liberating the heart to establish a new humanity based on love through a truly open heart.

In opening the heart all the masks fall: you have to come to terms with your truth. It might be that you are scared, feel vulnerable... there is weakness in you. But there is no other way to truth. That is there and needs to be taken care of. So you heal yourself. The masks were there just stopping your experience of yourself at the levels of pain and you didn't want to suffer the unprocessed stuff. So the masks came in. The answer is to heal them, not to use masks to pretend you are something you are not, or that it doesn't hurt. Be sincere; this is the way: naked you will go a long way. Because you will heal and then become truly strong but from within, not as a pretense having the mask of strength. And you will also be compassionate, something you cannot exercise with the rigidity and lack of love of a mask. If you don't accept your vulnerability — remember you hid it with a mask — you won't be able to accept that of others.

Often it happens that under pressure and pain masks fall because the heart is opening, Truth comes out under pressure. Under pressure the ego resistances often give in. This opens the heart in a request to know why and the truth therein is revealed. To act and communicate from a mask reveals that there is fear: of love, of God, of death. The fall of a mask is like dying to a lie we have told ourselves and a personage we have wanted to believe we were. It is about dying to be reborn to life, to God, to love. Then you will be free and happy; you will be truly powerful from the right place.

Change can happen in two ways:

Passive: "I have no choice."
Active: "I change because I want; I choose to."

Better to choose. The passive option is when you have reached the limit and cannot go in that direction anymore without destroying yourself; you have no choice. This is equivalent to saying you can take the masks off willingly or you can have them ripped off. Either way, you will come to face the truth. There is a great difference in the process, nonetheless.

Stargate Announced from Above:
Message from the Masters

In this message just three months before the Stargate opening, the Masters give the essential clues of an event that is inevitable. In these wise and loving words they masterfully distil the essence of the Stargate and its effects on everyone. They are clearly talking about it.

Message from the Ascended Masters on Stargate

"Identity is only divine. There is no other."

Frequencies of light arrive at you in the measure in which you make space to receive them. The violet light allows you to transmute and liberate the necessary to create that space turning everything into light. Feel your presence here and now as a presence of radiant light. Feel this clearly, intensely, with conviction that it is real. Do not be deceived by the vision of a dense physical body — it is also Light. It is the fancy dress you are wearing. In this moment you are a being of light that radiates Light. Feel it, live it, breathe it.

The light is the emanation of your consciousness; that is the face of God without a mask. Decrystallize your concepts and opinions — ideas — so that this Light of your Self — that God "I AM"— that you are can shine. Your job is to open the door, clean the glass so that the light there is behind shines through it. As you remove yourself from being in the way – dropping your concepts – you stop interfering with something which is already perfect, and you allow your presence of Light to manifest itself. Your identity in the Light cannot be improved; it is already Divinity. Your ego still believes it can improve something; what it has to do is renounce its ideas, give itself to the perfection of the light.

The creation of your divine identity is ready. You only have to recognize it and live it. What are you waiting for? How many more excuses do you want to have to delay the inevitable? The inevitable is your Divine Destiny — all else is avoidable. Avoid therefore the resistance to the Will of God, to Light and Consciousness shining in you if you want to know he who is behind the mask — the actor that represents the role — your Divine Identity.

This is the dance of the masks; the time for the dance of the light has come, the time of the Selves, of the true identities "I Am" where everyone is what he is: "It Self." That is why "I Am" — your true presence — the Divine Identity that you are, rules from now on liberating the masquerade: "I pretend to be." It is the time of truth. Stop making excuses for not being. The death of the ego is inevitable because your divine destiny is inevitable, and there, there are no egos. Your false identity is in its last days.

Do you still want to be in candlelight when the sun is shining? What is it you don't want to see? Be? When the lights come on, they won't be switched off anymore. You are going to have to recognize the pretension and your deceit, and your false identity as the vampire in the light is going to disintegrate. And yes, like the vampire, your false identity has sucked life away from you.

Our loving advice is that you do not delay this event and remove the mask now. If you wait for its disintegration through the light that is coming, you might undergo a period of great confusion and anxiety until you assume and understand your "death" and resurrection, until you recognize the Divine Presence you are and which is waiting for you, until you become accustomed again to the brightness of your Divine Presence — "I Am." This will also save you from wanting to follow darkness believing that it is you; the darkness of your false identity will have vanished; you won't be able to find it and you will have to turn to the other side, the one of the Light. This can be immediate or it can take you a very long time. It will depend on you.

The Violet Ray of light is the Divine Emanation that comes to transmute your identity and to free you; give yourself to it. Its mercy, its power of redemption and of manifesting the will of God knows no limits. It is Ascension and manifests your consciousness "I Am," the perfect ecstasy of your Divine Identity.

"I AM
THE LIGHT
OF GOD
IN ME."

Is your truth, your path and your mantra — your Divine Identity.

The Ascended Masters

•

*"Place the violet light in the crown chakra
and let it fill and inundate all your being,
with this ascended frequency."*

Rebellion Times

"I give no power to anything,
nor to anybody. Nothing has
power over me. I only bow to
God."

This is a statement of fact for all. Are you in this consciousness? Many times we "bow" so to speak, to many things as if they are greater than us, as if they contain some mysterious power that we cannot do without. Often the power contained there is a power that exists in us but which we haven't found. So we rely on outside sources for that power. That is fine for a short while if you are seeking after your lost power, and as long as you don't become dependent. This means that you can use sources of external power while you are looking at becoming free from them, since you are searching to find that power inside you. Most people are not on such a quest. They accept the fact that they need certain things or people to get power from and to function in life, and they don't question it. This is part of the equation that has kept things as they are in humanity for so long: there has not been a rebellion against outside sources of power, a rebellion against dependency.

It is time to rebel against the belief systems inside that keep most people living a lie of limitation and slavery about themselves. It is necessary to take distance from the belief systems to see what they really are and what they do to people.

"It is time to end self betrayal."

This status quo of accepting that "this" is the way things are and we just have to live this way is falling apart. The things we thought had power are proving not to have it. Many of those idols of power have fallen in recent years, and the ones remaining will do the same soon. At first it may seem crazy or impossible to accept that the power we think we draw from those idols can come from us. But as with everything if we have never done it, it seems very remote. One

STARGATE 2012: Earth's Imminent Ascension

of the things about the recovery of power is to become aware of it being there and then go within to uncover and awaken it. So practice is required for both. As we train ourselves to be aware all of the time and to go within, our effort will prove that things can happen as a result of it. More and more we will understand how to tap into our inner power, and we will see the effects of awakening it.

As with all rebellions, clarity, effort and steadiness are necessary. Let's call them all *drive*. If you have it, it will work. To shatter crystallized old habits that have reigned in all the departments of your life, as it is in the issue of power for most people, takes a very definite and sustained action and purpose; otherwise they will hardly move. They will certainly be shaken by the mere fact that you are on this planet, because the new energies won't let anything old survive. But this rebellion, which will either come from within or be forced and triggered by the outside action of higher frequencies, has to happen for the good of all. Conscious rebellion for a high purpose is often necessary as a way of evolution. This is happening to Earth; it is happening to humanity. Join this rebellion of love and peace through the art of fighting only that which is standing between you and Truth. Dare to be a rebel against the crystallized ways and assumptions of your own life; they are only taking life away from you.

Rising Against the Tyranny of Darkness

At present, humanity has a grave problem with the taking on of power. And it seems quite unable to get out of that situation. Humanity doesn't know it has that problem, and if it realizes there is this problem, it doesn't know how to get out of it. Darkness, individual and planetary, is who has the power. As far as it has the power, it is winning the match. Everything is a game of power. Whoever has it commands. This message of recovering power is a rebellion against the status quo reigning in humanity now and is going to revolutionize the planet.

What is the problem? The human mind is full of excuses and justifications, reasoning that impedes it from exercising its absolute sovereignty over itself and over its power. This sovereignty is the full state of freedom without conditions or intermediaries, the state in which there are no excuses, justifications, limitations to be oneself fully, to act in total freedom the genuine, pure and spiritually correct desires of the heart.

Darkness has the power. We mentioned this is the dark aspect inside each one of us, and that the global darkness and its lords are ruling the planet from the dark. There has to be a rebellion inside every human being; one of the retaking of power. A process in which through enough spiritual awakening happening in a man he realizes he has been giving power away outside of him, and then he understands that this cannot go on any longer if he wants to evolve truly and fully. Then a decision has to be made to recover that lost power, a decision which will be a rebellion against the present status quo of his life and the holders of his power. This is when the real battle begins for the liberation of every human being. Many have done it, most are in the process of awakening and many are still dormant to the fact that they do not have their power.

If a man acts less than what his heart says, he is not capable of acting out the true desires of his self. He has given his power to his dark side. Why this insistence on the dark? It is because human beings are afraid of the darkness inside of them. They avoid at all costs — often paying a huge price — recognizing and looking at their own dark side. It is there where power is lost. There is a need for an urgent reconciliation with the personal darkness, in which it is not seen as something to be rejected and denied but truly seen as what it is. Then it must be accepted and integrated in love, compassion and consciousness. This means with wisdom. If we are going towards a true and valid recovery of power, this has to happen. And since the pending issue in humanity is power, there is no other way to go: this is a must. So the sooner we all can say, "I have a dark side too," and "I am going to solve it," the better. Otherwise we are just putting back something that is only going to hold back our process of growth and happiness. There is no choice, given the evolutionary moment in which we are and the demands of the script. If something has to be done and there is no other way, the sooner we do it, the better. Precisely, all excuses and justifications and logic that you encounter in order to not take your power and act in freedom are supporting your inner dark side, and are used to avoid confronting it.

This darkness manifests itself as a belief system not based on light but on conditioning and yielding of power. A yielding to false beliefs that justify a behavior that is short of being free; a belief system that says that one is not able to or should not act in full freedom for such-or-such reason, which is considered very valid for everyone: family, society, the state, religion and all the rest; creating a complicity amongst everyone, one of not holding power. Because as soon as one emancipates from this state one is free and becomes a threat to the state of things, the present status quo. And in this way, he puts the game "everyone takes power from everyone" in jeopardy. That is the only viable alternative to the state of not owing power.

"In the moment in which reasons disappear in order to not do that which one wants, power is where it has to be: in possession of its owner."

Consciousness and Reality: We Are in the Final Times

One of the premises of consciousness is that the formed, the physical, is an illusion. Therefore the dismantling of illusion is also illusion. This means that there is nothing really being dismantled; no truth is being removed from existence since illusion was not real. What happens is that the higher energies remove the mirage from our world and open our eyes so we see the truth.

A set not real, right? It represents something; it represents reality, but it is not reality. It is like a movie. Our present reality is like a set. It is not real because it is formed. For the set to be removed is a normal thing to happen at the end of a play, but we have been with this one so long that we believed it was real and never thought it could be dismantled. It is not. When a play is over, they take away the set. This is the same: the play is over and now the set is being taken apart. This is what the Stargate brings to us.

Detachment = liberation

Detachment from the set means being free from the play and from the setting which have ruled our lives for so long. We are free from the fact that there is a change; we are not going away with it. We must allow change to arrive and not resist it.

> *"Everything is consciousness and energy,*
> *therefore it can change its form."*

We have the accepted the idea that certain things can change and disappear as they are, and we find this normal. Hence a piece of ice melts and its form disappears. But we don't have the idea that everything is made of ice. And it has been kept as ice due to the low temperatures of planetary consciousness. And if now the temperatures of consciousness increase and the ice starts to melt, is it going to freak us out? Probably. But the new energies bring this. This level of existence as it is, is not the normal state of things, not our real home, but we have become accustomed to it and therefore have believed it is.

> *"Does the size of the illusion make it real?"*

So we take that one, the ice cube, as illusion and the other, Antarctica, which is bigger, we do not. "This one is real." "Yes, because it's bigger." Do you realize how the mind is? Could not all of Antarctica, which is as big as a continent, melt? It is all made of ice and, in fact it is melting. That's something to really ponder. Size does not make

19

something real; a bigger size does not make something more real than something smaller.

If you have an ice cube and next to it another one, and another one and you raise their temperature, what happens? They all become united as the same substance, don't they? It is the substance they are made of: water. They become the same water. It is the same with everything now; everything merges with the substance of what it is made of: consciousness. That is why now comes a uniting of everything and everybody in consciousness. The defreezing of the egos, casting away the ego from the planet equals unity. This is what is happening the egos are melting, we are becoming spirit; that is where we find unity.

Because this reality is slow, in changing and moving, we have believed it was rigid, unchangeable, reliable. When reality melts, it becomes fluid, faster. When the ice cubes melt, they become faster; they become running water. Imagine that you live in a world of ice and it starts to melt: the walls, the floor, the buildings, the cars, the cities, everything. What is the thought that arrives?

Think for a moment.

"What do I hold on to?"

To nothing. You have to swim.

This is what comes with the Stargate. This is a symbol so that we understand the process. Buildings are not going to become water, but the reality and the processes we live with and the circumstances, including our thoughts, feelings and energies, are all going to become decrystallized, and therefore will start, as they have been doing for a while, to move faster and be more fluid. The very solid energies of our thoughts will become less solid energy, like everything else. Our bodies will also be less dense, although they will still appear physical, but since there will be more light in them and therefore a higher vibration, they will be lighter and more fluid in their energies.

This will apply to our emotional, mental and spiritual bodies, as well as to our physical body.

Thoughts will manifest faster, emotions will move more fluidly, events will speed up, and reality will start shifting towards a world of greater light, consciousness and peace. This is already happening — a world of greater love. When something accelerates it becomes light. Eventually, our bodies will be like light bodies; they will be radiant, like the halos of the saints. Light bodies mean ascension.

The nature of reality is becoming very changeable; events are moving at great speed. Change is occurring where things were previously static. The "solid" situations of our lives are likely to change and transform themselves, sometimes without warning and from one day to the next.

If I cannot hold on to anything outside, I have to find a hold inside. There has to be an anchor point, a reference somewhere. Until now, it has been outside: floor, ceiling, money, house, job, family, relationships. What is there you have not held on to? On what have you not become dependent? "I can touch everything. I can lean on everything." But we have seen that reality as we know it is an illusion: it can melt or be dismantled. So the permanent truth, that which is unalterable, is inside. This is the true, permanent, solid state we are looking for. We must establish ourselves there.

- *I suggest this practice in order to prepare:*

See everything as illusion, as that scenario of cardboard and wood that at any moment can change. This way, you free it and you free yourself. Don't see house, tree, person anymore; that is your mental concept and you impose it on reality. But it is not reality. You all create your reality with your mind. If you change your mind, you are going to change reality.

See, instead of that "concept" house, tree, simply *see*. What you see is consciousness; don't put a name to it. You will be surprised. Understand that "that" is consciousness, God manifested in that form, and consciousness is not attached to a specific form; it can change. In fact He takes on all the forms you see.

With this practice, you are going to decrystallize you mind and become liberated. You are going to see the concepts that you project from your mind and that you then come to believe, but they are not reality. Consciousness is reality; it is the only reality. This way you will start to perceive it without becoming attached to the form you see. Eventually, you will see a world of consciousness, a world that is alive; this is the true world.

Get ready and get going, because the minds, your mind, are strong with resistance and will want to keep seeing the same thing. Don't pay so much attention to the form. Relate to it as such – this is necessary to function – but go beyond. Remain in the observer part of yourself; keep the distance from it and see a beautiful manifestation of God.

Time for a Paradigm Change

Opposites and their servants cannot live together any more. Those for the light will be able to live in a world of light and love. The others who do not want light will have to leave the planet. As the Earth raises its vibration more and more — it has been doing it for many years now — it will fully enter the realms of light and love. There is no place on her for the dark. So the people who want another reality, that of the dark agendas, will have to find another place. They will literally be removed from Earth. How and when that will happen is not of this work. There are other places in the Universe where beings who do not want peace, light and love can go to learn their lessons in the way they choose. So they will eventually be able to develop in the way that they recognize for themselves, the way to God and to their Higher Self. They will gain the recognition that essentially they are that light they are rejecting now.

Isn't it time that the people who want to create and have a world of light, love and peace, and share it with others alike, have it without the interference of forces that disrupt that and want the opposite? Yes, the time for that is now. Those who do not want to play this game will have to leave.

This takes us to us. How do we live? How do we serve? Where are we going? Do you pretend to be a good person? Are you a good person? Is the greatest good for everyone your main concern? Or is your own good your main concern? Dear brother, sister this is the time to ask yourselves these questions. If you thought there was something more important than this, I tell you now, there isn't; that was a wrong appreciation. It is the time to do that which should be done, to live as we should live, from love. It is the time to leave everything else and focus on this as a priority, There is not much time left before there is a change of paradigm on the Earth. There is no other time to do this. It is now or who knows when. The steps in the right direction now will take you very far. There are times when the right investment should be made with the right assets. This is that time. The returns, in terms of your evolution, can be immense.

Practice
Feel how you expand to the infinite field
of all possibilities and merge with it.

Times of Crisis

Due to this intense higher dimensional energy coming in, everything is being shaken. Inside human beings, this is like taking all the contents of the physical, mental, spiritual aspects and shaking them intensely. This process shakes all the structures of those levels of the human beings and makes the inner structure collapse. And it brings all the hidden issues to the surface. All this creates a crisis. This crisis is a permanent crisis, because the fall of paradigms and adjustments happen constantly in a process to get nearer, every time, to the new satisfactory status quo, and this goes through many steps and levels as a constant update of life.

Structures fall, but so does anything in the life of anyone that it is not based on truth, love or light. Many couples are separating. There are more divorces than ever. The number of people changing jobs or moving to a new profession is immense. People are entering a phase of reconsidering the way they live and seeking new ways for living.

Look at your crises and the areas they are in and you will see what power you don't own. See in what areas you give power away. Crises take you to recover your power. A crisis is an absence of light, a lack of power. You have to increase your light, your power to come out of it as you get near the state of light in the process. Light gives you definition. Darkness, twilight is all undefined.

The energy now produces crisis where there is darkness in you.

God is definition of light. His ways are always defined in light and love. That is the definition human beings lack. The more light, the more definition, the more power. That is why in experiencing the light – Stargate – there is more power. You are becoming sovereign in all areas of your life with a crisis. See yourself that way. Eradicate the conflict of the crises.

> *"A crisis takes you to recover the*
> *power in the area of the crisis."*

Cosmic Signal Broadcast

In these times, as the new energies are coming in, shaking up people's lives, there is redirection taking place in everyone. Everyone is finding their true path, their true purpose in life. This path is often different than the one they have followed until now. But it is time to become actualized in one's truth, and, therefore that which one yearns for inside and has hidden is coming to the surface to be realized.

There is a signal for everyone coming from the Stargate energies, that awakens that personal mission. It is the cosmic signal broadcast. You are getting that signal. It comes for people as an image, an urge to do something with their lives.

What signal are you getting from the Universe?
What image are you receiving from the cosmic broadcast?

Do you see yourself traveling far to support a compassionate cause? Do you get the image of yourself giving conferences in new leadership subjects? That image is what you have to go after. That is the path to follow, which is your joy. That is your life's purpose, your mission.

Many times people have chosen a life path based on education, circumstances, reproduction of some model or ideal they have wanted to follow. That choice wasn't the best choice for themselves, their life's purpose or their mission and, therefore it has not brought them the greatest fulfillment. The cosmic signal broadcast brings the greatest possibility for fulfillment in resonance with the soul's vibration. It is as if the Universe was sending the message, "Okay, you have lived your human life; now you can live your highest divine possibility here." Undoubtedly, this higher vision is the one that carries the greatest possibility for happiness, satisfaction and fulfillment. It is the highest possibility of service once the new energies have awakened the Higher Self's consciousness, bringing the highest manifestation into action. And the realization of that vision will always produce satisfaction in the person and benefit for others.

Heart Times: Logic of the Heart

This message from the Ascended Masters just few months before the Stargate opening points the way to go with stunning clairvoyance.

Message from the Ascended Masters
The Logic of the Heart

Go to the heart where there is the logic of love and understanding. Listen to the language of your heart; there is the word of God. Listen to your heart closely. Let yourself be guided by it without manipulation.

To be in the logic of the heart you must trust. Trust in the complete wisdom that dwells there and guides you without falling for the need to analyze details, which fragment things and don't give you the complete picture — the result all of the distrust and insecurity of the mind. But you must be connected and remain in contact with the logic of the heart to avoid falling into the "natural" tendency to go to the logic of the mind and see it all from there. To know, love and be connected with others, you have to do it from the heart. Doing it from the mind you only classify, separate and define what is indefinable — you don't know; you only emit judgments and thoughts – yours – mental structures that separate instead of uniting. Here there is no love; there is no unity.

It is the fear of closeness and human contact that seeks the coldness of the distance and apparent control that the mental focusing provides. Fear of fusion, of dying to individuality, equals fear of love.

Follow your logic of the heart, without guilt, without doubt, without deviating yourself. The sweetness of the heart is your best weapon in life. It is your best protection, your best defense. It is your magic wand to perform miracles. Use the logic of the heart; live from there. The logic of the mind brings fragmentation, separation and rigidity, because it doesn't allow the creative infinity of life to fully manifest. It seeks righteousness and what is right to justify a vision, through a narrow way that does not allow the infinity of life. The logic of the heart unites and reconciles the difference; it brings peace.

Listen to the wisdom that emanates from the heart. Come close and listen carefully, from very near. The logic of the heart solves all problems. To move to the logic of the heart is to take a quantum leap in consciousness, to break structures, to liberate the inherent creativity of God in you. It is to vibrate. What resonates inside you is the truth that you must listen to. God is inside, not outside.

To use the logic of the heart you must learn not to question and to know that what you feel is what is right. The intuition that resides there is wise and complete even though your mind doesn't understand it. The mind will never understand or embrace the infinite of the intuitive world, which is beyond references: linear time and space. The intuitive wisdom of the heart dwells in a plane of consciousness superior to the mental plane. The mind, its logical function, is not the superior function. You have lived in deceit for a very long time about this, due to fear and the disconnection with your divinity.

Trust; it is the insecurity about your divinity and fullness that constantly makes you depend on the mental logic to function, giving you a false sense of security. Because you want to affirm your ego nailing in a stake on which to hold, in the infinite ocean of consciousness, instead of looking for your security merging with that ocean — your true SELF. There, there is the true security and peace.

You are afraid of immensity, of dying to smallness and being born to the infinite. It is the hour of the metamorphosis, *of Christed transmutation, of letting go of the old form and expanding with fullness, into the new being of total consciousness: your "I Am Presence."*

You only have to dare to die to the illusion; letting go of your ideas about what you think you are. Do all this; you will have a great liberation. You will be happier, more like a child, fresh, innocent; you will enjoy more life. You will forgive yourself and others. You will raise your consciousness: ascend. *There, there is freedom and joy.*

This is what you yearn for in your heart.

The Ascended Masters

There is No Tomorrow

The frequencies of the cosmic moment are making us focus more on the present, and the past, the subconscious, has to be resolved, actualized. It disappears. Life is now, so do it now. That which you want, do it. Don't wait to do it. Time is being compressed, accelerated. Everyone is aware that time is going faster than ever. And it will keep going faster as this is a key effect of the Stargate opening. So there is no time to waste. Something cosmic is going to happen: a change of vibration. The relevance of this is that it will mean a change of consciousness and a change in the way humanity lives. And I mean here the way every human being lives, so that has to do with you and with your life.

We have to be ready, free. We have to forgive, liberate, let go, and we have to do it now; there is no tomorrow. We must be getting ready today and every moment. We cannot leave things for later; later there will be many things to take care of, and we will run into a jamming situation if we do not keep processing the present when it is here, with the things it brings. There is no time to waste, we are going towards consciousness. Everything has to be resolved. Consciousness does not allow anything to be pending.

Pending is past and consciousness is present, and due to its high vibration the consciousness we are moving to will not accept the low vibrations of the crystallized past; it will send them on a trip that will make them face us, so they are resolved immediately, or we cannot continue to function. It will put anything that is not vibrating in clear consciousness — anything that holds some unconsciousness or unresolved issues — right in front of us so that we give it the attention it needs, so that it becomes conscious. This is the intensity of living in the present. Once we have the concentration to be focused on the present, it doesn't require effort and things flow naturally in perfect present time for us. When we are fully in the present, that which is not important doesn't stand a chance of taking our attention away from important things, from the essential. And in this way we are up to date with all things the new frequencies are bringing us, because they are providing us with the best opportunities to evolve at this time.

We must understand that part of our consciousness is in the past; that means it is not resolved so it must be brought to the present. The new energies require that we forgive, let go and close the past. All light and strength must be brought to the present for us to see and use, to have more light, more consciousness, more awareness to get ready for the jump in consciousness. That is why processes are so intense now, and they will be so for a while until we simplify our lives, bringing all that is in the past — unconsciousness — to the present — consciousness. That will manifest a tremendous evolution for all and it will bring the opportunity to focus on being in the light.

*"There is only time
to be in the light."*

Moving Out of Time

"The time of God is the eternal present;
this is where things happen."

As you evolve in the process of realizing that time is going faster every time, you will have to develop a great concentration to stay focused in the midst of such acceleration, with so many things that have to be done... and there is no time. Eventually there will be a quantum leap in you, and you will stop feeling like time is going by. You will feel everything is happening at the same time and everything is happening in the present. This means you have moved out of time. It is the sign that you have moved to a higher frequency and your vibration has increased. As time accelerates you drop what is not a priority and focus on what really matters to your life and your evolution, and if you are in service, to the evolution of others. The higher you vibrate there is less the experience of time and more the experience of eternity: all one moment.

Time is relative. It depends on where our consciousness is situated. The higher it is, the less time goes by and the more we are in the same moment, in a continuous present. Keeping focused is the way to stop time, the way to not be taken by the acceleration of time. Since time is relative, we have to increase our consciousness of the present when there are time accelerations. In this way the perception of time will change for everyone.

Part of our mind is concerned with many things that do not belong to the present. Our minds are hardly in the present, and they are dwelling in the past and the future all the time. We are doing something and we are thinking about many other things that have nothing to do with what we are doing and with what is happening in the present. We must move out of that, even though we think it is a normal way of functioning. In doing so we will gain a tremendous amount of presence, power, and effectiveness. Among other things we will have more control of our life and its direction, and we will not be surprised by outcomes generated by idle thinking that we created and we were not even aware of doing. Also, we will be lighter and connected with what our heart is telling us; its voice will be clearer and its guidance more perceptible, so we will navigate better in the events of life. We are so mentally busy moving away from the present that we hardly hear its voice. Then we run into situations that could have been avoided and would have been different if we had been alert. This is a key stance:

> **"Stay alert in the present. Move out of time
> to move into the present."**

The acceleration of time is such that we have to honor and value the present more. We need to realize what this means so that we do not concern ourselves with anything else except what is going on here and now. This way you stay focused, concentrated, and practical. Of course, you plan for the near future but according to how it relates to your present life; you don't start buying food needed in three years time or worry about Christmas gifts in May.

So we are moving from being half asleep to being fully awake — fully awake in the present. This is the way to be, and it does not admit any delays. Delays in being in this presence of consciousness will only bring us problems in the form of maladjustments and their sometimes intense consequences. This is because the energies are becoming more intense every time, and therefore more accelerated. If we are not in the present, we won't be able to keep up-to-date with the fast changes they bring in and around us, and that will keep us running into conflicts. If we are in control of our minds and our energies, we can create fabulous things; we can go beyond anything we have reached in our lives to date: we can hit the extraordinary. This is what we need at this evolutionary moment.

Being fully in the present gives us a tremendous amount of concentration; with it, we can focus our awareness on the right things, those that are necessary for our present evolution. This is fundamental because we need to be alert to stay in the vibrations of love and compassion and avoid karma, so every day we move closer to the frequencies of ascension. We need to live every day with the intention of advancing towards becoming ready for our ascension. Nothing is more important than that at this moment. This is the time to get actualized in your life and move in the direction that your Higher Self sees for you through what you feel in your heart. The pressure of the Stargate energies is pushing people towards the greater life they can live. Resisting that will only bring extreme desperation and total dissatisfaction. The call of the higher energies is bringing out the best plan for all, in everyone.

At the speed at which time is going now, you must make sure that what is important is done. What is most important is love and spirit. Thus, make sure that the unimportant things do not take up your time, because there is no time for that. Since if you entertain too much of the little, non-relevant things, time will pass and you will have missed this great opportunity for evolution and doing the right things for it. Time is so fast now that it is crucial to seize the moment. It is the opportunity to act, to make a change and to advance in the new direction.

The urgency of the priorities is taking a new dimension now, as the acceleration of time and processes reaches a new peak. Now they cannot be left for later; they must be done right away. This is part of the plan, that they are taken care of. This is what ensures your evolution, and all together doing this ensures the global evolution of humanity and the planet. Nothing is more important than that at this time, individually and collectively.

**"Everything becomes out-of-date,
except love and truth."**

What is Reality?

A friend of mine said to me recently, "This is my reality," referring to a situation in which she felt could not do anything and felt powerless; not a very positive situation to be in. I answered her, "You have just ignored an important detail: you decide what your reality is." She had accepted that reality. What amazes me is how people can believe a reality happens just like that, as if it just appeared out of nowhere. What happens is that people have bad memory and often suffer from acute amnesia. If people started to think hard about what they thought and felt, about what they did and said over the last months and years, especially how they lived life, most would understand why that is their reality.

This is why with the Stargate energies, people are forced to face the reality of their lives and stop looking elsewhere for the cause of it. They will be taken to find that the cause of everything is themselves. There are no powers outside creating havoc for you. You are the one doing it. I can only say to you: realize that as soon as possible, for your own good and that of others around you and beyond. Then, understanding that your thoughts, feelings and energy coming out of you have created your reality, you can start to think and feel in a new way to create a new reality.

The New Rules: Quantum Metaphysics

Change metaphysics for high vibration; this is Quantum Metaphysics: high frequency light. The highest are blue and violet light. Blue light is the light of Divine Power. Violet is the supreme spiritual vibration that the blue light is helping us achieve on the way to ascension, the Stargate mission. This help of the Blue Light is the support of power recovery. Power is the essence of the Blue Light. The Blue Light helps with the Violet Light work, since violet light consciousness is the aim of the process of ascension; reaching the highest vibrational state: the violet frequency.

Traditional metaphysical laws don't work as they did before. The new times and the urgency to get things into the right divine working have change all that. Now what goes is what is best for oneself, for all and for the whole, in the vision of the divine plan: what is best for everyone in unity. In other words: what is best for the global ascension. Hence the relevance of being connected with sources of high vibration, like the violet light. They manifest that truth, that "best for all" at great speed, burning karma immediately and moving things and people to the optimal evolution point in a very short time.

> *There is only one thing going on in*
> *this planet: the rising of vibration.*

This is for everyone, and everywhere. This alone will produce the change we are all looking for, individually and globally. If what you ask for is not at the appropriate level of vibration, the highest, with the most light, and hence the most beneficial to all, it won't happen. High vibration is nearer to God's intentions — God's Will. So what you ask for will need to have a high vibration in itself. This will be in terms of the intention behind it — loving intention — the amount of true service it will produce, and the benefit of vibration it will send out to all life.

Knowing that is not easy, especially if you are not spiritually trained. That is why the easiest and most accurate way is to work with high-vibration light, like the violet light. Everything you work with will increase its vibration at the mere touch of the violet light. The way? Put violet light to everything, and it alone will manifest the perfect divine outcome. More details on how to learn about the violet light are at the back of the book. So we have substituted average metaphysics for quantum metaphysics: the one that creates quantum leaps towards the manifestation of divine plans: perfection — the only thing that will work for everyone. With the use of quantum metaphysics, you will get the best for you and for everybody else, too.

Ascension is not Another Option: It is the Only Way

"In a very concise way, ascension is opening ourselves to the light."

Thus, opening ourselves to the light is the only way. What other way is there for humanity? For a humanity that being away from the light has created a sick world? What is left then? There is not another option. And humanity has exhausted the path without light. It has done it so much that the planet and the life on it are in great danger. The opening to the light is ascension. And this is the option available to any human being and humanity as a whole now. It is the only way, because it is the only way that makes sense. Returning to the worlds of light the worlds where God is, where love and peace exist. It just there isn't anything else in life. The sooner we all understand and accept this fact, the sooner we will enter into the light and peace that is so much needed on this Earth, and the better it will be for this living planet and every sentient being.

The light allows our change of frequencies and vibration, and therefore an intense manifestation of light in us. This is a reconversion to it because we are light. This light has lowered its vibration so much in some areas that we have become crystallized and we have lost consciousness and, therefore, light. And from this eclipsed state of awareness humanity has created the world it has.

"We have stopped shinning."

The process is simply to retake shine, the luminosity of consciousness, and elevate our crystallized parts to their original state: that of the light. This work here brought by the divine energies of the Stargate, is a powerful and very appropriate help in that process, help that like a map points the way. Besides, it activates us, placing us in it. It is a spark that gives us a considerable ascensional induction. We must all follow it for our own good.

Power & Joy

Raising the vibration towards unlimited joy and freedom... This is ascension. Why increase vibration? To come out of suffering, to enter into joy, into the consciousness of peace and unity. Power and joy are love. So ascension is about being in love with power and joy. Love is what makes people evolve. It is what liberates; it is what illuminates. As you love, you evolve and make other beings evolve. The greatest power is in love. In fact, only love has true power. And true power is a sign of love, a product of it.

We must react to everything with joy. How would God react? With joy. God reacts with joy; the ego reacts with unhappiness. All reactions of unhappiness are from the ego. We create reactions of unhappiness and we create unhappiness. People are codified to a great extent with the negativity of the ego to create misery. This is giving power away. Only that which is joy contains true power. So by remaining in joy, we are remaining afloat with power. This way we are tuning into ascension.

Happiness is the kingdom of God. Unhappiness is the kingdom of ego. The more unhappiness, the more ego. This way ego reaffirms itself in the belief of its own existence. From ego consciousness we believe in our own misery and create unhappiness that confirms it. Joy is high vibration; unhappiness, low vibration. High vibrations have power. Low vibrations are a loss of power. So remaining in joy is to build up the ascension reality in us. For our ascension we need to vibrate high because this gives us the passport to the high levels of existence and awareness: where we go when we ascend. Ascension is thus a process of moving away from ego and moving into God.

The coding of the ego makes the programming in our nervous system and makes it react in that negative way. When a person reacts with rage, anger or fear, he is blinded by his screen of unhappiness — unless he is a spiritually realized being and that act and feeling comes from an enlightened attitude, which seeks liberation and blessing. Otherwise, such a person reacting is not in reality or in present.

> *"Joy is reality. All else is illusion.*
> *Only in reality is there power."*

God sees everything as joy. God is only in a joyful place, and being there is the way to attract Him. We have to create actions and reactions of joy – without negativity or ego – with everything: body, emotions, mind, spirit, words, actions, thoughts, feelings. We have to generate so much joy inside, be so strong in joy that the ego doesn't touch us. And neither do its manifestations: fear, anger, sadness, pride. So you see them and see that they have nothing to do with you, that all this is from another world foreign to the world of joy and peace. In fact, you are free when you choose joy. Choosing joy is conceiving it as the only reality; it is to open up to ascension.

> *"Everything is a simple choice: love or darkness.*
> *You are in the light when you choose the light."*

Ascension is Happening Now

The energies sent to the planet by the Stargate's influence are increasing the vibration of everything on it, including things, all forms of life and human beings. You and everything else are ascending now. You are protagonist and witness of ascension wherever you are. You are ascending yourself, and bringing other people with you. Feel and see how you are all ascending. You promote ascension; it is already happening. Feel and see that all the people you know are ascending with you. It is a global ascension; you and all the people you are in touch with relate to make a network of ascension.

Any time you can ask yourself, "What can I do now for ascension?" Quiet yourself; emanate a field of high vibration for the Earth and humanity, a field of love, peace and violet light.

Ascension Matters

Every body or energy field of our global consciousness focuses on living in complete consciousness. They seek the unlimited, permanent expansion of joy, truth, eternity, bliss, consciousness; in other words permanence. Thus the physical body looks for another, unites with another body and wants this to become a permanent situation… and attachment is born. It is in that fusion that it finds more of the above list. The emotional body identifies, relates and unites with another emotional body energetically, creating an energy field where there is more joy, unity, expansion… and attachment is born. The mental body contains realities as ideas, projects and things that maintain "the reality" subjective of course; it seeks a similar mental body to relate to in another person. Attachment to that reality and union, and therefore to those ideas, is born, as with the other bodies, in a lack of higher consciousness. That attachment seeks to maintain that vision of reality and how things have to be.

From all three the idea of *mine* is created — those things that belong to those bodies: physical activities, possessions, emotional contents, feelings, emotions, and their attached objects, mental ideas, concepts, and beliefs, as well as people. All this is what a person is in his conception of reality and of herself: the field of the ego identity. But they are all limited states of consciousness because they are limited bodies. They look for fulfillment and eternity, which is the right search and a compelling drive of all consciousness, but the direction is the wrong one. Those bodies are limited in their capacity, size and life. Designed with limits to experience consciousness through limits, so that the person's overall consciousness can grow... they appropriate for themselves that idea of eternity, believing they can achieve it independently and attain that permanence we mentioned. They end up believing they are the purpose itself, and thus want to manifest it, but in a realm of limits. It doesn't work. They can't. So there is suffering. They seek eternity because they are consciousness, although limited, and all consciousness looks for freedom and limitlessness; it seeks to become whole: a search for the unlimited state of God.

They try to experience the eternal on their own, but they can only do it while looking for the higher body: the body of light: the Higher Self. They need to lose their individuality as different separate sections of a being with their own projects and schemes, to become part of the instruments of the Higher Self for his purposes of evolution, which is their function from the start. They just borrowed consciousness that was for a higher purpose and made it their own for their own purposes, separating themselves from the original unity. In that separation they thought they had an identity of their own and wanted to live it out as if this was the reality; it wasn't. It was just an illusion and therefore they lived an illusory reality paying the price: suffering and death. They have to wake up to the truth and to the fact they are serving their master: the Higher Self.

It is the Higher Self, the real consciousness of the person, the one who has access to the original list: bliss, joy, consciousness and eternity. In uniting with it, they experience the eternal, and in God, they satiate from their search. In this way, they renounce the ways of attachment and manipulation to maintain their individuality, to obtain joy and the feeling of permanence from the wrong place. All the bodies or fields of consciousness have to ascend to the consciousness of the higher body or spiritual body: the light body. They have to open up to receive its grace, but here the great obstacle is fear.

Since there is a limited consciousness, the "I" in each of these bodies, this implies an idea of death. This feeling of disappearance is fought against intensely. This is what maintains the status quo in all the bodies. They contract before the vision of this reality, due to that fear. This is the blockage; it impedes the access and openness to grace. Grace is seen as the bringer of that death. Grace will inevitably awaken the bodies from their self-absorbed dream. That very acknowledgment of the need for a superior energy, of a superior consciousness, creates that fear. From it comes the resistance to grace, as the enemy that will terminate the illusion they are living. It is a menace because the bodies have the acknowledgement that they are not complete — all mighty or eternal — and they recognize there has to be a cessation of being, a death, which has to be accepted; and a resistance to that is inevitable. The relationship and union with other bodies, as we saw earlier, is just an intent to experience expansion and move away from that fear of cessation.

A fictitious world is then created in which the body, as an entity, is the protagonist: a delusional world with made-to-measure rules, all conditioned to create a false reality based on the attempt to believe in eternity, by excluding from that reality the idea of an ego, made up of those three bodies, which has to die. Thus creating a play where death is excluded. It is not a death, it is a cessation in order to become something superior, the winged being — Quetzalcoatl — the serpent with wings in the Mayan culture, which has evolved from an ordinary serpent and ascends. The serpent doesn't die as such; it evolves into a new being. It is not a serpent any more: it resurrects into a higher form of existence. This is the same with the ascension of man.

The creation of systems, ideas and belief systems that talk of permanence promote the delusion that one is here to stay, and a world that supports this has to be created. A world of consumerism, comfort, of consuming for comfort, when there is the most ridiculous parody imaginable: constant consumption of perishable products to give the impression of constancy and permanence. But as we must realize:

"The infinite possibilities of the mind do not take you to infinity."

And therefore neither do those of a world created by it, even if it is to escape the idea of limits and cessation. Neither of those infinite possibilities takes anybody to eternal existence. The only path is to get out of the mind as a field of operations and venture to the unknown territory of Spirit. Without inner work, meditation and openness to grace – and this requires work – it is not possible to come out of that fictitious world and to awaken from fiction to Reality. The growth, the training is to train the bodies in the truth of their limitations, while the grace of the superior reality is accessed. To understand, in that self-effort of gaining consciousness and training, that one cannot be stuck or be physically united with another person constantly, to balance the anxiety of separation and loneliness; that one cannot depend emotionally on others vampirism of them, possessing them or chaining them as a belonging with tyrannical emotional demands disguised as love, good desires, desire to help, and even service to others. Also we must understand that it is not possible to throw bombs at another country or neighbor, literally, just because people there don't think as us and do not sustain and support our belief system of how we have decided reality must be, because such difference scares us, threatens us, and shakes us. This is not possible. And when I say "not possible," I mean not possible without paying the consequences.

To impose a reality, be it through the physical, emotional, mental or spiritual aspects, is undoubtedly something coming from the distorted and scared vision of the mind, seeking to satisfy a sick vision to make of reality something that is not. With structures and unfounded philosophies that are only impositions with rules full of holes, such a mind forces a reality upon the world and others; something that only causes separation and pain that afterwards must be healed.

The only way is that of openness; the fact is that deep down there is an openness of the heart, an openness to the wisdom of the heart, that sees and knows what is real, that feels and thus knows. It is a heart refined beyond the emotional sphere, becoming a superior and conscious compassionate heart, intuitive and truly loving, beyond the weak and superficial idea of love and compassion so extended in the world today. Something that is only possible when consciousness and superior grace have touched it with their magical touch of light, infusing true power to any being. This has a beginning – initiation – that starts a process of liberation and expansion in an ascension to one's higher consciousness. It is a process of inner development that inevitably goes through the step of taking on power.

All this happens because of a lack of power awareness in the human being. Such lack creates a dependent human society, suffering and chaotic, which has lost its direction and searches for truth in the wrong, manipulative ways that make this world what it is, and one which desperately needs to awaken to the source of power in God, to turn to it for fulfillment. Such a turn will bring peace, prosperity and ascension. This is the key, the crossroads in which the world and humanity are at this very moment. We are going towards ascension.

- You may go now to the *Support Section* and look at the list "Ascension Essentials." You may also check the list *Guidelines for Your Consciousness Focus,* a great reference for any time.

Light Body: The Resurrection of Man

The light body is a field of light, a body of light related to Christ Consciousness: it is the field of light that holds the Christ Consciousness. Having the light body active is necessary to ascend, and Stargate energies develop and activate it naturally. As man ascends to his higher dimensional consciousness through spiritual development, he enters into communion with his divine nature and increases his light. As this ascensional spiritual process develops, a human being intensifies his light until he merges completely with his divine presence. Then the light such being emanates is very intense. He has become a saint or a holy person. But this is not something reserved for special people or those who would want to become saints. This is the standard path for every human being. Everyone is destined to merge with their divine light presence. The saints we know have done it quicker than the rest. The halo of the saints is a representation of the light body. Most of humanity has been very sleepy regarding spiritual matters and spiritual realization. But man is God in essence, and the spiritual development of any human being has as its end the realization of his unity with God. And the light body is the means to that aim.

"The light body is the resurrection body of man,
the energy body necessary for ascension."

Using the Energy Correctly

One of the side issues happening with the new energies is that many people are using the energies available in the wrong way. Stargate energies are very intense; they act as an amplifier. When people use the energy wrongly, what it does is amplify their issues. The energy of high vibration acts as a wave amplifier, and when focusing on negative emotions, the only thing you achieve is making them bigger. They act as a magnifying glass, and wrong and destructive habits can be intensified instead of being resolved. This is why there is so much conflict on Earth now, and so many fights and extremes in manifestation, when things could be much better and harmonized with the present energies.

With the wrong use of these energies, if people feel anger they can be carried away by it. And the anger grows, and the same is happening with other unprocessed lower energies. The way now is to join the ways of love, and the lower emotions and energies will be mostly dissolved. The part that is not can be processed from there. It is important to process and live with anger or other negative emotions in positive, harmless ways.

Things can be lived and be released in a creative way or in a destructive way.

It is important to use the energies in the right way: to elevate consciousness. Elevate oneself in the vibration of love and from there, process and manage the negative energies. Then things can be seen from above and they lose intensity: they are not so important. In elevating the consciousness with them we move out of the problem and are not caught up in the illusion of negative emotions: they present a false world of misery and self-pity. In this way the high energy is not used to set off intensely negative emotions. Then the light available can be used to be lifted to higher states like love, peace, cooperation. It is there for that. That is the focus the new energies should have and the way they should be used. And when there are unresolved issues, then high vibrations should be used to put love and light to them.

One must use the new energies available, and with determination go for the negative habits and low vibrations and dismantle them. With courage and resolution, you should break limiting habits and ways of life — acting, thinking and feeling — and reach a new way to live, expansive and free, that with this light and effort catapults people to a new sphere, a new platform of being and existing, in power, love and wisdom. Go for your fears once and for all and reinvent yourself.

The present frequencies of light must be used to resolve issues transmuting everything that doesn't vibrate in the light, and to amplify good feelings, love, unity, and bring peace. Importance should be given to positive and enhancing emotions, and other low vibrations and negative emotions must be disregarded; process them as necessary, without harm and let go. Take importance away from them. Don't dwell in them, as if they were the reality. They are just illusion; they must go. They should be dropped. The solution is not to get into destructing habits more intensely. A closed alley will not become a road to somewhere just by going around in circles in it.

People must find a center of serenity and peace inside. It is time. When emotions or pending issues come up, they must have the consciousness that this is part of the script, a scene in the play, and live them that way. In this way the issues are processed and released: they have been brought to consciousness. Then they must be forgotten, left behind. It is done. Don't give them importance. Those things are being left behind as humanity evolves towards ascension. Forgiving is necessary as an act of letting go to move forward and be free. This is essential on the way to change the paradigm.

> ***"In these times what doesn't***
> ***work must be dropped."***

God's Alchemy: Divine Transmutation for All Life

Power? You don't dare. Fear — you continue crawling like a snake. Don't get up... Your mind, your ego. But the snake grows wings... And what do we have? The winged serpent, and it is able to fly.

The ego and the ego mind do not believe in greatness; they cannot grasp the greatness of the power of God. They only know their own limited power, by which you have been doomed all these years... lives Before such immense power of God coming into this reality now, a being can be transmuted in a deep metamorphosis and become a powerful being capable of rising above its own misery and ashes as a winged serpent. Such a being is no more a reptile that finds its way low on the ground, but a being that conquers the beauty of the heavens and the high realms, which are its true home: close to God. God through a mighty descent of His power touches us and transforms us beyond imagination in a way that only He, the great alchemist of the Universe, can. This could be a perfect summary of what is going on, on the planet right now. A big event.

- *Take a moment to let this fact and truth*
  sink into your being, if you will.

Now you rise like an eagle; symbol of transmutation. It is no longer about thinking that this poor human is incapable of doing anything transcendent. You are God; He is making you so. You are God in your divine self. The "I can't" and "I shouldn't" are gone forever. All that low life is manipulation, power control; that is why as kids, we were brainwashed… and we perpetuated it. Not anymore. There is no need; other facts are coming into play, other reality manifesting, the dream is broken… we are being awakened from the longest and craziest lie of all time: "We don't deserve," "We are sinners," "We don't have power," "We are cast away from the kingdoms of glory and joy of God." No, my friends. We return to the facts: we deserve everything, all the good and goodness there is in the Universe, because God wants us there. And no force can oppose that because it is the Will of God for us, for you, for all.

Opportunity to Evolve

We are presented at this moment in time, with one of the greatest opportunities to evolve that humanity has had since its beginnings. The great thing about it is that people can evolve tremendously at a speed unknown on Earth before. People can do all that which they haven't done for their evolution in a long time, even in lifetimes. The energies are so strong now and so accelerated that people have the most incredible opportunity to evolve and ascend. This is more than pure gold. There are no words that can express the great possibilities of this moment. It is just something not to miss. And to go for it fully, with all focus and determination. There won't be something like this again for a huge amount of time.

There is a unique opportunity now on Earth
to acquire the highest evolution.

In consciousness you get what you earn, not what you deserve — meaning, what you work for. Because this is a Universe of free will. If we were to get what we deserved, we would all be enlightened. We deserve it; now we have to work for it and earn our stripes. This is the most precious circumstance to do it. We deserve everything, but what things and what level of power awareness do we each want to embody? This is the thing. Everything is there. How much of it do you want? The opportunity now is that you can earn the whole of it, if you want it. The energies of Stargate are here for you; you have to decide how much of that you want. My advice is that you go for the whole lot.

The End of the Innocence

The new energies are bringing a dramatic change in paradigm. They are changing the reality humans have lived with until now, and changing the inner consciousness to see something new: the truth that has been hidden. It is the end of the innocence, of the "I don't know; I can't," and therefore the "I am not accountable." We are knowing, powerful, loving beings, and we are being reborn to that truth.

The end of the innocence is about ending the lies about being good boys and girls. It is about ending the belief that "I am not bad; I am not a bad person," and taking responsibility for the evil inside oneself. This takes guts. But it is the only way to reality. Not doing it is to confine oneself to a life of superficial passion and power, a half-truth life that makes no one happy and serves no good purpose.

The end of the innocence is to stop believing we are "so good" that there is no evil in us. Believing that this is something reserved to criminals who appear on the news. We all need to look much more seriously at the trail we leave behind us, since "You will know them by their actions," actions that many conveniently forget the moment they have done them. We must have the honesty and the courage to see if the trail we leave behind us is a blossoming garden of peace and harmony or a battlefield of disruption and broken hearts.

The human being believes he is "good" without questioning himself deeply. He believes he is good, and his actions show evil, and he doesn't want to recognize them. He is blinded by the idea of being a good person and is unable to see that in his acts there is no love, that those are not acts of goodness — those that come from enlightened love, free of evil. He exercises a mediocre love because he has not illumined his shadow side within: his goodness is tinged with his dark side.

On the other hand, being innocent is a state of not assuming one's power and not using it, with consciousness and maturity for the good of all. Being innocent means acting as someone who doesn't have influence on life because one has rejected the power inside. That creates a being that is at the mercy of things, an irresponsible person who feels and acts powerless. A being that doesn't want to own his power partly because of the responsibility it means to do so. He needs to realize the fact of his own power and use it for the good. The end of the innocence is the end of the lie in which most of humanity still lives: the pretension to be powerless and thus acting in detrimental ways thinking they are doing a "great good." While in fact no good action comes from powerless ways because they cannot be committed to the highest good. And often those actions are seen as good when really they are a compromise: they lack commitment. Total commitment can only come from total power.

To know if one is doing good or not takes a really awakened consciousness, because that is the only way to have real discernment to know if something good is really good. Many times people do "good" things that are really terrible. Then the reaction is, "Oh, my intention was good." But as many already know, good intentions are not enough; they can literally bring you to hell. There has to be true love. That love has been forged in the inner fire of personal spiritual growth and is very strong; it is fool proof; it has a deep wisdom; it really knows what is good and what just appears so. One then is not fooled any more by what appears good but is not. That false goodness is produced by the dark side not being enlightened. By enlightening the dark side in that intense fire of spiritual growth, ordinary love becomes enlightened love.

The end of the innocence is becoming awakened in the truth that there is an immense power inside granted by God, and that it must be held and used. In other words, it is becoming a responsible agent in life. Not being a responsible agent is to count yourself out of situations that happen before you every day, that happen to you. Whatever is in your life is your responsibility. It also means being responsible for life at large. It is too innocent to think that what is not inside our front door is not our problem, or it is the problem of the government or other people. Fortunately, in the last few years there has been a global move towards involvement in personal and transpersonal — global — issues by a great part of humanity. But still there is a long way to go individually and collectively towards the end of the innocence and the taking on of power. The influence of the new energies is awakening people to their power and responsibility in a way that we are getting near that end of the innocence.

Death and Resurrection

As people move into the awareness of their Higher Self they discover the truth about their power: it lies there. With the awareness of the

Higher Self people can stop believing they are their ego. This is a great liberation since in the ego lies very limited power. That is why there is suffering and death in it. While people remain in the awareness of their ego, they will suffer. They need to stop believing they are it. And get to know the Higher Self: the source of True Power. To do that, meditation and spiritual practice must be done to shift that perception and awareness from ego to Higher Self. It is a major thing, it doesn't happen just like that, although with the new energies it gets easier all the time.

Take into account that the ego is mainly what you think you are; so your mind won't let go of it that easily. The change implies a death and a resurrection: you die to the ego and are born to spirit. From then on your identity is in the Higher Self, where it should be. This is what you truly are, not your ego. It is the spiritual practice, constant and focused that gives this discernment, the true vision and the right perspective on things. This requires an increase in vibration which is what this whole book is all about, because ascension is all about that. Meditation is crucial because it is the way to gain exposure to higher energy, the most direct way of doing it and the way that most impregnates that high frequency into your awareness, your body and your whole being.

When it seems that everyone and everything has abandoned you — something that more and more people are experiencing these days — it is for you to find the truth of God within you; you are preparing for the final jump: dying to the false in you; resurrecting to your higher truth.

Synchronicity

There is no cause and effect. They are synchronic events. This might seem hard to accept, especially since humanity has believed otherwise for a long time. But things look one way when looked at from one level of consciousness, and a different way from another. What the worm calls the end of the world is what we call a butterfly, says Richard Bach in his book *Illusions*. It just depends who is looking and from where. For a man rowing placidly along a river everything is perfect, but a man flying above it in an airplane can see that a mile ahead there is a dangerous waterfall. Things depend on your state of consciousness: the more consciousness you have, the higher you are looking from and the greater your perspective. The more you see, the more it makes sense.

For the man in the airplane, the waterfall is a present reality, but for the man rowing, it is a future event. We see here that time is not a fixed reality: for one man, the waterfall doesn't exist; for the other, it does. The waterfall is present for the man in the small airplane; it is there now. So the man rowing and the waterfall farther along are happening at the same time for him; it is a synchronic event. For the man in the river, the waterfall is something to come to in the future, after a process of moving along the river: cause and effect. So cause and effect is the appearance of a Universe that is synchronic but that we cannot perceive from this standpoint: the state of consciousness in which we are.

As you move higher in consciousness, you move from karma to synchronicity. Then you see things happening at the same time and being part of a Universe that is synchronic in its operation. The Universe, its consciousness, is everywhere so it can act and manifest at the same time everywhere: it doesn't need time or cause and effect. Synchronicity is an element of power. As you realize this is the case, you develop more your power. Power doesn't depend on events to cause a situation; it simply acts and manifests synchronically. Certainly the more you move to your higher power, the more it will be so. Everything is an interrelated system. When you move higher in your consciousness your perception changes and you don't see cause and effect, you see synchronicity. Change is synchronic; it happens everywhere at once. As something shifts, everything moves and you do as part of the system, too.

The Universe as the field of God is not foreign to you or to anybody. This divine universal field is everywhere and reacts to consciousness. It answers calls. It has solutions, resources, power for you and everyone. As you make your calls to it, there is synchronicity happening, and that is the response. So you meet the right people, find what you are looking for, experience an inner change or an answer comes to you.

❖ *Try to be aware of this fact:*

"I am in the total conviction that God has the solutions to my life in this moment, that He will bring to me all I need to get out of the situation in which I am with the right solutions, because in this moment He is creating them for me. And what I can do is have faith that this is so, because it is so."

This is to accept the synchronicity between the power of God and you. As God is, so are you and there is no time, no separation in this fact: it happens at once. You do not need to wait or to become worthy of it. You have been created and sustained with power, with the attributes of God and the Universe. The fact that you might not be aware of that, or might not experience it is another matter. We must become aware and enter a life of synchronicity consciousness. It is where things are happening. It is how things are happening. While we are not in that consciousness, we are missing a great deal of reality and we are caught up in time, limits and space. It is a life of no power. Synchronicity is the reality because power is the reality for us all. Synchronicity is the reality because God has no limits. Synchronicity is real power.

Effect of the New Energies

The new energies are touching all areas of human consciousness. These include the physical body and all the levels of the aura:

emotional, mental, spiritual areas. We will have a look at them and how the energies are making them behave. I remind everyone that whether you are aware or not, this is already happening.

Physical body

Emotions blocked in the organs will be moved and released. So they might manifest as a condition that will probably draw attention to that organ demanding some sort of healing. So through the healing, the emotional blockages are released, and the organ is liberated. This will improve the functioning of the organ and its associated energies producing a greater global balance.

Energetic or functional imbalances in the organs are going to become self-evident so they can be healed and corrected. All these will result in the increment of the vibrational frequency of the body. The physical body will eventually feel lighter due to these liberations, and because of that, it will be able to assimilate and contain more light.

Emotional field

The emotional field is the area of our aura that holds our sentient contents: feelings and emotions. Unexpressed emotions are going to want to come out; they will claim their space, their identity. This no doubt has been happening to most of you over the last few years. For some, this process has been going on for a while; for others, it is starting now in a big way and for others, it will start soon. Everybody has their own time and moment for the processes to occur. But if something is there blocking light and truth, liberation will occur with the influence of the new energies. As emotions and feelings claim their space, allow them to express themselves; now you cannot hide any longer the things you feel. Always do it with respect for others and for yourself. Seek inspiration, the vibrating high of your emotional body, to reach the bliss contained in it.

Mental body

In this area of our consciousness there is going to be a breaking down of fixed ideas and rigidity, concepts and assumptions. False beliefs are going to fall for truth to be known. False identity and the elements that support it — "I," "mine," the mask — are on the way to collapsing. As the individual mind disappears, as we have known it, universal mind is born in every individual. Such a mind contains universal truth that is divine and eternal, and it gives rise to a divine mind and a vision of life and process of thinking which have nothing to do with the logical, linear process we have known for so long, and that so many difficulties and limitations bring with it. Such a divine mind is more in tune with everything and all life forms. And it is based on intuitive knowledge — a far happier place to be in and to come from. The idea of the limited planetary "I" will start to fall once the mind is free from the rigid components that have made up its configuration to date. And the higher energies coming to the planet will transmute it to a higher level of existence and a limitless configuration. Before that state, its limited contents will have to be cleared. Then, such expansion can take place. The cosmic "I" is born.

Spiritual level

As all the other levels are liberated and freed from a deceiving limited consciousness, the spiritual consciousness is manifested. Since all the other bodies have been set free, the soul is liberated from those constrictions and can manifest freely. This will produce the manifestation of the divine in you and everyone; the manifestation of your Christ Self known as "I Am."

•

To access the Stargate frequencies with the different bodies and to make them resonate with the divine plan it brings, you can connect with these truths:

- "My emotional body aligns itself with the divine plan."
- "My mental body responds to Reality and becomes enlightened."
- "My physical body manifests the consciousness of light."
- "My spiritual dimension resonates with the higher divine frequencies—Stargate. I enter into spiritual power, love and peace through the unity with it."
- "I become God in my unity with God."

Illuminating the Shadows Within

The following year after the Stargate alignment, Archangel Michael gave me a new vision of the event, a vision that would be going on for the following years. It is a key update on the Stargate information. It has been included in my courses on the Stargate since then.

Planetary alignment update

The alignment is the entering of a new age of light for humanity and the planet. There can be no light if you are giving it outside, to the tyrants of darkness — inside and outside — you do this by valuing them. The key is inside, where the tyrants of darkness are found: guilt, fear, jealousy, control, insecurity, because they keep you in doubt — a lack of faith. Then you give your light, your power, outside. You become dependent and chain yourself — you become a slave and servant of darkness, which controls you freely in your absence of light.

To give power away is grave; it is the worst thing that can be done, because the tyrants then tyrannize you, dominate you, and do with you what they want. To avoid fear, you do anything. With your light, you can confront fear; without it, you obey the master of darkness and you do what he wants because you fear him. To give power away is the worst thing — without power you have no freedom, because you renounce consciousness, and in unconsciousness you are slave.

The new entering of light – alignment – casts light upon the tyrants for you to confront them, recognize them, and claim your power: the one you have given them. This new light raises the frequencies of vibration and obsolete structures fall, those that tyrannize you inside and outside, and the tyrants of darkness outside won't be able to continue controlling humanity, because humanity will claim its power. The coming light will show what is happening and what has been happening, and the play that has been taking place here for such a long time: there are going to be a lot of surprises. But the light will be able to bring to light this fact, and people will be able to see for the first time in millennia, what they have done with their power, with what purposes and who owns it.

The final battle, the fight for the power of humanity, goes hence from the hands of darkness to the hands of light. From the hands of darkness inside of you to the hands of your light, the ones of your Higher Self, and to the hands of the global light, instead of being in the hands of the reigning obscurity.

This awakening happens activating the consciousness of the Inner Self, or Christ Self, of each one. As the veil that separates each person from light, keeping him in unconsciousness goes away, his light activated through the grace of God and free from the structures that chained him, he will radiate as the most brilliant sun and with his sword of Christed Power, he will cut the veils, the cobwebs, the structures, to bring freedom to every human being and to the planet. The system cannot be freed if every human being does not claim his power and his freedom. The liberation has to be done from within. Otherwise it would be a free system but every being would still be slave of his inner tyrants and would always look for something or someone to whom to give his power.

The light entering now is going to allow each being to realize what he has done and what he is doing with his power, and from his awakened Christ Self, he will act in consciousness and end the deceit that he has accepted and in which he is immersed. Structures fall and all this process of light will allow to create new ones based on Love and Truth. This will take some time and it will be done not without resistance by some, those who insist on living in fear.

In the union with light there is no fear. It is the union with the Source, with the Father, with the Creator. The path from this moment on is to recognize fear – unmask it – confront it, to resist fear with faith, decision, courage until it abdicates – backs down, and surrenders – and you are free. We must always unmask fear. It is what makes you act in those "strange" ways out of balance, harmful – for yourself or others – without love. That brings more and more fear and keeps you acting that way. Whoever seeks to be free from fear will receive my help and assistance, my support and my strength and that of Saint-Germain.

Confront fear and you will see who it is. It is like a frightened child who turns into a tyrant, and directs like puppets, his partners and their children — guilt, anger, control, frustration. Those are your inner ghosts, the ones you have to eradicate and cast out forever with the sword of Power and Freedom, the sword that I bring you.

Beloved ones receive my initiation, my assistance with an open heart. I am your great ally. Act with faith always and you will live the rewards.

Always in the name of Freedom and the Power of God.

I Am Archangel Michael

•

You can now go to the activation of power from Archangel Michael section, *The Jewels of the Stargate*, or you may wait until you get there following the book.

We Have Stellar Origins

As we should know or perceive at this moment, we are stellar beings. Earth is a planet that was created at some point in time. This means it has not always been here. So if life is eternal and our souls are too, most of us come from somewhere else in the Universe. Some of you might clearly know this; others might have some intuition about it already. Whether you know it or not, you have cosmic origins and connections. To track these stellar origins there are a number of things you can do. You can mainly ask your Higher Self for information or revelations, or even activate that stellar contact in you. Later on in the section *Practices for Ascension*, there is a meditation to activate this connection.

The Equation of the Universe

"The Universe is not defined;
what defines it is your faith."

This means that you introduce an element into the equation of the Universe and create, from what you believe. Creation is power. Power creates. The more power you have the more you can create. If the Universe was set – a closed equation – you could not create, it would all be already done, predefined and you would just join it and follow its pattern. We have the power of creation given to us as part of our divine gifts. So we are creating all the time. If the Universe was not an open equation, there would be nothing to do, nothing to add and life would be useless. It would become a process where thinking would not be necessary, a system in which humans would have no power and therefore would follow rules and patterns; they would be like robots. That's not evolutional. Such life would be pointless. Beings have choice and create. Sometimes they create goodness and a wonderful reality; other times they create hell. We are creative beings in a creative Universe in which everything is possible: the limit... you set it yourself. This is obvious but not to everyone with this clarity and conscience. I mention it because if you are more conscious of this you can really use how things are, rather than looking at life half-heartedly and missing out on using all that is available to you: power and unlimited possibilities. Power and unlimited possibilities? What more could you want? Everything can be done with that.

Live the reality that you are the power, and the Universe an open equation that can manifest your vision. The equation has two elements that combined produce a result. One of the elements is fixed: there are certain conditions to every situation and the Universe has an order. The other element is a blank space for you to place your call; the result is unknown. But if you are doing things right it will be close to your dream.

Imagine that the condition is that whatever is introduced in the equation, it will be multiplied many times. The open option is what you are going to put in it, and that will be empowered. So if you put in good wishes, you will get loads of good wishes back. Let's say that the fixed part has a variable side: you can define how much your own variable will be multiplied by. And then we are getting very close to how the Universe really works; it is a field of prosperity. It is a fertile field: you sowed something, you harvest it multiplied. You say what you want and you have faith in that. The Universe creates it; it generates abundance in that direction, as the fertile field of prosperity that it is. So you already have a tremendous power, although you might not realize it. The way the Universe is configured gives you all the power. It is a powerful game. And the Universe is a powerful system of reality creation. This way everybody gets what they create, what they have decided to focus on, and depending on the faith they had in it. People are creating their own realities all the time without noticing what they are doing most of the time.

"The Universe is a field of prosperity"

So how do you use the equation? You define the amount of times you want something multiplied by; this is your faith. You decided what it is you want to have expanded; this is what you concentrate on, where your mind is: your dream. It might be goodness; you will receive goodness according to the amount of faith you have. You want to focus on fear. You will have abundance of that according to how much you believe in that.

The Universe is a quantum equation; it is unlimited. The only one limiting it is you. Since it is open one of the results you can get in the equation is limits, since that is one of the possibilities. You can play the game you want. You create your own version of your life with the limits you set for the Universe.

Ascension energies are removing limits in people so they can perceive with clarity that this state of the Universe is real, and to realize they are creators and can create the reality they want.

The Way of the Enlightened Universe

As we have just seen, most people have believed that the Universe is set and fixed: a closed system already defined. And because they ignore how things are, they live a reality of limitation and despair. But due to the great number of people doing this and their slowness and often inability, to change their paradigm, a paradigm change is being motivated from above, from the spheres of Spirit. This is the Stargate. It aims to awaken people to the fact that power is theirs, and resolves the present need to recover what they own. So they are free to create from the power of a liberated consciousness, the type of reality that will most benefit them. It is not that choice is not true anymore; it is that an awakened person will always chose what makes sense: goodness for all. And that is true service, the way of the enlightened Universe. So service comes from awakened consciousness and the right use of power.

The awakening is about taking people to their real potential state, not choosing for them. But in that they have the true option to stop believing that they are limited and without power. Since that option is made available to all, they can all choose again the type of reality they want. If awakened enough they will chose to create a reality for the benefit of all. The way they do it is up to them, and that will be very welcomed by the Universe as an act of individual creation that seeks the benefit of all. And it will fulfill the individual's drive and personal style of living, and that which makes him or her tick: if he feels a musician, he will do it creating music. So there is a fantastic choice open for all in this New Age: to realize one's dreams by serving in the personal style through the use of the recovered divine power within. We see that the issue of how the Universe works is intimately related to the issue of service: they will happen together. It makes all the sense: such a huge system would have to go in that direction because it is the only way it could perpetuate itself, if it was going to manifest as individual consciousness with free will and power. It is the only way to maintain itself, generate love and motivate unity.

The Downfall of Human Power

Most of humanity uses power for its own interests. People use power to dominate and for selfish motives — too often to attack others. Human beings in their wrong vision of life, use power against others and to acquire things in wrong, non-divine ways. Throughout the history of humanity people have wanted to accumulate power to dominate others. So in this humanity disconnected from the divine, there has always been slavery. Slavery has always been present in one way or another. In the human madness, people have thought for too long that if they had power they could use it to attack others, destroy them or make them slaves or prisoners. This is happening today. Amazingly there are still too many people and some nations using power in this abominable way. One of these situations is

China's attack on Tibet, which started decades ago and is still going on.

Now perhaps the obvious slavery of not so long ago has been abolished, but there are other types of it, just as terrible, that are hidden away from view And the most generalized slavery is that of the Matrix of the Dark, which has humanity as a whole enslaved in the ways we have seen. Power comes from God. Human beings get power from this loving and benevolent source. But one cannot use this divine universal supply to harm the life of other divine creatures, who have been given the same life by the divine creator. Acting that way shows the most abominable blindness, produced by ego's self importance that has ever been in the Universe. Using divine resources like power against the life God Himself has created brings a terrible karma.

In this era of change, more divine power and light are constantly manifesting to set things right on the planet. Those manifestations of misused power are being brought to the light, one by one so they can be widely rejected, condemned and stopped. There is a long way to go in this respect, but it is happening all over. Hidden, obscure agendas of power are being frozen by the beings of light and the spheres of divine will for the good of all and the ascension of Earth. Many of those are unseen actions that are happening as the spheres of light move what is necessary to free humanity from this terrible use of power and from the dark agendas of the Matrix of the Dark. There is a lot more going on than what people can see happening. That is changing the planet and shifting dark agendas for those of the light.

Everybody has to start using power for good. There are many people already doing this, who have understood that power is to be used correctly, and many have become merged with divine power to a point where they let it act and lead their lives without ego interference. They don't try to act with power; power acts through them. This is when they become really powerful and influential for the good of all. They are pure and have no ego agendas. So divine power supports them for the manifestation of the divine plan through them. People using power in those old ways are being pushed aside and progressively isolated until they either leave the planet or they transform to the ways of the light.

It is mad and sick to use power to destroy life. Power should be used to create beauty, goods, joy, life, to help people to get ahead. Nations should help others to move ahead and advance. Power is a wonderful tool for life. It should be used correctly and then we will have a wonderful world of peace, joy and evolution.

I Am: The Return to the Higher Self

"I Am" is the higher spiritual presence, what has been called your Higher Self. It is the highest part of you and contains all the divine attributes for you. In reality, it is you. The ego awareness is a small version of yourself, not what you truly are. It is indeed very diminished. All spiritual paths talk about going to and merging with the "I Am," the Higher Self or True Self. This is because we are experiencing and manifesting much less of that Self experience of being that which we truly are. And because it is the only sensible place to go: all the resources lie there. We have contracted, lost a lot of our spiritual experience and therefore have become limited, deluded and confused. The return to the Higher Self is the recovery of our true state of being and of consciousness; the return to truth, power, clarity and love; in a word: true joy. "I Am" is the individualized God for every being, and the part we must get to know and own. There lie all the powers and divine gifts. It is what Jesus manifested as a divine presence because he had realized his High Self. The Christ and the Christ powers reside in it. Only when we realize this truth fully we will be experiencing ourselves as we truly are: perfect, luminous and immortal. This is the place where we are going in the Ascension, and we are getting there with the impulse of the divine energies of light brought to us by the Stargate.

With them we are returning to the mighty presence of our spiritual selves, the place where we will be fulfilled, where we will recover our full power and we will be free from all limitation and lack. It is the door to infinite bounty.

So as our Higher Self holds everything for us we must go
there to get whatever we need. It is our source of everything.

If I need confidence, I ask for it from my "I Am" presence.
If I need faith, I get it from my "I Am" presence.
If I need realization, I ask for it from my "I Am" presence.
If I need clarity, I receive it from my "I Am" presence.

The Play is Over:
Returning to God Consciousness

Everything in life is God in disguise. Everybody is God with a mask; everybody is acting the disguise, instead of acting God through it. The consciousness of God is in a state of unconsciousness, sleeping inside everyone. The play is over. The new energies are here to change that. Those energies seek the divine part of each one and activate it. The result of this is that people will progressively start to recognize they are divine. This process is a process of divine realization. The acquisition of divine power inevitably comes with it. This truth is not new; it is in the old spiritual texts of India, especially those known as the Vedas. It is contained in the teachings of most religions in a veiled way: God is everywhere... So He is in everyone... So everyone is God. This is the new "religion" the true one: the same for all, and this one is real. People have the opportunity to move from human consciousness to God consciousness — the truth about themselves. This is Stargate: the journey to the fifth dimension

Prayer

"Divine Father I open to receive your
blessings in the divine, perfect way in
which you manifest them for me."
                    - Amen.

Summary of the Present Situation

As a result of entering into the planetary system of high vibrational energies, this is what the scenario looks like:

- High vibration in the Earth — Due to high spiritual energy
- Strong emotional crisis: polarization of emotions
- The mind is set off; it becomes extreme in its attitudes
- Light separates from obscurity
- There is no longer a grey planet as a result of communion of light and dark
- The planet goes to the light — The dark leaves the planet
- It is the moment to decide on which side you want to be — no "buts."
- But beware of the darkness inside you, because according to how you act, you might be an accomplice of the plan of obscurity without noticing it
- That is why people are polarizing to the extremes:
- Those who want war; those who want peace
- Those who want light; those who want darkness
- Those who serve the plan of the light
- Those who serve the dark purposes
- Those who serve the ego; those who serve God

THE DARK

*"Darkness just wants the power
for itself, for its purposes."*

The World Matrix: The Prison of Power

Power is not present in the human being. This is not a normal
situation. Power has been taken away from people for eons of time
on Earth. Where is this power? There is a dark system that has a dark
agenda based on keeping people in ignorance. To do that, it needs
to hold people's power, so they can accept the terms of the system
without questioning. And this is what is going on. For if you take a
step back a number of things stand out.

We are immense beings created in the image of God. Why, then, do
people die? Why is humanity so helpless before illness, so vulnerable
to weather conditions? Why are there constantly millions of people
dying of hunger when there is enough for everyone and everybody
knows it? Why do most people have to work a lifetime, often in
extreme or hard conditions, to receive enough to live or survive?
And who do they work for? Mostly systems with the main objective
of enriching themselves creating goods and services, but that make
people dependent on them. So the system is perpetuated. Doesn't
that look from outside like a herd of millions who are supporting a
system that milks them? It is a big system of slavery that is so big
that no one questions. So big that everyone seems to accept it as the
reality.

How much of all that the world offers is really needed? How many
of those needs are created, false? And don't those have everybody
going crazy, trying to fulfill them? And is not all that taking people
away from God and the spiritual reality? This is why there is life in

the first place…but who doesn't want to emphasize that, and why? Once you start asking, the questions keep coming and it is scary. That is also why most people don't ask them. The big question is:

What is really going on in this planet?

How can a system do something, create goods and have everybody going crazy over them? *Power*. This is the answer: by holding people's power. The system is a prison of power. The agenda that rules the system, the forces and beings that are behind the system are the Matrix of the Dark. This is the hidden agenda that moves everything on the planet. It is invisible. The people behind it are unseen. Politicians, financial institutions, and governments are mostly serving those dark agendas. Many don't even know it. For a Matrix of the Dark like this to exist we must understand that there are people and beings that want it there.

People go after anything new that the system creates because they seek that lost power and live the illusion of living a life of power with them, feeling they have power through them. While the system goes on creating things that give little drops of power to people so they feel happy. In this way, they are controlled.

"Lack of power creates fear."

This is the way people are controlled. People need to acquire things to feel some power and stop feeling the fear. But that is not solving the problem: the essential void of power inside. But it is a deceit that most people fall for. In this way the system has made people forget a great deal about God, the real source of power, taking the place of God, by giving people toys of power. Real power is not there. Real power is in the connection with the inner energy, the real consciousness, the divinity inside: God. It is in the sovereignty that comes from a connection with that power source, the sovereignty that comes from a *real* free will that only comes from that connection.

You have it all inside. I mean everything. All the power, all the ability to create from that power, to be happy and fulfilled. If you live it, then you become still and peaceful and the world outside holds no power over you, no appeal, no attraction. You have harnessed so much power going within, that you have found this is the real power, the real you. And it is all inside: infinite treasures of ecstasy, love and freedom that manifest in the way you are, the way you live. So you look at the world in a different way. What can it give you when you are independent in your power and joy? Your supply of them is free; it is independent from the world and so is your joy. So you don't need the world's creations to fulfill you; you can enjoy them or leave them or both.

If everyone found power inside, can you imagine what would happen to the world system? Yes, it would collapse. It is of no interest to the hidden powers that control everything and the world itself to promote and expand such truth. That is why power has always been hidden and people programmed to find, buy and consume things and power outside to make their lives "full." This emancipation of the individual and humanity is inevitable now; and it will be the downfall of the planetary system: the World Matrix of Darkness, the prison of power.

The Matrix of the Dark: The System

*"The Matrix of the Dark
is what rules the system."*

We are inside the Matrix of the Dark. All that you can see is unreal. It is a hologram; we are inside it. We need a three-dimensional, physical body to enter into this world. There is karma inside the Matrix of the Dark. From the moment you are born you give the power outside to systems, rulers in the dark. This is part of the equation of being born here.

The Matrix of the Dark is an energy structure like a grid. You are inside it; you don't see it and cannot act outside it. This structure contains the global belief system and holds people's power. When you are born, you are born inside a planet with this structure. You acquire it energetically; it is part of the subconscious mind. Parents and educators teach it to you as if it was the truth; they believe it is. They cannot teach anything different because this is the truth for them. They are faithful to it and live for it. Inside this matrix set up, there is a program of loyalty, a parameter that says you have to be faithful to her. And when you are not you feel guilt, you feel treasonous, you feel that you are not being good with others, with the system, with what they taught you; you feel that you are going against the system and against everyone. This is so strong that is unbearable, and you renounce going against it. But keep reading... there is light at the end.

All this creates people's behavior, dictating a way of being and living. In this condition people feel "this," think "that," and they act in certain ways, living a number of assumed truths that are not but which people defend intensely as if they were. Remember that it is invisible... this is very hard to see. They believe that they are deciding, thinking and feeling their own things, and they are not. It is the matrix in them which dictates their thoughts, feelings and actions through that programming which is fixed in them as a belief system, that presents several possibilities within its limited range, but that it is not free thinking; it is conditioned thinking. It affects everyone's behavior and behavior creates karma, your reality and your destiny.

This is quite hard to accept. It is essential psychology of the subconscious. The belief system is the program everyone has as humans. This program says what goes and what doesn't. It has the definitions of what to believe, say, accept, feel and think in life situations within a certain range, but that doesn't allow anyone to go beyond those assumed false truths. It defines what is good and what is bad; what you can do and what you can't. This is not a very free state. It doesn't mean you are a robot. You have a consciousness and a will; it is just that they are in a big part sleeping. That part is taken by the belief system of the matrix.

How it works

Since this programming happens when people are born and in the early years, it is unconscious. You believe it is you, the way you are, until you start questioning what you do and why you do it. Then your consciousness increases and you awaken. You start recovering that part which is sleeping and regain it from the matrix programming making it yours. And you do that by deciding consciously what you want to do, why and how in every area of your life. Essentially how you want to live your life. As implied before, that takes a lot of work, courage and pain. Because you are facing supposed truths assumed as such for all your life up to that point of questioning; and because of the guilt and pressure from the matrix in you, which resists the change, and around you, which is manifested essentially in the way people live and behave. So there is a considerable amount of resistance inside and outside, to becoming free. That is why not many people have done it fully, until now. But the final result is a power and a freedom that has no price and brings a happiness impossible to be reached in other ways.

The systems, political, religious, financial, educational and the rest are the pillars that maintain this entire matrix: they dictate the directions everyone must follow as a herd. Until a person does not become free from this matrix, he doesn't have his power, and he cannot become illuminated, be happy, give true love and ascend.

The Will Retained

*"Only by having your power
are you loyal to yourself."*

The matrix system has made sure to implant enough fear and guilt in the psyche of each human being born on the planet, so that his will is not free. With fear and guilt it is assured that you are not faithful to yourself but to the interests of the system. A free will would be a will without fear and guilt. Such a will would create a revolution like that of Gandhi or Jesus. If there were millions of people like that, they would change the system; it would collapse. A free will would never support a belief system based on control by fear, guilt, manipulation.

Your will must not have partners. The only partner should be God. All partners of your power that are not God will be partners out of interest. And their interest is having part or all of your will. God is the only partner who doesn't act from interest. He only acts to give everything to you. He doesn't want anything from you.

"Your power is only yours; don't negotiate with it."

You want to do something from your free will… you want to be free but you find you have fear; you feel guilt. Your desire, your want, your will is retained, you cannot exercise it freely. It has partners; it cannot act on its own. The will must not have partners. Your will is your property. In having fear and guilt, it is granted; it has been handed over. It has strings that create dependency. It is not an effective will any more. A will with partners gives credit to the partners, it listens to them, and if these partners are fear and guilt, what advice are they going to give? "Careful, don't do this. Don't act. Be fearful." "Don't go against the conventional." This way, you cannot do anything. With a retained will you cannot decide freely and life is lived without questioning oneself.

Maybe the values and the way of life you have adopted as yours and have considered normal, are valuable for you because you have given them a value from what you have seen and learned. Maybe if you reconsider, you will see that doing some or most of those things is not the greatest life for you. This relates to all areas: family, the way you work, what work you do, where you live, what you eat, how you spend your time, who you spend it with. Why do people live in so many ways that don't bring them happiness? Why do people do so many things that damage them? And are so well accepted by society… but are killing them? There are many assumptions, many ghosts, which people don't want to face. Each ghost you don't face stays alive. And if it is alive it acts.

To take your power and resurrect your will is to take everything you do and question it. In doing it, you actualize it and decide if you're doing it because you want to or because they taught you this was the way, and you are doing it out of habit. Then you can be the one living your life.

Belief Systems

A belief system creates a specific destiny. That is its power. A belief system configures a structure, an internal galaxy that guides us through life. It is like the map of people's lives. When you believe a certain thing, power is given to that belief. That power is not in you anymore; it is in the belief. That belief is being held as truth. That limits you because it will be that belief that will define your reality. In a word: you are limiting your power. Your power is total, infinite, limitless. You are capable of creating anything with it in you and in your life. Why? Because you are a spark of the Creator and for Him, everything is possible.

**People give their power to the outside,
through their belief systems.**

This outlines the way of seeing and living and therefore of experiencing life. This will determine your experience, and thus your destiny. Jesus said, "According to your belief, it will be." So giving power to a belief system or to a force outside is very grave because it creates a destiny. A specific belief system creates a specific destiny.

This is what it believes and therefore what it creates, thus giving power to its condition and accepting that condition it means it is the one life is going to manifest.

A belief system creates conditions. It is an intermediary, a usurper of power. You allow it to act instead of you acting directly from an openness and neutrality. It stops you from following what your heart says. So you follow mental logic, not heart logic. Mental logic comes from what has been learned, and from being faithful to an acquired belief system, not from being faithful to oneself. Coming from the heart is to be faithful to oneself. Observe how much of your life is ruled by limiting beliefs. Observe how your belief system takes power away from you. Start breaking those beliefs and change them for a belief in power in which there are no limits. Use the new energies available for that. The truth that belief systems offer is not the real truth. It is a partial and distorted vision of reality. They were created by the Matrix of the Dark to outline a limiting reality and freedom to control people and humanity so they would not be free.

The reality, the truth, is a field of all possibilities, complete and without limits. This is where we are going with the Stargate. This is the option that opens to humanity now. But when you enunciate something different than this, it becomes a belief not a truth — a limiting belief of that reality. What happens in your life then, is what you allow. And that is what you accept as possible through your beliefs, and you leave out what you don't accept. And that can be your greatest dream or the highest possibility of life for you... but you did not conceive it as possible.

"You limit your power through a limited belief system."

From a limited belief system comes guilt and fear. You must believe in all possibilities. Simply believe; don't limit what you believe. Believe in life, believe that everything is possible. This is what you are going to create. And above all, believe in yourself. This means that you can do anything and create the life you want and be what you want. Believing in yourself does not place any limit on the full manifestation of your divine power. You must seek to be aware of your belief system of limits and change it for a system of power: one that puts power on you.

Keep alert

Being alert allows you to tap into your power and avoid falling on obsolete beliefs. It means keeping alert to realize when you adopt limiting beliefs or continue living those that you have accepted from the time you adopted them. It means being alert to see what makes you feel guilty, when you act like a prisoner of guilt and fear and when you give your power outside. Being alert is the key.

Guilt & Fear:
Instruments of the Matrix of the Dark

Guilt and fear are dark instruments of the matrix. Guilt is the perfect example of giving power away. Guilt kills you. It breaks you down, destroys you, corrodes you; it finishes you as a human being. Guilt is a way to minimize your self-esteem and not love you. Give your guilt to God; free it. What frees you from it is releasing it; don't hold it. Stop accusing yourself and seeing yourself as impure; stop flagellating yourself and give guilt to God and surrender. He makes you worth it; He returns your power to you. But you have to first let go of it, saying in this way you don't want that. You must give yourself in to your inner innocence. To become free is to have the courage of not judging yourself, allowing yourself to be in peace.

**Guilt is the best invention of the matrix system
for getting people to give power outside.**

Fear convinces you of things that are not true. It convinces you that there are reasons to doubt; it convinces you that you are vulnerable. It is the instrument of the Matrix of the Dark. You are invulnerable in God. Your faith convinces you of the good and tells you what is true. People who are full of doubt are full of fear. Between fear and guilt people live in paralysis. What people are most afraid of is being free. In truth, what you are afraid of and what you feel guilty about is of being free.

If you are not faithful to yourself hundred percent, you are giving your power outside. And guilt and fear don't let you be faithful to yourself. Thus allowing the external world and others to control your life and will. The inner tyrants are the ones that don't let you have power and be free, you give it to them, to fear and guilt. And you don't use power because you leave fear and guilt to decide for you. People don't generally decide to go against fears; they allow them and don't want to assume their power: they fear that. People must start to dare to have their power. People need to trust and to surrender all fear to God. Surrender all worries — do not hold them — to let them go in peace and serenity.

People must recover power, freeing themselves of the beliefs that move them to renounce it, and thus, they will start to hear and recover contact with their inner voice, changing belief systems for inner voice guidance. This is the voice of personal power. All this happens on the way to recovering who they are, freeing themselves from fear and guilt that are the denial of what they are. Free from these weights we recover faith and confidence in ourselves to be who we want to be and make our dreams true. This way people stop going against themselves and support their life and happiness, instead of destroying them. This changes the belief of what they have to be and replaces it with the truth of who they are, so they can live it. In recovering power you recover your capacity for discernment and say no to what you don't want and what is not for you. You are faithful to yourself, which is the key to happiness. You value yourself and acquire confidence, independence, strength, clarity and serenity with which you live life. Assuming one's power is the way to be who you have come here to be. You will be *you* with all your potential; you will be in peace. And you will make the greatest creation you can of yourself and of your life.

If you find negative emotions when you want to act what your heart says, that is not the heart but the dark side that covers it. If there is no motivation in you to act for the good, you need to purify your heart intensely. One thing is the heart and another the layers that cover it with resentment, pain and fear. Those are the layers, not the heart. Those must be cleaned first. When acting what the heart says, you might encounter negative feelings; what you feel is in the emotional body, not in the heart. And the emotional body of most people is full of negative emotions. You must differentiate what is truth from what is pain. Acting in pain just creates pain. Acting from love generates love.

Notice that when you feel guilt, you feel guilty of being yourself, of doing what you feel in your heart, of following what comes out of it. And we are talking about good things that you deserve. Freeing yourself from fear and guilt is one of the key steps in your process of ascension.

●

"Fear doesn't let you surrender."

Evolution of the Matrix System

The institutions, often so apparently compassionate, which were created to solve all problems humans have, are there solving them... But because those problems are created in an absence of power, and that is why most of the institutions are there. So yes, there is compassion in this world, but my dear sister, brother there is a higher compassion that wants you to have the power that you can have, so you do not enter into most of the problems human beings have at present, and so you do not need those institutions to solve your problems, whether they be financial, religious, political, health or something else. When humans recover their power, those institutions will be transmuted into services that will enhance people's power through the recognition of it globally. Whereas now they support the system of lack of power because they represent big daddy, which is going to solve people's problems, those created precisely by the global absence of power. Yes, dark forces are at play behind the world systems, for as things remain as they are, power is in the hands of the dark rulers: servants of the Matrix of the Dark system. A system fed by people just like you, who still believe in it and keep feeding it with that precious power. It is dark because it takes light – power – away from people, and thus it lives at the expense of them.

But as long as every human being is not awakened to the awareness that he is the sovereign of his life and power, it will be so, and there will be self-appointed managers willing to take and administer people's power for their own benefit. This is what has been and still is going on on this planet. Not for long.

Collapsing of the Matrix of the Dark

The intense influence of the Matrix of the Dark has diminished considerably in the last few years. It diminished before the Stargate opening, with some important preparations at the higher energy levels of the planet, and has diminished intensely since 1999, at the opening itself. This has made the Matrix's influence weaken to the point of not being enslaving and limiting like before. But the residual world it created is still there. And it continues to influence in an important way. Nevertheless it is receding, giving space and freedom to create another paradigm. Now there is the weakening of the Matrix of Dark due to the new energies of the Stargate, and it is possible to look at the other side, that of the light. The intense light coming in through the Stargate opening is literally shaking the dark structures and the Matrix of the Dark is collapsing. New energy and light structures are being built in the planet. There is a choice on the planet like never before. People can keep looking at the old world or look at the new world. People can chose to look at the new possibilities of light. Many people still want to look at the old ways, old habits, the contracted ways devoid of love. But for those who want a new world of light, love and freedom it will be there; they can choose it and have it. This will not be an easy task generally. To change one reality for another is a huge mission, which requires sustained effort, to retrain the mind and also commitment to change.

Still the dark agendas are there. The codes infiltrated into everything in the planet keep playing their part. But it is the time to recode the whole thing and to do it with light and truth. So it is so important to look inside oneself and see what is going on there, what has been put there over the years, and see those dark contracted ways, thoughts and belief systems based on pain, fear and limitation and discard them. All that doesn't serve any good purpose any more. It is like waste that has to be eliminated and substituted for new structures of light. Certainly, there are many who have no interest in things changing. They are happy to live in the ego with how things work, with the toys and sensations of the third and fourth dimension, with material possessions and not opening the mind and the heart. But as with everything, there is a choice. The ways of the light are there opening for everyone. This is a time of global opportunity for all.

The whole world is in this process of turning over the dark ways for new structures of light. The old planetary structures were based on fear, control, lack of power and absolute lack of truth. Now new ones are being created based on truth and light, literally. The inertia of the old ways is still keeping the matrix functioning, together with the rulers of the dark, those beings that still want to hold the dark systems for the planet and don't want to let go. Like a big ship that stops the engines but is still moving, the Matrix of the Dark still holds onto planetary control. But every day the hold of power, the sustaining of the dark agendas, is weakening progressively and people are finding a new space to function and create another paradigm.

It is as if some wild horses had been closed in, surrounded by a fence for all their lives. One day the gate opens and they can choose to get out. The fence is still there, but the possibility to get out is there for every horse that wants it. It is the same with human beings. Now the door is open and one can get out of the known world, the matrix, to another world, more expanded and better with more possibilities. This is so for whoever wants to get out of the old paradigm. Power is retaken and one can come out. A new paradigm can be created; freedom is available. As with the horses, not everyone will choose freedom, but it is there for those who want it. This light will eventually bring a freedom in which people will be able to completely choose a new reality. In this new freedom you will be able to actualize your life and create the world you want, for yourself and others. Let's see more of that.

THE LIGHT

A New Age of Light

"What Stargate brings is light."

Stargate is bringing a new light that is completely changing the Earth and its functioning. That is a huge thing. It means freedom from the Matrix of the Dark. This event, brings changes in all planetary structures based on fear and absence of light and designed to take people's power from them. Stargate is acting to create new planetary structures based on light and truth, and it will empower the individual and the whole. It will create structures to serve people instead of the present ones that enslave people. This equation of freedom has two parts:

The liberation of the system: Freedom from the *Matrix*
Illumination, Christification: Entering the *Light*

Freedom from the Matrix of the Dark

You have to increase your vibration, your frequency to be free from the matrix. This is the essential you need to know and to focus on. Nothing will do as much as this. In doing this the energy grid of the matrix inside you weakens, and you start to come out and start to see and be amazed. You go on acquiring power. The matrix is inside and outside. Inside, it is configured in your mind, and outside, it is placed in the etheric, the invisible energy field around the Earth. It is also inside the energy fields in which all of humanity moves. You have to free it inside you, and then you will start to see it outside. As you do so, it will loosen its grip on you.

The high frequency energies of the Stargate shake and dissolve the matrix inside your mind. Then you start being filled with light and consciousness. The awareness brought about by the Stargate shows you the wrong beliefs and gives you initiations for different aspects of your consciousness, to grow and liberate yourself. You must want to be free with all its consequences. This means your will must be in line with this process to succeed. You have to desire your power above anything else, above anything inside that will say, "No, no" – the matrix trying to survive in you. You need to free yourself of all the comfort that presupposes staying there and not coming out free. You have to be prepared to say no without negotiating and not do what you don't want to do, to face the manipulation of your mind. You have to be prepared to listen to your heart and your truth like never before. You have to be ready to question everything, revising the way you live and act.

The matrix manifests in things like "I cannot do this; now I should be doing that." You can notice it is always the denial of the individual will. While you are faithful to something that is not you, the matrix will be safe. Beware, since if you are faithful to yourself and start having power and thus freedom, the matrix is in danger and starts to spy on you. It watches you. How? Through all its keepers: your belief system and the outside, through the belief system in others, which will react to you behaving with more power and freedom; and through the people who behave as "it is supposed to." The belief system of the matrix is suspicious of anything that acts differently and thinks differently. As you recover more power and freedom, you will question many of the things of the matrix and its behavior when you see it in people. You create a distance from the common places of the matrix, its ways and places. You will seek your own space and time to be with your inner self and to listen to it. You will need to be with yourself and your inner voice, your solitude, your feelings. You are hearing a different voice inside: the one of your truth. You are alive.

While you are thinking what everyone thinks, you are close; while you are where others are and do what others do at the time they do it, all goes well. When you start acting differently, you start being "far;" you create a distance from the matrix and its system. When you behave differently, you become a challenge to it. This is good.

Getting out with your power

If you have to recover your power, where are you going to get it from? What is the source of power? Where does all power come from?

God Source.

Thus power recovery turns into a spiritual issue and is inevitably a matter of connecting with God. It is a theme of turning to God. And for that, you have to turn inside.

God and the Matrix of the Dark are opposed.

One takes power away from you; the other gives it to you. This gives us a different view of God as an ally and best friend, different from the dogmatic vision of control, rules and separation of the distorted, classical and false vision portrayed by some religious convictions.

*"When I recover my power, I
fear nothing. Fears don't haunt
me, don't give me insecurity."*

Entering the Light

"The issue is the state of being"

A log is inert, opaque, still. When you put fire to it, it starts getting hot. When fire goes, coals remain: its matter emanates light. Then it is luminous; it has become crystallized. We could use the term *Christified.* This is entering the light, becoming it. This is an alchemical process.

Human beings go through the same process: they become Christified through the action of superior energy. In the case of the log, it is through the action of an energy superior to its own: fire. The log increases its vibration and becomes more illumined through it. When this happens with human beings we talk of ascension: spiritual ascension. Then people become filled with light, emanate light and increase their consciousness, and thus their power and love. They become free and experience peace. It is a similar process to that of the log. Higher spiritual energy increases the vibration of a human being, filling him with light; the vibrations increase his frequency so much that he emanates light: becomes radiant. That is what the halo of the saints exemplifies.

In this ascension, karmas disappear; they are burnt by the intense light. We need this ascension, this Christification. This is what is happening on Earth with the energies of Stargate. What is the situation of the human being? Low light. The issue is the amount of light you have as a human being; that tells how high you vibrate. The more light the better things go and the better you feel. The more light, the more spiritually evolved you are. The Christification we are talking about is like the one of Jesus in which he becomes Jesus the Christ. He became Christified in contact with the light of God. He became luminous, thus showing the way for every human being. This is the way for everyone.

It is a matter of being in the love, in the light. Goodness and love. Staying there. That protects you from low vibrations. Everything is according to how you vibrate. You allow fear and doubt to enter; you lower your vibration and you go down. You are in love, peace, light, and forgiveness, and you go up; you elevate your vibration. Light conquers all. You think of someone positively, and you help them come out of their problems. You think in the world with love and send light to it and it comes out of its crises.

If you resist darkness, it becomes stronger.
If you send light to it, it dissolves.

•

Now the time for Christification has arrived. We go to the light.
This is the mission of the Stargate; this is the destiny of humanity.

Considerations About This Planetary Moment

- The system is breaking down – you are dismantling it. Your structures fall; they also fall outside to liberate you.

- Now the system is based on the individual giving his power outside.

- Do you need all this consumerism? To be somebody?

- Consumerism: "I acquire from outside and I am. I have my identity, based on consumer habits."

- You need support from outside on things that should be coming from you.
  "I lean on all and I am."

- Now the I am is "I Am," which is Christ Consciousness.

- This is the increasing of vibration, the Christification of man.

- In it, man becomes light.

- Now things are different: you are given the sword of divine power.

- So you cut the ties of dependency upon the external and you are: free – divine – powerful.

- So you take on and assume all responsibility for yourself — all freedom.

Questioning Everything: A Matter of Freedom

In order to gain freedom from that equation of limited power, the Matrix of the Dark, and from its life within every individual, as its dark seeds were planted inside everyone at birth, a number of steps are paramount.

- Question what you do and why you do it.
  Is it what you want to do?
  Is it what they have taught you?
  Is it what you believe you must do?
  According to whom? Who are you serving?

- Are you serving your Higher Self of freedom, power, and consciousness? Or the system, the ego, the mind — the matrix?

- Are you following your higher plan?
  Or a dark plan manifested as an unconscious way of life that goes nowhere?

- What is the purpose of your life?

Contemplate

In what areas of your life have you given your power outside?
In which areas are you giving it presently?

*Write down the answers as a reference and make a point to be aware
of how and when that happened or is happening. You can and must,
for your own good, recover your power in those areas.*

Following the Call of Inner Power

You must break schemes, concepts, prejudices, duties imposed on
you from outside sources. You must abide those ones you have
chosen freely. You have to honor your free will because God honors
that, and if He does, no one else can minimize the right of being that
you have been given by the Creator Himself. He has appointed no
one to limit you or to weaken your divine power: a seed of light and
love given by the Creator from the origin of Creation.

The key to this process is self-observation and questioning
yourself. Observe, as you act during the day in your daily tasks and
relationships, how and where you are accepting your duties and
tasks as given by outside forces, or when those duties come from
your own authority and willingness to take them on, as part of your
co-creation of realities with other human beings. Observe how the
best outcomes come from non-dependent co-creation of different
parties that enter a situation for the benefit of the many, including
themselves. See how in those situations, there are no selfish forces
coming into play. Those are the signs of people acting in freedom
from their liberated powers. When that happens everybody is happy
and there is no resentment in the outcome, because everybody acted
in the understanding that the responsibilities taken were a free act
of choice. And everyone assumed their part knowing the necessity

to come into the play from that awareness, to create the beneficial outcomes that were projected from clarity of purpose, responsible freedom and teamwork with the perspective of mutual cooperation and empowerment.

Affirmations

"I am the power of God in me."
"I am the freedom."
"I am the power."
"I am free choice."

"Here and now, I am completely free, in
all areas of my being and my life; from
my cells to the totality of my consciousness."

Power is Non-Negotiable

"Don't give your power outside.
Don't give it away under any pretext or reason.
Don't give your power outside under any circumstances."

If you want to be free from the influence of the Matrix of the Dark you must observe the above. Your power must be from now on, non-negotiable.

Many public personalities — power figures, so to speak — hold a tremendous amount of power. Some are priests, doctors, lawyers and, of course, politicians. The power they have is because people give it to them at first. Then many abuse it and take more of it from the collective. Of course, this comes from the belief that they know things or have faculties others don't. They know as far as they have been trained and practiced. They don't know everything. Their knowledge is limited. I have seen doctors being too quick in going for drastic solutions, strongly recommending radical treatments and things like that. I have also seen the results of that, and they weren't good. You might not know about medicine as an ordinary person going to them, but you know about common sense. And things in the body are there for a reason. There is God medicine. Sometimes it is a life-or-death decision, and one should consider this when acting. But in most cases, there is time to explore and try other alternatives. If you go to a building contractor, he might want to pull your house down. If you go to an architect, he will redesign it. Both are solutions to the same problem. But often the radical solution brings another problem.

Whose decision is it? Let's ask it with another question: Whose power is it? A power figure will act as the holder of power in the situation, a power that ultimately is the person implicated who holds it. The power figure does not have the last word on life, no matter how revered a doctor or priest he might be. I am not against any of those professions; I just use them as a good example because of the power they have been attributed. I want to warn everybody from this standpoint of the abuse and confusion that not owning power has taken people into. We must take away the false reverence of false powers and unmask those who pretend to hold our power. Holy cows are out in these times. So don't make anybody an idol of power. Power over such issues is ultimately yours. If it is given away, it will be taken. So the one you have to watch first is yourself. Doctors, architects, priests, or politicians don't have the last word on anything; they know it. Doctors and lawyers are okay. But they should be used as a support of our own good work in taking care of ourselves. Our health is our responsibility; if the doctor is your best friend, you are becoming dependent and passing on the responsibility which is yours — unless you have an acute condition that needs constant medical supervision or are elderly and quite ill.

There will be readers in those professions, I am aware. If you are one of them, I just hope you are at a level of personal growth that will give you the detachment from many of the standard practices of such power-holding professions, so you can see beyond them and have a greater perspective – wiser and more compassionate – more infused with divine wisdom that makes you an outstanding professional, and that will make this book worthwhile for you.

When someone stands before you and tells you about something as an authority in that field, you should question him and feel in your heart what is valid for you. And that includes myself. Maybe you don't know about that field; that is why you go to an authority. But what you know is whether that feels right in your heart, and when you hear it, you can say, "Yes!" Feel what is valid for you in your heart; you are the sentient authority in your life and have to see for yourself as you reach your own conclusions. Look around; see it for yourself. Validate things from your own core being of knowing.

In feeling, you have truth. You all are the sages of your lives, not the supposed power figures in any field. They will help, advise and point out possible ways. But decisions are yours; responsibility is yours. I might guide you towards yourself. That will be the mark of a true leader: one who won't take your power away. A true counselor will give you the power over you; he will return your power to you — will empower you. This is why feeling has been so lowered and repressed in humanity — eclipsed thanks to the manipulations of the Matrix of the Dark. Feeling is the way of knowing. It has been minimized because, by eclipsing the importance of feelings, people are not in contact with their truth. The truth is in their wisdom, and without it they are able to be manipulated, because they don't know and have to look for wisdom outside.

This is the Matrix of the Dark.
We are changing it for light and power.

"Unmask the idols of power
you have created and be
responsible for yourself."

Salvation is Active

"You save yourself..."

Since humanity is inside this dark system, there is a need to come out. But whether there is such a system outside or not, the fact is that it is inside people's heads: the belief that things are the way they are, and that this is the reality. Human beings need to be saved from this belief; this is what makes their reality.

Salvation is not going to come to you just by sitting there doing nothing. You have to move your heart. God's grace is there. You have to open up to it. If God's grace was enough, everybody would be liberated and saved by now. But it is not enough. God gave us free will. So our intervention is needed. Our part is to open up to it, let darkness go, let go of pain, addiction to bad things, wanting things that don't help us, things that harm us, things that don't bless us. For if we choose those things, God is not going to impose His law forcing His Will on us. We see humanity is a mess. That is not God's Will; that is people's will. It will happen when we choose God. That happens when we have faith in Him, then we get involved in salvation by surrendering, which means we open the door to Him. Then it happens, He enters, we are saved. We are receiving His Will then, His Holy Spirit. It enters but it is not all done. Our salvation is a process; it doesn't happen just in one night. We have to be active in it; we have to keep our focus on salvation and not be convinced by the dark side again that it is the way. We have to work very hard to keep on the right path and also work intently to change, to support and sustain the work of grace inside us, so with it and our effort we can sculpt ourselves to be divinely shaped.

The Holy Spirit enters and purifies us and sets the house in order; that is true growth: spiritual growth. But that takes time and as a process, it has good times and not so easy times, because our addictions are strong and many things have to be ripped from us: attachments we don't need, but which have to be removed if we are to be truly saved. You have engaged with God; God engages with you.

Salvation is Possible with Power

"Ascension is salvation."

The only truth is that you are the whole power; there is no other way to total peace: salvation. There is no power that can take peace away from you. Do not acknowledge any power other than the power of God in you. But we are always doubting, and doubt destroys us. Faith is power; to doubt is to kill faith – believing in you. Therefore power is the way. Your salvation has always been the belief in yourself, your rock in the sea of waves. If you don't believe because you doubt, you already sank. What happened to Peter with Jesus? He was on the water and suddenly he sank. What did the Master immediately say? "Why do you doubt?" He who knows the metaphysical law better than anyone sees it clearly: it fails you because you doubt.

The ignorance and suffering of not knowing what you are, who you are, of being limited, thus without power, is not a good place to be. Salvation is recovering your complete potential in the knowing that you are son or daughter of God, and you perform as such with all the power, not halfway like until now. It depends on you. Thus you have to make the effort to hold the machete and cut the lie within you. The lie that something or someone is going to solve your existence for you. And when you start that job, see what is there: beliefs and dependency on outside forces. And you have to cut your way through them, because it is like a jungle. You have to do the work to reach your freedom. If someone did it instead of you, he would have power over you and that would be total dependency; it wouldn't give you the experience and wisdom that comes from doing it yourself and it wouldn't work. God did not create dependency in his sons; we wouldn't be like Him if he had.

For this to take place you need your power acting; you need to believe in it. But if you don't believe, power won't be there. If power is not there, love cannot work. Thus nothing is happening; life is not happening. So even to love truly, power must be returned to the individual and be active and conscious. If you don't exercise this principle of love you are denying its fact, and you are going nowhere. You deny it and deny yourself, because this is the truth that lives inside yourself: you are love and power. It is like saying, "God has not given me everything." You are deceiving yourself. This is condemnation.

Salvation depends on you; doing what is right for you: recovering your power of love. The most secure and best way of saving yourself is to invoke the power and love of God within you. Recovering the spiritual sovereignty that God put there in the first place. And that is love and power without limits. God is independent. He created you with power and independence through that power. Deny that and you are a zombie at the mercy of more awakened powers, which by their nature can be merciless.

God made you free from the origins. In God we are all free already. It is man who has condemned himself by tying himself in chains, believing in false gods that had something valuable to offer him. Man has deceived himself. God has done nothing to him. Accepting salvation as a power you have been given by God Source of Power, gives you, of course, all the responsibility for your life and evolution. It is for this reason that it has not worked, until now: you placed that responsibility outside. Neither God nor any true spiritual figure will want you to be weak and dependent on them. They will support you, but only on the way of you becoming like them: divinely powerful. Christ himself said it when he spoke the words:

"This and more you will be capable of doing."

There is no point in being a follower of a mighty spiritual figure and being a disciple forever. Even Buddha taught to question him to his followers, and sought to enhance spiritual mastery in them. The point of following a spiritual path or a spiritual leader is to become a spiritually realized being: learning that from someone who has achieved that mastery. Otherwise, what is the point of following a spiritual path? The only sensible answer is to become spiritually realized. At that point one is free and has acquired all power in his union with Divine Power. One then becomes a spiritual path, hopefully to be at the service of leading others in the same way one was helped to get there. From salvation we can show the way to it.

When you place any responsibility outside, you place your power in the hands of others. This has been the great fall of humanity and what has propitiated the state of humanity in utter dependency of external powers. Placing power outside can never work. If you don't do it yourself you do not become saved, since no one can do it for you. Jesus said:

"It is your faith that will save you."

Do we want it clearer? This might generate a certain amount of confusion due to the fact that we have grown with the belief that Jesus or other spiritual figures are our saviors, and we must commend ourselves to them. Yes, but there is a small detail that has been overlooked: you commend yourself to the spiritual power of grace that a spiritual figure embodies, and that is the same spiritual power that resides in you. And to that is the true invocation. That is what can utterly save you. That is a mighty power: it is God in you. In other words, Jesus Christ embodies the realization of the same Christ consciousness in you, which you still have not realized or do not embody fully: you still have to own all your spiritual power. You have to earn your title, of course, through spiritual work. When we say that Christ is in you, in me, we are talking of that light essence of the divine in each one, which is what Jesus attained. Some other people call it *Buddha Nature*, or identify it by another term. It is the same essence regardless of the name used.

We worship Jesus or Buddha, but the true worship happening there is to the spiritual state they have realized, which is the same state I am to embody as an individual. And I worship that state — not the personality — which is the same in me as in someone who has attained it and represents it for me, until I can embody it for myself. I honor that which is highest in me and seek to consciously merge with that higher reality in myself. It makes sense. I want to be free; I invoke freedom. I want riches; I learn from the rich. I want spiritual realization; I invoke spiritually realized people.

But salvation of what? Of the limited condition of a human being, which takes us to a life of misery, lack, suffering and death. Salvation from an illusion we have believed was our reality and true condition. We have to be awakened, saved from such madness. This will only happen with the total, full awakening of the divine in us: divine love and power — by awakening the God seed dormant within us. The grace of God can help; the assistance of Jesus, Buddha or any spiritual master who has the power, the wisdom, and the love to help us get there can be extremely helpful. In that divine awakening, and later divine realization, we cast off the limited human identity and see the unlimited, all powerful reality of our divine state and start living it. Thus creating blessings and bounty from our awakened divine power.

If the human being would recognize the power in him, he would not give it to anyone asking for it; he would reject them. You have the power to heal yourself, of manifesting in your life everything you want, of changing your life and everything in it... but you have to awaken it. Because it is sleeping or partially dormant. Archangel Michael has said for these times:

"Here starts the final battle for consciousness"

The battle to recover our power, our consciousness. Consciousness is the result of recovering our divine state, the result of recovering our power. The battle is so because it is a fight against your inner ghosts, those that take your power away. And it is the hardest battle: it is against yourself; against your ignorance and deceitfulness which is what makes you unhappy and brings you suffering. But they are coming to our aid. This teaching is a wonderful way of receiving this help. Here we are. You receive the keys and an extremely powerful initiation to divine power brought by the very Archangel Michael, later on in the book. He is the archangel of Divine Power.

It is not even you who does it; it is the power of God in you, but you have to open up to it, recognize it for what it is, and allow it to act in you, instead of allowing your ego power to act; it cannot do anything worth mentioning.

"Stargate is about salvation."

Message from Archangel Michael: The Will of God

Let's get into this enlightening message by Archangel Michael about becoming free of darkness by assuming the power of God as His saving Will.

The Will of God

"You only have to open the door to me... to Power, Faith, to the Will of God.

You open the door to faith with faith. You only have to say, "I will." Then you are illuminated with the Will of God. Something you don't see clearly? Difficult? Irresolvable? Offer it to me, to the Will of God. The Will of God restructures all your energies. It is what feeds the flame of fire, of life. The Will of God balances and reestablishes your state of harmony and strength, clarity and vision. Ask:

"Your will be done."

In these times everything has to be offered to the Divine Will to keep afloat. It is equal to renouncing the ego, to recognizing God within and surrendering to Him. It is the wisest thing, the holiest thing. This shows your faith in God; without faith in God there is no healing; without it, where are you going? Without faith in God, you believe in the limited, in darkness, in lack, in death. This is terrible, it is suicide: the denial of life. It is to believe that you are abandoned, alone, lost, condemned. Without faith in God... He doesn't condemn you; you condemn yourself. You choose the lowest levels of existence and you manifest misery in your life: you open the door to it. You enter into fear and fear destroys you: your cells, your energy, your light. It finishes you.

You have to open your heart to faith in God. The moment you recognize He is the Power, you have peace, you become free; everything happens. In faith, everything happens. If you believe in darkness – the opposite of perfect power – you are full of fear and don't have faith. If you have faith and love, the Universe is at your feet. This is why the Violet Light is so great; it is faith and love.

To overcome the darkness in you, you have to have Faith. This is my message, because faith illumines and the dark disappears. God is who can; He is the one who has the power; if you don't have faith in His power, what do you believe in? And then you place yourself at the mercy of darkness so it does to you what it wants. Depression, abandonment, fear, decadence and death follow.

Never move away from Faith.
I am here.
You only have to open the door.

Everything is possible in faith.
Jesus said it: "Everything is possible for he who believes."
Now I remind you: "Everything."
Be in peace.
This is the infinite love of the Father.

I Am Archangel Michael

Prayer
"Archangel Michael protect all humanity.
Awaken the Archangel Michael in all."
- Amen

Invocation
"I am the power of Faith.
I am the strength of Archangel Michael."

- You can continue exploring the ways of freedom from the Matrix of the Dark in the entire book. All this work is to set you free. Essential elements here are *The Warrior of Light,* and the essential connection to activate inner power in a mighty way, section: *The Jewels of Stargate - Initiation on the Sword of Power by Archangel Michael.*

THE DARK SIDE

Your Personal Journey to the Dark

The Inner Dark Side

"Integrate with all of yourself. Be one with it all,
all that there is in you. Do not reject evil in you.
Recover it and heal it in love so there is only love."

We all have a side that doesn't want the light, that resists goodness. It is a great achievement of will and sincerity to recognize it. As in the dream of resurrection, later on in this section, we have a dark side and a part that wants to know; a part that doesn't want to see and another that needs to be liberated and come out of that oppression, that chaining, that tyranny. Thus the dark side doesn't want the other side to see and be free: if the other sees, the dark will end up seeing since they are tied, they are part of the same being. We are divided in an inner fight: liberation and chaining, two forces that oppose and if they are not resolved create chaos inside anyone. The mediocre life of a great part of humanity is due to this unresolved conflict: not having given itself fully to goodness. It is due to still having areas in which the ego doesn't want to yield, give up and let go of that which is grabbing strongly: a power that doesn't do good and that wants to continue holding on by the mere fact of believing it has power. This power is not power; it is resistance. And as we see from the story, the dream, it is very passive. True power is free.

The ghosts are ghosts while they are in the hidden. If they stop being hidden, they stop being your ghosts. They control you; they scare you in the hide. In taking them to the light, they stop being a hidden force over you. When you have become one with the dirt in you,

99

then you will become light. This is the way, the path to follow to freedom. It won't happen by rejecting the gloom inside. Darkness has to be integrated into the light; it has to be illuminated, leaving aside labels and fixed ideas about what you have to be, because you cannot accept that *you* also have a dark side. Rejecting the dark in you makes you a very shallow being, it is like your virtual image, a fake self, and it doesn't feel; it isn't alive. What feels is the other side the imperfect one, made of flesh and bones, the real one, the wounded one which contains the virtues. The heart is in it; it is the one that is alive.

You have to be in the line of the shooting arrow, the one that gives the option of the direct experience of the present. Then you vibrate with life and with what is happening in you. If there is pain or hurt in living it, it will be released and will leave space for love. If not lived, it will be repressed, and the unprocessed feelings will eventually give rise to the dark side and a fake self. This is the one unable to feel; it is not real.

- *"We all have a dark side. It is part of human condition. There is nothing terrible about it. It has to be illuminated, brought to the light."*

The transformation of the dark journey

- Inner immersion
- Regeneration
- Resurrection

After having gone to the deep, dark, painful place of your own hell, like Jesus, then resurrect, ascend.

This alchemy of transmutation creates a process of recognizing, welcoming and integrating our dark side, by which we recover our power and enter into true compassion.

Shadow Manifestations

*"The dark side reacts badly
to the presence of light."*

The dark side, as the inner shadow has a tendency to keep itself alive; it will reject light. This is a paradox: that which will free it sees it as its worst enemy. This is what has created the eternal battle of light and dark so present in the history of humanity, in its literature, films, tales. In fact, dark needs light, but it is so afraid of it that instead of seeing it as its ally and savior, it sees it as its worst enemy. This will be so until dark is ready to face the light and become liberated, becoming what it really is: light.

There are unmistakable signs of the presence of the shadow. They are shadow manifestations. Shadow reacts badly to the presence of light, and those are some signs that detect its presence. This happens in the presence of light or that which represents light. It makes one think of Dracula and legendary vampires that lived in the dark, and the light literally dissolved them. This is because they are symbols of concentrated darkness. Well it is like that; those entities are excellent representations of the qualities of the dark side. These unmistakable shadow reactions happen when people are afraid of something good, for instance, God. Blessings and good things come to you and you become suspicious, or are afraid; you don't trust. It's too much light for the dark side. There is an almost automatic response from the shadow side before these manifestations of light, as rejecting it and declaring it the presence of evil; there is too much light facing it. It is also a relevant sign of shadow presence when people want to overprotect themselves or protect against good things. This is the shadow acting.

Shadow manifestations occur when something happens that challenges the comfort of the personality — when truth comes in. You cannot expect truth to come in and not upset the personality; you cannot expect it to come in silently and not wake everyone up. Truth comes precisely to wake everyone up. That is why Jesus said, "I am not here to bring peace; I am here to bring war." So that truth is known. Personality just wants everything to be nice and comfortable; it does not want anything to be upset. Those are the masks of false comfort the ego wants to live with, in a blinded state of avoiding doing the work of going into the light.

How the Shadow Works

The inner shadow is what makes you not have control of the good. That makes you act impulsively, without reflecting — in unconsciousness. You cannot control it because the shadow has to liberate the tension of being repressed, and then it does things against the will of the conscious part. The shadow was created as an ensemble of all those repressed qualities of consciousness that were rejected, especially through education and conditioning. Basically we repressed being vulnerable, sensitive, soft, tender. Our parents wanted superman and superwoman in their kids; we were not accepted in our natural and spontaneous way of being. All that went to become the shadow part of our nature, and we became divided and therefore unhappy — maybe not consciously. All that happened particularly, as we tried to fulfill the vision our parents had of ourselves, together with the vision of our educators and society. We had to hide and repress a terrible number of things and aspects so we would fit into this neurotic world, and we would become one of them: separated, divided, unhappy. They could not allow someone to be different from what they were. So the cast of unhappy human beings separated inside into good and bad, created a shadow side that minimized our light and perpetuated the unhappy and tensioned race that has populated the Earth for thousands of years.

The other option is too tough for most: being a crusader that grew defending his ideals and feelings to the last consequences, and then he was in a constant battle, being constantly rejected and separated from the rest. A rebel, considered to be someone undesirable, extraterrestrial; probably not far from the truth. I know some of it. But the power, freedom and realization achieved were worth it; that is the path to becoming a free being.

As the shadow was created, tension inside was created too and there started an inner fight. Impulses that do not conform to the conscious role keep pressing to be recognized and keep being repressed. But consciousness is whole; you cannot divide it without paying a toll. It seeks completion all the time, so it returns to its natural state: wholeness. That division is a time bomb; sooner or later the repressed side will have to be recognized and liberated. Until then, it will keep pressing the consciousness for its integration, while the many different problems that arise in the life of any human being, including difficult relationships of any kind, manifest as a "vengeance" of the shadow for the treatment it constantly receives: a lesser kind of being. It will not accept the status of "monster" that darkness often gets and will claim by all means to be accepted as a member of the light. Hence the many different tricks it plays against the will, the manifestation of goodness and the plan you might have for that evening. It has no other way of being recognized, it has been repressed and expected to keep silent; nobody counts on it. But the truth is that the only reason for this fight and revenge is the legal urge of a part of consciousness that has been removed from its right to be. That is all it wants: true recognition. When this happens, the dark side is freed from the terrible dark, monstrous mask, often like that of Darth Vader in *Star Wars*, to show the sweetest and most gentle nature and aspect. As if the mask of the witch when removed, revealed the beauty of Snow White, the true being inside.

Devil or Saint?

"There is no angel without devil."

You feel you are a good person. You try to make everything okay, no matter what. You feel you are holy, in the sense of good, and others see you as a good person. Beware. Are you not faithful to yourself, with all the consequences? Then you should stop having holy feelings about yourself; it is a fictitious holiness. You need to start working on your shadow side; you do not have it recognized and integrated it in order to get to real sainthood. Work on your shadow; see it, accept it, integrate it, because you see it in others but do not recognize it in you. It is a projection; you are disowning what is yours. You project it onto others, thinking it is theirs. This is the way the subconscious works.

Deal With Your Darkness

"You have to reach the point
at which you are able to look
darkness in the eye without
winking."

It is crucial that you stop turning your back on it, your dark side, and see what is in you that you don't want to see. Allow that to manifest in you; don't resist it. Give it recognition; see that this force or presence — be it anger, hatred, bad feelings, jealousy, envy, whatever — is part of you, although it is hidden and repressed. This is not someone else's stuff; it is your stuff. Accept that without fighting it. Just accept that fact. Don't resist it. You are not evil or bad. This is human condition, not an enlightened one. You want to enlighten it. We are doing this now.

Once it is looked at and accepted for what it is, allow it to live in you so you don't repress it, and therefore you can see it. This is the beginning. As you can see it for what it is, it becomes less intense; it stops being an unknown problem. Allow the feelings to be there; feel them. Cry, shout, hit the mattress. Do not be aggressive to another; this is against you. Now forgive yourself for those feelings, for repressing the good things about you that created them as a reaction. Love them, love that part of yourself that is hurt; love that inner child that was mistreated by repressive and confused parents and teachers; love him and understand the mistakes of others and your own, seeing that everyone acted in the best possible way not knowing any better, including you. Put violet light to all that; release it and be free. Feel light and have the consciousness that you do not need to carry any of that any longer. Feel relieved. You are free. Give thanks.

As you give your attention, with consciousness, to your dark side, it will be brought to the light, which is what darkness needs; and it will be released.

> *"As long as you keep darkness in the dark,*
> *it will not be resolved."*

It will get worse. So you must do this to become free from it. Then it will stop pestering you and making your life hell. The way to heaven is to bring everything to the light and light to everything. You are always blessed. Embrace your gifts freely. Amen.

Dark and Light: The Two Sides of the Mind

On the resurrection day of some years, ago I had a dream…

Two women lived in a small room, confined to that small space and shut away from everything. One was quite young, whereas the other, being older, was quite aged. This woman was lying on her bed, facing the wall. The other was up with an active attitude. At one point, the young woman said to the other, "I am tired of this. I need to find out what is beyond here."

The older woman did not want to know anything or come out of that situation. She didn't move and stayed there without wanting to become an accomplice of the other in her drive. She moaned some words equivalent to, "I don't want to know. I want to be left alone. You are crazy."

The young woman said, "I have to do something about this now." She went to a side of the room where there was a huge locked door. There was a huge key tied to the wall above it. She took it with resolve and opened the door. Immediately after it there was another door. It was bolted up. She released the bolts and opened the door. She walked some steps and there was another bolted door. She did the same. Then she found herself in a dark corridor. It was quite dark; she could barely see anything. She walked to the end of this short tunnel and saw on the back wall, a door with a faint painting of a face that was incomplete. She couldn't make out what it was. She opened the door. Then she found herself in a dark alley with some dirty old windows on the left side. It was very gloomy but she could see enough to appreciate the space she was in. She walked to the end of the alley to see the same face on the back wall … but she could see it clearly now as she was brought to her knees. She put her hands on her mouth while she let out a sigh of awe in her amazement, as she contemplated the face of Jesus clearly printed on the wall, staring at her.

Notice how the young woman represents the Self's consciousness, and the older one represents the shadow, the dark side; she is full of fear. The consciousness represented by the younger one, seeks freedom, seeks the Christ without knowing it. But her drive puts an end to confinement and limitation and looks for resurrection: truth. The door out was always there. Even the key was there above the door. All they needed was to take it and open the door; if they wanted to, of course.

This is a perfect story of resurrection, and of the conscious part having the drive to be liberated. Then she can bring light to the other side. The two women are the same being with the two sides of the psyche: consciousness and the dark side. It is a perfect example of liberation: the conscious part wants freedom and truth.

Which one are you?

Do you pretend to be a princess? Can't stand witches? Do you pretend to be a witch? You can't stand princesses? That which you reject is your own shadow. We are all princesses and witches at the same time. We have to realize that and integrate both sides: Snow White and the witch are the two sides of the same woman. They reject the other side. That is the state of human consciousness when it is not integrated: it is separated. People are divided inside; it is like having two beings, two people inside: they need to become friends, they need to become one. We are in that process. But every day, a witch becomes a princess and a princess a witch, and wherever that happens, light shines and a person has found happiness, because she has found peace inside: there has been inner integration. This is necessary for ascension. It is happening on the planet at large; everyone is having an inner crisis because they are having to face their dark side. It is all about ego expectations or Higher Self expectations:

"Serving love or serving fear."

Important…

*"I recover my full will, the free exercise of my free will.
I posses myself fully. I expel from my body and mind
the ghosts, identities that pretend to posses me."*

Shadow Dynamics

Become Aware of Your Dark Side: Changing Your Destiny

How Darkness Happens

God is light. There is no duality, no shadow in Him. Light, when it hits resistance becomes divided; it creates light and shadow. That light is less than the original light. When this resistance is the ego, light separates in consciousness and unconsciousness and creates the part called dark side or shadow. That part of the divided consciousness is the one that contains and develops the dark contents we have seen before. By understanding that humans are divided into this separated consciousness of light and shadow — conscious and unconscious — we can understand that we have a situation that is not enlightened: there is a dark part that needs to be integrated. And since this is human condition, it is a situation that has to be evolved out of, since this condition is not stable and not whole; that divided consciousness will always seek to return to integration, to whole consciousness. It must be integrated by making it conscious. So the step towards dark side integration is a step in evolution and enlightenment.

Shadow Reflections

The higher and purer someone's vibration is, the more it is a mirror for others. The more loyal is the reflection. If you start running scared, you are not prepared to face yourself; it is your shadow that is projected; it is the side that is in you that you don't want to see. The subconscious is projected upon the crystalline vibration of a great presence of light. In that light anything that is not truth, the subconscious, gets reflected. Such intense presence of light can be a very high spiritual energy. It is like the one that is in the planet now, with the Stargate influence. It can also be a spiritual master or someone with very high vibration. A pure presence of light that can act as a mirror for you is your Higher Self, when it is activated. And it is, as now it is activated by the Stargate energies. This means you are most probably seeing things about you that you don't particularly like and didn't see before. You probably are having a hard time accepting this is you or part of you. Those are your shadow reflections. They manifest in a very crystal-clear mirror that in this case, is played by your higher spiritual side being awakened by the mentioned cosmic energies. Other people too can act as a clear mirror if they are clean of the personal darkness by having integrated their dark side. In fact, people are becoming clearer mirrors for others since the inner light of the spiritual self is greatly awakened and shining more than before.

This is the reason why there are so many personal and relationship crises; things are being shown, things that were hidden before. The global purpose of this is that each individual takes the opportunity to look at his inner dark side and brings it to the light and process it, to release it. By opening to forgiveness, understanding and compassion for oneself and others – everyone is having a hard time – humanity can change towards a more forgiving and loving attitude towards others and thus change the planet. Once the inner dark side has been released, there is true ground for goodness. Evil is gone. It is important to take this process into account and be gentle with yourself and others. We are all evolving to a greater global state of peace and harmony, although the process is quite hard most of the time, especially for those who haven't worked their consciousness or seriously looked within to see what was there, creating some true spiritual growth — which is most of humanity.

Shadow reflections are the daily menu of this planet at this moment. Although delicate and critical, this moment is a blessing for humanity. A liberation process is happening in a very intense way, which means a lot of work and thus spiritual evolution, which can take place faster than before. The amount of stuff being processed is immense. This is the way to go to the light and love consciousness once and for all. It is those shadow reflections what creates…

The Play of the Dark Side

Darkness will manipulate and use anyone to have its own way. You cannot trust it; it is the devil itself. It will always sell you to get what it wants. Darkness always wants another victim to fall into its claws, another person from whom to take energy and favor; in a word: power. Everybody is of value for its purposes. It will ask you for favors that will allow it to avoid looking at its truth, imploring your compassion. You fall for it… you are serving evil. It is using your power for its purposes. Don't fall for it; don't trust it, even if it hurts it. There are hidden issues. It is all a play in which you are one of the appointed actors, by it, all to get everyone dancing around it. That darkness can be a side of the personality, or a person who has repressed her unresolved issues so much that she has been completely possessed by her own dark side. This is what happens when the repression and rejection of one's darker aspect is so total that it ends up taking over. The personality is then a mere puppet in the hands of the repressed darkness. This is the way it has to operate from the dark and send its contents to the conscious part. But since it is not through conscious integration, this whole process and manifestation won't be conscious by the person.

The dark side is often disguised as a poor victim and wants you and everyone to feel sorry for it. In this way, it controls everyone inducing feelings of "compassion." Everyone not awakened falls for that. It takes a real awakening to be able to distinguish false from true compassion. Darkness takes advantage of its minimized condition. With its deceitful ways, it will keep everyone tied to it as "someone in need" and use everyone's power for its own purposes. While it keeps comfortable in its sleep without wanting to face the truth: its own hurts and dark areas. Until someone or something brings an awakening wave and does not behave as expected in order to keep that status quo. This is the end of darkness. The moment you bring light to the dark side, it will rebel. It will reject it and declare it the devil himself. This is the first reaction. But darkness is being weakened and awakened by the light. Eventually the light will do its work and the hurtful feelings of resentment and hatred that kept that mass of dark alive, will soothe out and humility will start appearing as the recognition of the true feelings manifested.

Sooner or later, that dismantling has to come, probably from someone who can see truth, act in truth and promote truth. This person can take the figure of someone professional, like a psychotherapist, or someone awakened enough, who happens to encounter that situation. In this way the record is set straight. The disruption will send a message of awakening to general darkness and people to acknowledge their power and truth, provoking the setting free of everyone one step further. Consciousness is all united.

You must be aware that darkness wants you to feel compassion for it, be it your own dark side or that of another. If you do it, you just perpetuate the situation. If you don't, you help in the liberation of someone that can perhaps be yourself. That doesn't mean the person will like it or like you, or that he will be conscious of what you are doing. But you will, and that is all that is needed to start a healing and awakening process. Darkness doesn't want to wake up. It does, but it doesn't. It is a strange paradox, a contradiction between the pull of the dark and the force of freedom, the need for it. It is the need for light and the force of passivity avoiding to face the truth that hurts: the pain that is keeping the person in the dark.

Darkness inside or outside, will often have a good kick as a reaction, resisting the vision of truth. It will almost always try to have a last blow and do as much damage as possible before letting go, especially when it sees there is no way to go, when it has reached the end of that possibility: it is against the ropes. There is no way out. Darkness wants you to move away from your center, to have you leave your position of power. If you don't, it will react badly. Pay attention, at that moment it is showing you its truth, the truth of where it is coming from. If you are rooted in your light, you won't concede darkness a step forward. True power is in the light. If you doubt your light, you are serving the dark; you are supporting its cause. You have to hold the light for the good of all. It sends darkness a message. A message of liberation.

This is what darkness plays at. This is what goes on when it acts. This is the greatest evil in the planet. This dark side not integrated is what has been the enemy of peace and goodness in humanity for thousands of years… but we cannot stay with this, otherwise we would be fooling ourselves. We need to move on to another perspective…

> **"Illuminating the dark is the only way**
> **to become immune to it."**

Your Best Friend: The Dark Side

"Without the witch there is no power."

Contrary to what most of humanity believes the dark side is our best ally. In it are contained the hidden treasures and resources we need to become fully realized and therefore, happy beings. The greatest secret to be known about it is that it contains our power. The way to deal with the dark side is to consider it our best friend, because it is. Treating the dark side as it has been done mostly in humanity's history, with repression does not resolve the issue. The proof is that it is still there, and people don't have their power. Dividing the shadow side from the good side is sending power away. The dark side is evil in as much as it will act in evil ways. That is all it knows. Remember, it is in the dark. But if it is integrated, it learns other ways and becomes a powerful ally: all its power turns over for the good.

"Keeping the dark side separated from consciousness is what makes it so evil."

This is the dangerous thing. The two sides of the person divided will be in conflict and will take it in turns to have the control of the will, and therefore of the actions of the person. The person is not good or bad but both, at different times. The dark side knows ways of the dark. But we know better. Our conscious part knows other ways. Ways of caring, support, help, respecting others until it is taken over by the dark inside. Then people turn evil, clearly manifesting a change in behavior or personality, having two sides. The classic story of Dr. Jekyll and Mr. Hyde is a representation of this reality of the two sides of a person. This taking over by the dark side is what happens every day to most people in a given situation, when they discuss intensely, when they shout, when they are mad, when they defend their mistakes, when they don't want to see they are being selfish or hurting someone because of it, or when they are not honest and want to take advantage. To many, this happens for a short period of time, it doesn't go beyond that, and the person returns to his normal state of being but still needs to integrate his own dark side. To others, this happens most of the time, and some take it to the terrible extremes we see every day on the planet. All that would depend on the intensity of their shadow repression and how much they recognize their own evil. Recognizing evil in oneself is good because it doesn't take you by surprise and it is in the light; you see it. So you can control it more and act far easier in the ways of goodness, the ways of the light. But if we make the dark side our friend, we are not taken over by it. Then we can act in light and goodness all the time and our will, will be free from dark pressures and evil ways.

113

All this is important because the way to treat the dark is not what it would seem. Now, having considered all that, we must understand the attitude towards darkness is not repression. It must be understanding and reconciliation: the reconciliation with ourselves.

**"Fighting evil will keep evil, evil
and the fighting on."**

There must be another way. We need to understand what the dark side is doing there and what it wants. Then, understanding can truly happen and reconciliation can manifest. Most people are not used to psychological truths, and therefore it might seem strange to know that the dark side has its own will. What is happening here is that the psyche is divided and part of the will is in the dark side too. So the dark has its own consciousness and can act with enough independence from the conscious part to create havoc. So reconciliation is a must because that dark side is part of us, and also because it holds a part of ourselves that is very important and necessary to be well. Because consciousness is divided, what solves the issue is unity. The dark side is not to be trusted and we have seen why; but it is not to be hated. It is to be understood, loved and forgiven. Essentially brought to the light. Then the door will open for integration, liberation and peace. The dark side holds the key to our life, *the key*. A key opens the door. That key is our power. This is why the dark side is our best friend.

The Alchemy of the Dark

The dark side needs to be released, freed. Repressing something only makes it stay there; it doesn't solve it. In fact, it makes it stronger. But transmuting is a way of changing things. So by this alchemy transmutation brings, the dark side stops being dark and joins the light, and we acquire our power. This happens by making the dark side conscious with the help of light — high vibration energy. Thus you recover your power, and in exercising it, you make decisions and follow life paths based on freedom and the acknowledgement of your right to be what you want.

**"By making the shadow side conscious,
you change your destiny."**

When the dark side is integrated and made conscious, it doesn't act against the will any more. It is not a dark side any more; it has joined the conscious part, and they work together as a team. It has acquired light, and in that transmutation it shows a very different face, one that is very interesting. It provides the conscious side with depth, resilience alertness, and power. And it liberates it from false sainthood and innocence.

Someone with a well-integrated dark side is not fooled easily, and his ways are commanding. In fact, the dark side is full of treasures. When away from the conscious part, it served evil purposes. But once integrated, it gives the other side personality and life and makes it very attractive and powerful. So it turns into a very powerful ally. When the dark side inside has gone through the alchemy of illumination, it makes you very commanding; you acquire a great power for good. This is the way you will always support the light, the highest in you and in everyone. It is the only way to light, to ascend to the light.

*"Your commitment with light is directly
proportional to your shadow liberation."*

Witch Hunt:
The Inner Inquisition

Projection is happening in everyone's mind. The personality reacts and judges according to its distorted view of the world and complains in a myriad of ways, about the world not being what it wants; it wants its own self-centered view of it. And often it goes to great lengths to get it. Witch hunt has started.

We need to find the cause of discomfort and annihilate it inside, not outside which is what witch hunt is for. We have to embrace our darkness, not deny it and see it in our neighbor and want to obliterate him. We don't want to blame others for it and start a witch hunt to wash away one's own guilt of evil. Unconscious unresolved issues are projected upon external life and seen as something that belongs there, whereas it is something one owns. This is how the personal dark side is projected. Then there is an immediate accusation and pointing out of that external evil and the need to finish it off. Examples abound in the history of humanity and in modern times. What we must be concerned with is our daily life: the witch hunts we perpetrate every day. Jesus said in a well-known passage:

"Whoever is innocent can throw the first stone."

We can use that as a mirror in our daily dealings with situations and people. Often we are chasing some sort of evil outside which is nothing more than our own dark side projected. When things are not being dealt with straight, there is room to hide. Pretension arises and we have lies and masks. Then we are completely deceived by our own dark illusion. Our evil starts when we resist good and doing good to others; whatever that means.

The Transmutation of the Shadow

This is an appropriate message from the Ascended Masters on the subject of the dark side and the resulting witch hunt its presence produces. You may look at it with the awareness that this is an enlightened vision on the subject.

In your dimension it is difficult to forgive, love, open the heart and keep it open without a communication with the higher reality. The ego always finds reasons to close the heart. Your work is to invoke and meditate on the higher presence constantly.

Transmutation is the key word for these times. Transmutation of the dense to the light, from the low vibration to the high. Transmutation of the human shadow — the personal darkness accumulated in the subconscious. Transmutation of the collective shadow. It is imperative to transmute your darkness and to help others with theirs. For this the Violet Ray of Light has been sent out to the planet. It is the greatest frequency accelerator, which takes everything to the light, to its liberation. This transmutation is salvation. Salvation is forgiveness: it saves you because it liberates you from low vibration, where there are fears, suffering, obscurity. Those are the vibrations that live in the shadow side. The high energies like the Violet Light transmute your low frequencies; it forgives you from them on the way to ascension. Forgiveness is the Divine Vision. It is the act of liberation through the reestablishment of the Divine Vision — through its intercession — through the Holy Spirit; by elevating the vibration.

Invoke and open yourself thus to the transmuting light of the Holy Spirit. Only by raising your vibration will you obtain the correct vision, in it, forgiveness is immediate, spontaneous. In God there is no condemnation because there is no separation. How could it be possible where there is only One? In God there is only love and peace, Light. Therefore, in God there is no shadow, but you need to return to unity and, with it, to peace, integrating and transmuting yours through this high forgiveness granted by God. This is the

117

miracle of your transmutation. Returning to Him is to return to the shadow — free state.

The shadow not recognized, not transmuted in the human being gives rise to its persecution in others through different forms of the so-called "witch hunt" of the past and the present. The shadow is projected to the exterior, since the consciousness, in not recognizing it inside, projects it outside, where it tries to eliminate it for not being able to accept that it is its own reflected darkness. As the Master said, "It sees the splinter in the other's eye but fails to see the log in its own." Forgiveness is the process of unity, of liberating an unrecognized, unaccepted darkness to arrive at peace.

Transmutation illuminates everything and thus darkness stops being such, allowing harmony, unity and peace to reign in the heart of every being, as God; reestablishing the Divine and the Truth inside. The human being is being taken to meet his truth face to face: his hatred, fear, aggressiveness, intolerance, arrogance, and the effects of this darkness, to liberate it through his acknowledgement and to purify his reality through forgiveness: transmute his blindness to the Divine Vision."

Beloveds, this is the way.

We are the Ascended Masters who guide you and love you.

POWER

Recovering Your Lost Power: The End of Self-Deceit

The Truth About Power

*"When you give your power away
anything can happen to you."*

The other side of the dark is light. But there is an element without which light is not what it could be. This element is power. Power, as we have seen already is retained inside by the dark side and outside by the Matrix of the Dark. So power needs to be brought to the light. It is a fundamental element of illuminated consciousness; and for light to be really light, power has to be integrated into it.

It is therefore essential to understand the essence of what power is and the power dynamics that are part of us and of life. This section contains the revelations of true power and the most relevant aspects of power itself. All these are essential for ascension. This also serves anyone to see what he is doing with power, to realize the true ways of power, and, if needed, to correct those ways and move that power to the light in the correct way. By seeing the truth about power, we can move more freely to the Stargate objective, since all its energies are moving humanity towards the recovery of power from the dark. Power is the most essential element to go to new spiritual states. This is the importance of this element, and all the sections here are to prepare you in the right understanding and use of power for that aim.

"If you want your power back, you have to move away from ego."

❖ *While power is not in the light, there will always be a dark side. Power belongs to the side of the light. So to make the way towards ascension, this has to happen: power has to be returned to the light.*

Inner Authority: Independent Power

"Recovering your hidden power, is the end of self-deceit."

We must embody the fact that we are total power without conditions. Not any area in us is lacking power. Power is continuous without cracks. Power is there for you; you are that power.

To have conditions for your power is to accept that it doesn't have continuity and that, in some circumstances, you do not have it. This is to accept that your power is dependent. Then it is not power anymore. Power must be independent for it to be power. The power of God is there for you to take it. *There* means in you and in the Universe at large. You must have total conviction that you are the power, that you are the power in your life, and that nothing happens to you without your consent. From the moment you cannot generate independent joy — peace, love, power — you are dependent. You depend on an external supply for your peace, power, well-being: this is addiction. And you go on seeking others to take power from them. This happens when you don't have the realization that the power of God is there for you, and that He is the source you must go to for it.

Taking on your power is a thing of turning to God
Power is in God. To own our power we have to turn to Him.

On the other hand, when you own your power you live a life of responsible freedom and sovereignty in which "I am sovereign of my power, God gave it to me," reflects the loyalty to your inner truth: you are true to yourself. That is a manifestation of having correct power dynamics: you go to the source to get power. When you correctly exercise the sovereignty over your life and others' schemes are broken by it, that is a lesson to their power dynamics. If others get their plans, expectations, or ideas broken or don't like it, it is their predicament. They have a problem with their own power dynamics. And I am not talking here about doing what one wants regardless of others. I am talking about one's use of his life, time, dedication, what one puts his energy to: how he wants to live his life and what he wants to do with it. Not what one does to others. Everyone should understand that everyone is free and should allow everyone's freedom. We are not here to fulfill other's agendas or infringe on people's freedom and rights.

"When there is dependency, you give your power away.
When you give your power away, there is dependency."

If you, or anybody don't let people be free in their conscious and free decision on how to live their lives — provided that doesn't affect the freedom of others — there is a problem with your power source: you are seeking it in the wrong place. And there are too many people in the world trying to tell others what to do with their lives, when those people are perfectly happy with the way they are leading their lives, instead of focusing on becoming better and more truly compassionate human beings. This is necessary to move to the higher dimensions opened by the Stargate.

You should be able to live this truth with the considerations I have mentioned before: "I allow myself to be free and do what I want," without harming another and respecting the freedom and power of all.

❖ *To help people with their fears and insecurities even
 in a dying situation, they need to feel connected with
 the source of power, life and love. They have no fear
 when they feel the power of life and love with them.*

How to recover your power

The first thing you need to do is to become aware of your own lack
of power, those areas in you where power is not manifesting. You
will recognize those areas where power is not available, because
in them, you will feel things don't depend on you. Some things
truly don't depend on you. What is meant here is: those areas in
which things don't depend on you but they should. And the ones
that depend on other people and circumstances outside you but are
yours — you have given control away. Control should always be
yours in the areas of your own life. So if something major is going
to change at work and you are just an observer because it is a general
company change, you have to deal with *your* situation in it. Here, as
in all situations in life, you only have a few options: you accept it,
you don't and change it or you leave the situation. This is holding
your power: you act from your center doing that which you can do,
being true to yourself.

If you cannot freely make decisions in your life, see why that is.
Maybe you are married and some decisions have to be jointly
made, but are you happy about how the equation works? Are you
truly having your share of power there? The issue is very deep and
complex in each individual case, and you will have to use the wisdom
of this book and sharpen your perception to investigate deeply what

is going on with the issue of power in your life.

Commitment to Excellence

There is a force in the Universe, an energy field intelligent and giver of life that makes everything work. We call it God. We know very little about it. It is the power of everything. We function with a certain amount of power, a limited power, because we do not unite with this universal force of all power. People's condition is this because they have separated in identity and consciousness from this power. To surrender to this power would be to accept its presence and renounce the limited power. The union with this force is the way to excellence.

But for that we have to enter into surrender and commitment. Surrender of what? Of our limitations and limited conditions. Commitment to what? To excellence, to that which works. What works? Unlimited power. What doesn't work? The limited power, the ego. And this commitment to smallness is the cause of the situation on the planet. There has to be an ascension in the attitude people have towards power, an illumination about what power really is and where it can take all. If you commit to excellence, power flows through you. If you don't commit, you never find the power to improve yourself. You bet on mediocrity; that is what you have.

Excellence is about seeing and believing in a possibility and taking it. It is a matter of seeing that possibility for you, the best you can conceive for yourself. Ascension requires that you see this possibility for yourself. It is about not letting it pass as if it wasn't for you, because you do not see yourself that way or there. It is about seeing yourself that prosperous, luminous, healthy, full of peace, joy, success. It is feeling that you deserve it. You commit yourself to that possibility, accepting that possibility for you. Then the doors open for you. The Universe moves it because there is a space where to manifest that, a space that attracts it into manifestation. You have invoked excellence for yourself, from the powerful Universe; you have made the space for that. Of course, you see it, but you also work for it. It doesn't land on your doorstep without you going after it.

"It is the space that attracts something into manifestation."

A new possibility, one of excellence, is one in which it is believed and the Universe creates it. There is a space big enough — welcoming — because it welcomes that idea. It is a space of love; hence the Universe cannot resist and attracts it to you and your life.

To do something new is to go beyond your limits. This requires investing more power to change a given situation. If more power is not introduced into it, the situation remains the same and there is no change. There is no movement towards that level of excellence. More power needs to come into the equation. This entails a change in attitudes. Your attitudes now generate the situations in your life. A different situation needs other attitudes. But if you don't change the attitudes you have now, there won't be a new result. To do it, more power has to come into you to implement a new way of being. To maintain a condition energy is necessary. You can use that energy to create the opposite, to leave that condition. You have to stop feeding it and put the energy in another direction.

"Excellence is giving the best of yourself, being impeccable with yourself, life, people."

Excellence is available now. Why comply with being a vulgar terrestrial? Shine with divine creativity and create an original, fun world full of the life and magic of the higher energies by using your divine power. This is exactly what we can do with the new energies.

If you are not committed, you will never achieve excellence. Why? Something came up. There is always something that stops people from getting there. Thus whatever it was you wanted is never achieved. Those are excuses. When power is on, there are no excuses. You achieve things regardless because power is on you. You cannot be sidetracked from the essential things in life now and be distracted. This time, distractions can be your worst enemy. Your highest evolution possible at present is what is at play. The difference between achievers and those who don't achieve anything is that they keep power in them. Achievers only see the goal; this is commitment. People who get there do not have more luck; they have more commitment. Hence power for that comes to them, because they open the door to Universal power.

"To get to ascension you need to commit to excellence."

This is because you are asking the Universe for the best you can have. There are people that everything they do, they do it well. Everything they do has a level of excellence. It is because they do not settle for less. Excellence is their minimum, thus they invoke the power to manifest it in their lives through their attitude. And in one way or another, they always achieve it. But he who stops before excellence does something he doesn't realize: when he sees something less than excellence he says, "Okay, it works for me." He accepts it; something the other never does. He doesn't identify with that. He has a divine vision of the result, and the divine comes to his aid. It is a vision that everything must work perfectly, that the best will be for all; it is a vision that gives life. It is a non-selfish vision; it is the good for the sake of the good. This is very powerful. If you seek the good of all, your influence is greater and the Universe supports you with more resources because your task is greater and your responsibility bigger, because you are serving, because the good you seek is greater.

The vision of an ascended being is the vision of excellence. So it is in your interest to consider from now on, excellence as a way of life. We should commit to excellence, to unlimited power. At the end, not expressing excellence is a lack of power; it is an expression of limited power. Seeking excellence is seeking all the power of God. It is recognizing there is a power in you that comes from beyond the personality that can make your life soar, and touch others in a way that the greatest chord resonates in them. This is the aim everyone should have in life.

Excellence requires surrender and commitment. Those who live excellence have become committed, have accepted the responsibility, have surrendered to the best, to the biggest. Those who don't, have not accepted the responsibility and simply, more power is not given to them: they don't need so much to fulfill their objectives. It is an investment: how much are you going to invest? How big is your project? The bank is going to give you according to it. If you go to ask for a million, it won't give you ten. If you ask for twenty, maybe it gives you twenty. The Universe is the same; it is a source of power and resources. What is your project? How much do you need for it?

Commitment is also necessary and foremost for evolution. If you want to live the realities that are mentioned here, the new world of light and joy, all the wonders that the Stargate brings you are going to need commitment to excellence. Ascension needs commitment to excellence.

**Your commitment to your vision is going to move
the resources; your commitment to excellence.**

Power should be used for good. Excellence is inside you; it is in giving the best of yourself all the time. And if it doesn't produce good results, a good crop, don't accept it, don't stay there. Sow better, improve until what you give is of quality and brings good to one and all. What is true moves hearts: it comes from the right place. It is God source manifesting through oneself.

Prayer

*"In union with the infinite possibilities
of manifestation of the Universe for us,
for all, we enter into surrender of our
small power in the name of Divine
Excellence." – Amen.*

Declare Your Freedom

*"I am freedom,
I am the power,
I am free choice."*

"There is no power, authority, control outside myself. There is no force external to me from my divinity. I am the lord of myself." This is what we recover: we have lived ignoring this truth. The only law is the law of God. The law of God is love, peace and respect for life – it respects all life. San Agustin said, "Love and do what you want." The law of man is there in order to control and manipulate, because the law of God is lost. If you live the law of God, you don't need the law of man. The law of God is beyond the law of man. The law of man was created because the law of God was lost. But you can recover it. Everybody can.

"The law of God is love"

This says it all. The only law is that of our Divine Father/Mother, the One, the only one, the Creator, God. All the others are either in Him, in His law, or they are not the law; they are manipulating to take away power and control. And in this way, they create guilt. They want to open a branch of heaven and define themselves as managers of the branch. There are no branches of heaven — *there are not.* There is only one heaven, one Lord: the Lord of heaven, the Lord of the Universe. The Celestial Father. Everyone must have this very clear to go where we are going as a planet.

"I am free" is your truth, with all the consequences and in the full meaning of the sentence: without conditions and without limitations. So you are free. If you act in freedom, ignoring the only law – the law of God – you will leave the consequences. And most probably they will be very hard on you. So remember that in declaring your freedom, you have the greatest responsibility too. And this means respecting life and the freedom and power of all. You need to break, undo, dissolve everything that is against your freedom, which is in your dark side. Then progressively, you will break free from the limitations of the Matrix of the Dark outside. As you break free from the dark side inside, life will present you with more choices, according to your greater state of consciousness and therefore, freedom.

"Here, now I Am completely free, in everything, in all areas of my being and my life, from my cells to the totality of my being."

Say this until it becomes a truth you live and embody. Feel its effects in you, in your life and in others around you. Cut with the sword of truth guilt and fear, designed to end your freedom of expression and happiness in all correct ways, and try to end your peace.

Idols: Power Robbers

When you disconnect yourself from God, the golden calf is born: you create idols. God is all; if you are not with Him you need a substitute: a figure to which you will give power. That is the figure you will expect to have power to draw from... just that this power is the one you would have given it first. It might be money, work, a person, circumstances, the stars, symbols, sciences, or techniques that can become your own personal god. Without a good relationship with God, you are vulnerable. Placing your power away from Him, in idols, makes you very vulnerable. Idols are never to be trusted as something to be dependent on, as a reality to draw power from, as a way to live life: they will always let you down. But pride makes you believe you are invulnerable. Pride can be your downfall, especially if it is associated with idols and their power. Even worry is a substitute for God. In the lack of a good relationship with Him, worry has the perfect ground on which to thrive. Many people make worry their main idol.

As a reference, when something obsesses you and God is not there, you have created an idol. Your own ego is the greatest and more unpromising idol. Man has substituted God for the ego. As all of them it has to come down. If you fail to see that behind that discipline, ceremony, element of power, what is behind and what you invoke is the power of God, that has become an idol for you: a substitute for the power of God. And you are giving it a power that it doesn't have, a power that is God's since He is the one that has power. All other power sources draw their power from Him.

Remember that the power of God is for you and it is available to you through your Higher Self, and through the opening of the gates of grace in you. You do that by purifying yourself and coming close to your heart and your spirit. Also by wanting it passionately; it is then when God reveals Himself. But you have to want Him more than anything else; He will not compete with your other "gods." He will let you enjoy that fake and weak power until what you want is the real one. And therefore you go to Him in the recognition that He is the source of *all* power.

> *"And you shall seek me,*
> *and find me, when you shall*
> *search for me with all thy heart."*
> - Jeremiah 29:13

You might use elements of power no doubt, but you will be okay doing it if your relationship with God is good. Otherwise you are at risk of easily believing that such elements of power are your source of power, and that is when problems start. A good relationship with God will keep you in the awareness that there is nothing more powerful than the Holy Spirit. And that will above all be, where your true relationship with power lies. As soon as a symbol or idol enters into your mind with the belief that it is more powerful than the Holy Spirit, you are off the mark: you are moving away from power, from God. That is never a good thing since in Him is where success and true protection lie. The good thing about this is that God, contrary to what many might believe, is not a controlling force. God is pleased that you take all the power He has available: it is for you and for everyone. For ascension, all idols must go.

True Power: No Imposition

Power is not dominance, rigidity, imposition. That is insecurity. Divine power imposes itself without intending to do it. It does it through its own strength and vibration, without really doing anything. True power comes from inner confidence. True power is a state of awareness from an inner development of light. You show your true power in your freedom and light. That power does not impose from the ego; it comes from the Self — strength is from the Self. It is a power that does not want anything. Divine power only seeks to bless.

One should discern between ego and divine power, and see where one is acting from and what or who is really acting. It is fundamental to recognize who is acting inside oneself, the part that serves the light or that part that serves fear. Fear is a path that creates havoc, because it wants something from the wrong side: that which does not bring blessings.

True power is tranquil, relaxed.
It doesn't have anything to prove.

When you have true power people trust you and want to add their power to yours to make a bigger power. This is true leadership: people recognize a greater power there. Imposition never gets this recognition since it wants to impose power and control from the ego. True leadership comes from inner power, not from external power. External power is a yearning for control to obtain the power one doesn't have.

True power gives clarity, serenity, self-control, wisdom, love. When you have true power you follow your hints, your intuition, your dreams, your feelings. In a true power state you synchronically attract events to your life; synchronicity happens. Your true power comes from an alignment, a connection with the Universal Source, which gives you an acknowledgement that you are eternal, your essence indestructible. If you are indestructible you don't need to accumulate external power; your spiritual essence is constant power. The way is to awaken your reality of inner infinite power and use it for good.

Ego reacts; it has to demonstrate the power it doesn't have. This power we are talking about is another power different than the power of the world. It is divine power. True power never goes out with the intention to dominate another, because that power serves love. That is the sign of true power. It was cast in the truth of freedom and therefore it seeks the freedom of others. That is the highest power.

To have that power active is necessary to have gone through a great number of battles inside against one's owns phantoms, and have cut their heads off, one by one. They are not interested in serving love and if kept alive, will oppose it. To wield the sword of that power one must be immune to certain things. The main one is the allure of power. Because that power will never seek the increment of its own power when acting; it will have the clairvoyance of seeing power traps and will recognize the ways that awaken and develop power in all beings. The other one is that it won't feel insecure supporting the power in others. That power is not easy to come by, but it must be achieved. All other states of power are false. The delusional mind makes people believe they have power, when in truth that power is not serving love. Such power is always false. True power is at the service of the Highest. Everyone must turn towards this state of power in order to have access to the ascension waiting for all.

"Everyone must use power to serve love if they want to ascend."

The Spiritual Warrior: The Ascending Man

*"The spiritual warrior is he who has
confronted his dark side retaking his
power from it, and uses it to serve
love and compassion."*

The spiritual warrior is undoubtedly the personification of the Stargate process. He who has retaken his power from his shadow side inevitably becomes a spiritual warrior. He is someone to be taken into account for the compelling force and energy that emanates from his mere presence. He is an agent for change wherever he is. His restructured radiation of power awakens power where it is asleep and changes every kind of energy to move things towards honoring God and His truth. Thus he acts for the benefit of all. This is inevitably the highest compassion, the state all humanity is moving towards.

Archangel Michael gave us a beautiful and powerful message about the spiritual warrior a few years ago, right in the midst of the activation years for ascension, after the Stargate's opening. The clarity and meaning of his words cut like a sword through any nonsense and confusion we might have about becoming a serious spiritual being: a spiritual warrior. This is undoubtedly a teaching that should be followed by anyone having true spiritual aspirations; in fact it is the true beginning, the corner stone of such aspiration.

The Spiritual Warrior

"The Will of the Father is the greatest joy that can exist. Since in Him there is no other intention – other vibration – than peace, blessings, love. Any thing or intention that opposes love, opposes the Will of God. He has already foreseen all – there is no will that can improve it. He is the biggest joy, His vision is infinitely high, His gifts unlimited; He is the supreme attainment. To give oneself to His Will is therefore the only sensible thing; it is the total liberation from smallness, limitation and the spheres of fear, which only keep the

slavery of consciousness in the absence of love and of the knowledge of what the Divine has for you.

This is why today I want to talk to you all about the spiritual warrior.

This is a being that having seen, lived and experienced the ways of the limited self-directed will, and seeing that despite all the effort and work from there, he has not reached any good place, he has understood that the opening to the Highest is the only way and has decided to undertake it. And maintaining the vision in his ideals has placed them all in the hands of God. With complete surrender and humility, he has opened up to the divine and has renounced, consciously and voluntarily, his limited power and will. The battle is over for him. Once he has given himself, he is in peace. Such being experiences an alchemy worth seeing, a metamorphosis that radiates through his eyes, his presence, his movements, his acts, his light, his sweetness and his strength. His persona transmits an emanation of the divine beyond his earthly consciousness, of his visible incarnation, as if he was being driven by an invisible higher impulse, wise and loving, that can only come from the will of the Most High.

Such a being is a blessing for all Creation. The sword he carries is the light of God, and his battle is that of the light. Discerning first in his own being that which is divine and that which is not, he defeats, with his lucid vision the traps and manipulations of his ego, bringing light to his brothers and sisters infusing them with the strength of discernment. The physical or emotional weapons are a substitute for the power of God, a poor substitute, one of destruction. The spiritual warrior is a warrior without weapons, with the power of God liberating and creating.

From the origin – where his perspective comes from – his vision is elevated, his purpose, noble; his love deep. But he has seen that the action from the ego's limited will, far from bringing the joy supposedly contained in its vision, provoked separation and pain and the result was not love. That took him to the humility to renounce his own ways to take on the divine ones, and it is that humility the key, that acknowledgement that there has to be a superior way.

Hence the action of the spiritual warrior as divine instrument – even though it might generate apparent destruction, change, unbalance, rejection, unrest, due to the resistance of ego to change – always comes from love, and the end result is always love. So the spiritual warrior is a warrior of love. Thus the rejection of Divine Will by the ego is a constant that is there while there is no giving in and renouncement of that one to this one, since the mere existence of the ego's will depends precisely of its opposition to God.

The spiritual warrior has, in the inner joy of his communion with God, the motivation to continue illuminating himself and to take light there, where the life lived in the suffering of limitation yearns for the divine; there in the heart of every being. His yearning and impulses are free from selfishness; his actions reflect the higher cause he serves. Hence, in the clarity of discerning the ego from the divine, he becomes his own master and inevitably, the master of others. The spiritual warrior makes his existence one of service; he does not live life for himself anymore, nor does he live for his individual wants, which go nowhere. He puts everything to the service of the Highest, since an individual want is a poor substitute for a life full of the Will of God.

When you doubt whether you are on this path or not, you will know since you will have no doubt, no reserve in acting serving the Father – that will be your joy. While you want to keep your fears and justify them, you are not giving yourself to the Father to avoid doing that which you must; to stop doing what you should. Keep alert because those are the ego's tools to not do it, to not die. The greatest reason that the ego will always sell to you is that of your own death, that is only his because you are eternal. And with that he manipulates you to keep controlling you and keep existing and thus with that makes you fear God and hence reject Him. It is of no use to listen to the advice of someone who bases his own existence on fear. You will know if you fully accept the Will of God, when in invoking it there is no sign in you of doubt or fear.

The question that I put to you is: Do you want to be a spiritual warrior?

You cannot serve two masters.
It is the time to choose.

I Am Archangel Michael

•

When I asked Archangel Michael for a mantra that I could use to connect with the Will of God, this is what he said:

"I will the Will of God."

The Warrior of Light: The Only Free State

"The warrior of light
serves true compassion."

The general state of humanity for the last thousands of years has been:

> **"You don't have power; you have to manipulate.**
> **You have to invent a source of power."**

When you have recovered your divine power you are a warrior of light. Then you act in true compassion. Until then you come from ego power, and that is a very tricky place to be. It is the source of ego compassion, a very weak way of dealing with life. In the name of being good, it gives power away. This is the worst scenario. Divine power is not weak. Ego power has the worst idol: false goodness, which is very far from being good: it leaves those without power, without power. This is because it acts from weakness. A person acting this way has not toughened enough in the purifying fire of divine grace and meditation on the high vibrations of his Higher Self that cut through the nonsense of ego power and its attitude of false goodness. A warrior of light is therefore a being that has been purified in the fire of God and has become, as a result, truly strong: a place where true goodness can come from. Sometimes that good does not look good to the ego's eyes. The warrior of light is free to act in the best possible way without trembling. That brings true goodness and he is a blessing, as we see in the message from Archangel Michael.

"A warrior of light is free of idols."

Whilst we believe we are the ego self we run into all problems: it has no power. So anger, pity, pride are part of us. The warrior of light does what he has to do, regardless. This is love, and it is so because it comes from love, and he knows that. He knows the results of his actions of power are blessings and love. The results of his actions are in the hands of God because those are divine seeds sown by Him through his warrior of light, seeds that come from divine power; it is not his power, it is God's power through him. That is why he is a warrior of light: his actions are not tainted by ego. But beware of acting as a warrior of light without having endured his trail, and thus acting from ego. The lack of purity will backfire and a person acting in such way will learn an important lesson in a hard way: impeccability.

"If you don't have your power, you have nothing to offer."

•

"Surrender is the victory of the warrior of light.
The warrior in this way accesses all the power
to battle with his own shadow and recover his
lost power within himself... Then he is free."

Compassion is Awakened Power

The love of God is infinite. Sometimes it is sweet, sometimes strong, tough, intense. It can be revolutionary, soft, solid, fluid. It manifests in the way it is going to work, depending on what is needed.

The right compassion gives the appropriate type of love response to a person or situation. That takes an awakened consciousness: the only place where true compassion can come from. The love of God alchemizes itself to have the appropriate effect for the best outcome. If you are neutral, are out of the way and flow in unity with God, you will manifest the appropriate love and compassion in every situation.

The ego is made up of structured patterns, crystallized energy. They have to be liberated, dissolved for it to function freely. Otherwise action is based on preconceived ideas, automatic and unconscious responses to life. There is no space for true compassion to manifest there. Just for the crystallized idea about compassion and that often is not a good service to anyone because it is filtered with the ego ideas, an ego that is not exercising power and therefore it will act in weakness and self-pity. In high vibration the ego loses structure and you can return to the Self. Then you function from the Self. The ego is the past. You either function from the past or from the present in the Self. You then love, because loving is the function of God. There is nothing else to do. Everything else is a distortion, it is an illusion, a wrong belief that there is something else – to do.

"To love is to experience oneself as God."

You exercise a level of compassion according to your level of consciousness – of freedom, of power – your level of love free and unattached. Consciousness is radical. Here is where its power lies. You are either with it or you suffer the consequences. Ego says that this is not compassionate. True compassion does not negotiate with evil: that which is not the best for evolution. Evil is what causes suffering and unconsciousness, even if it is disguised as some of the "wonders" of this world, which so many worship so much. Compassion doesn't allow for manipulation. It will do whatever it has to do. This is true compassion. This is divine love power. When we can live a life like that, we can count ourselves as beings that have recovered their power: "buts" have disappeared and only that which works is on. There are no excuses in a state of power.

True power gives you eyes to see. Before reaching that state, your eyes don't see. They are deceived by ego and its idols: God has not fully entered you yet. When He does, He sets the house right. That house is meant to be a temple of light and love and power. When those eyes are seeing you see deceit where before you saw wonders. Shining metal might be gold to the unlearned. But to the wise, only gold matters. Other ways are an attempt of the ego to want to preserve its self-deceit, its ego illusion, its ways it holds so dearly to keep its own fantasy alive: it is a death trap. The only paradise lies in truth, and for that one has to recover his mighty inner power. "Truth will make you free." Free of what? The fantasy land of this world which is not a fun fair, it is the world of limitations, chaos and suffering. But it takes nerve and power to want to see it for what it is.

"Compassion is the only way"

When you have power the illusory things are not appealing anymore. This is why it is fundamental to recover power: to get out of this world and enter into ascension towards a world of light. This is the most compassionate act you can do for yourself. People look outside to find and gain power. They want to access, buy, and take power. They crave things and others to acquire power from them. This is what everyone is after. It looks like something else. Well, it is a world without compassion.

True Compassion: The Highest Love

"Providing the support for the evolution and independence of other beings." This could be a good definition of true compassion. Independence in physical, emotional, mental and spiritual terms. This is regardless of personal opinions or advantage. So you have to be a clear channel to do that. You cannot have shadow issues and not expect a personal reward. Compassion is a completely ego-free state.

The truest and highest compassion is free; it doesn't get implicated. This is hard to accept. People are programmed otherwise about compassion. Compassion depends on your state of awareness. From a high awareness you discern what is compassionate at any given moment. In one situation, getting involved might be the compassionate act; in another it might not, it might be not getting involved. Compassion is not a set rule. It depends on many factors. The more developed your consciousness is, the clearer you can see this and the more truly compassionate you can be: you will have developed more discernment. From a higher state of awareness you have the understanding that this world is an illusion, a play in which we are all playing roles. You have more freedom to see things from outside the play. If your consciousness is not developed enough, this is impossible to see or even understand: you think what is happening is real. This doesn't give you choice. In the understanding that the world is an illusion you don't have the obligation to get involved; you choose. Of course, that choice will be enlightened by true love and power. If that choice wasn't enlightened, it would show a mean attitude and it would develop karma.

Power is in each person; it belongs to the person using it. If she decides to give it to suffering, it is her choice. If compassion doesn't get involved in the face of an apparent pressing situation, it is because that is the most compassionate response to it. Helping isn't always the best thing. Some people are used to demanding help from others. That could be abuse. Others might think this has to be done all the time; that is a lack of power and discernment. In between those extremes, there are many options. Not getting involved is often the greatest act of love; you allow someone to have her process. That is growth; it is an opportunity to experience something valuable for expanding awareness and going beyond limits. It might be that what the person needs is to awaken her power. If she gets help, often that option is gone.

Not getting involved from the perspective of true compassion, is an appropriate thing. If that response doesn't come from compassion, then it is not appropriate. Love will see when it is appropriate. Many true spiritual masters – they do have a high awareness – don't get involved in many ways. There is a lot to learn from them. Many times helping doesn't come from discerning compassion but from self-pity. From a projection of seeing oneself in that situation and feeling bad about it. This is not compassion. What a person suffers at a given moment might be seen as terrible, but very often that is a blessing that will save her from greater and more prolonged suffering later on. Everyone has her own personal path to freedom and peace; everybody's learning needs are different.

At one level, we might exercise involved compassion because that is what we need to learn and what the situation unmistakably is demanding. At another level, we might exercise higher compassion because that is where we need to go.

"The absence of something outside will invoke that from inside."

That is the highest compassion. I remember years ago hearing the story of the lost goat. A master and his disciple reached a village in which a family gave them food and shelter. When the master asked about their livelihood they said they hardly lived from the goat's products: milk and cheese. When they parted the master said to the disciple, "Go to the house and throw the goat off the cliff."
He replied, "But master that is not very compassionate."
The master said, "Are you a server of the master's truth or of your ego thoughts?"
The disciple threw the goat off the cliff. Years went by, and in one

of the travels of the disciple, now a master himself, he reached the same village. When he approached the house of the family that helped them years before, he was very surprised at what he saw. There was a new house, cars, abundance everywhere. He knocked on the door and asked them how they developed such wealth. They said: "We had a goat and we lived from what the goat gave us. One day the goat fell off the cliff unexpectedly and we had to find new ways of living."

The story speaks for itself. We know very well that in life prosperity often comes from hardship or at least the creativity that will produce it. Wouldn't this be compassion? Compassion is not what most people believe it is. It is a great teacher in the Universe. It is the highest vibration in the Universe. And for that it is a great master capable of teaching the greatest lessons, those that will take anyone to the best circumstances for evolution and prosperity. Often people miss the jewel inside that package of apparent hardships. Sometimes those lessons are tough, but they bring the greatest rewards.

But most people are not very good at understanding the meaning of apparent suffering when it is in front of them: they don't have their power with them. Jesus taught, "Teach people to fish instead of giving them fish." Doing something for people who can fend for themselves is not compassion; it is doing them a disservice. You need discernment. Many people complain when that happens because they don't like to leave their comfortable position of always using other's power – and good intentions – for their benefit. They don't want to get up and start working on themselves, on their own power.
The more power, the more compassion. In order to get ready for ascension people will have to move from fake compassion to true compassion.

- *The highest compassion will always make you independent, powerful. It is about invoking the power within you. It takes a deeply awakened awareness to exercise it.*

Surrender: The Way to Power

*"Until you surrender to God you see nothing, you
hear nothing. It is in surrendering that one
acquires power... power to see and to hear."*

Most people want to go to God and walk the path side by side with
their ego. That is why Luke 14:33 says:

"Those who want to follow me leave everything."

This is not a call for irresponsibility; it is a call for motivation, for
clarity, for truth. Walking the path in any other way doesn't take you
there. It is good advice. It doesn't mean leave your responsibilities. It
says, leave the search for God in the worldly affairs; leave the search
for power and bliss where they aren't and find truth in God. This is
what will save humanity: focusing on the right ways, those where
truth and freedom lie. Otherwise human life is a limited experience
because it is tied in chains. Sadly, most people don't realize they are
in them.

The message of Jesus in Luke declares, "Live ordinary life in an
extraordinary way." This is only possible when you seek God as a
priority and then living life from that realization. This is the message
of Jesus. Extraordinary people are people in true service away from
ego, channeling God not ego; they recognize higher truth when they
see it. They serve it even if they are not aware that is what they are
doing. And they are not necessarily spiritually declared people. Often,
they seem like ordinary people; they give and serve in mundane areas,
in ordinary activities, but extraordinarily. Extraordinary people are
people that whatever their position, high or low, are in surrender.
Those are the high ones: true power is theirs. Others think they have
power because they hold some power wand that is poisonous and a
fake that gives them the idea of self-importance. In not surrendering
the ego believes is in a state of power, and thinks it can exercise
power by itself. This is the downfall of man, believe it or not.

●

*"Surrender is the only way
to access power. In it,
we let go of everything
and true power fills us."*

Surrender: The Way to Perfection

*"The only thing that has to be
perfect in a human being is his
surrender; God takes care of
the rest."*

Of course, surrendering is to the Truth, God's Will. From that state of surrender, everything works, everything is possible. You don't have to seek the correct result; you have to seek the truth. You have to seek the heart. You don't have to seek perfection; you have to seek action. You cannot focus on the result, there is limited power here and this is ego. You have to act for the sake of acting. You must have as objective: acting, not the result.

God then makes man perfect. Ego seeks perfection in the no surrender. From there it tortures and flagellates itself for not being perfect. It is a tyranny. Man must stop seeking a relative perfection from being away from God's perfection. It will drive him crazy. Man needs to be saved from the distortion of wanting to make a perfect diamond from himself without the assistance of God. A diamond needs to be perfectly shaped and polished to cast real light. Only a master jeweler can do that.

And then you can immerse yourself in the experience of the heart. You cannot go to the heart with schemes and expectations, a script that has been edited. He rules; he is the king. You go empty, as a blank canvas and enter into communion with it to feel that which is your truth. "How can I serve you?" This is the attitude: kneeling down naked before your heart. Then it will take you to love – true love. And to an encounter with yourself which is necessary if you want to experience that level of love, and therefore of freedom and joy. God is there.

When are you going to stop opposing God? God wants you to be well why do you insist on the opposite? On punishing yourself? On suffering? You fix nothing; you don't come close to God – to the answer. You surrender to that which you give your love to. That must be something mighty. You don't surrender to an idol or to a human being; your true surrender must be the highest source of love and power in the Universe, a consciousness without ego. That consciousness you can trust completely because it wants your good beyond anything, without conditions, in which there is nothing in it for Him. That consciousness is your creator. It is God.

How can you not trust your creator? So many people don't trust God. He gave them life. What can God ask of them? Deep inside, the soul trusts God. It is the ego that doesn't. People think that God might want to take something away from them. Yes, their nonsense. They think joining God is for priests. They want to keep their little world of ego and misery instead of uniting with God and having the kingdom of God. Only in it there is all the bounty, the incredible bliss and freedom. People want to create a great kingdom on Earth when the kingdom is there waiting. God is sustaining it. People need to trust the Creator and surrender to the great will of God. Then they will see that the kingdom they seek is there. This is the paradise every soul yearns to return to, but they seem to only remember a faded idea of it and of where it is. It is not in your next holiday to a virgin island. Stargate is here with its most powerful and loving energies, to point the way, the way to paradise.

Don't miss the ship.

Responsibility and Power: The Key to Choice

Your responsibility is being given away when power is not there. Most people are always looking for the solution to their problems outside, in some kind of source, but they never find the answers. That keeps the person in a never-ending loop of desperation in which she cannot move ahead; although she might try many ways, many solutions and many techniques, she never quite manages to change. One cannot place responsibility outside and expect to have any control over the outcome. That is why the solution never arrives and the person keeps going around in circles, thinking the breakthrough hasn't come yet because she hasn't tried the appropriate technique. And thus she keeps trying new ones until the feeling that she is different and things don't work for her makes her abandon the search. Finally she stays the same, in the same place with the same mediocre experience of herself and life. She has missed a crucial element in the equation: that which kept her from taking part in the whole process, that which made her believe she was a mere observer of the process. Obviously she didn't realize she was the protagonist of the story, the problem and the solution and therefore had to get involved and be present in all the stages of it, since she was the sick person and the one to be healed. But that is the destiny of the path of not taking responsibility.

Whilst a person does not take the necessary responsibility, she does not have access to power in the situation, power to change. And therefore, she cannot change the situation or herself. When a person takes on responsibility she is able to change things and therefore evolve, improve, advance. More power means more choice. And choice means change. Having choice gives the opportunity to choose differently and advance.

> **Power leads to choice.**
> **Choice leads to change.**

Awakened power means choices, more ability to question and feel. Unwanted or inappropriate choices need greater exercise of power in the present, and this is able to change the course of life and destiny, by choosing light in the moment.

You have an individual responsibility for what you give to life and the Universe. With your acquired power you have a responsibility for blessing the Universe and all beings, all life forms, and do all that is necessary and what you are able to do for that.

Total Responsibility

The only way to assume all your power is to exercise total responsibility. When you ask yourself what you are responsible for, the answer is: everything. You do not have to wonder anymore what comes into it; you know that everything comes into it. Now, this sounds like a big statement, and it is, but let's look at it more closely. Total responsibility does not mean you are responsible for everything that happens around you and everyone there. It means you are responsible for all your thoughts, feelings, actions, words, for your life and what is in it: the happiness or the unhappiness. It refers to the role you play in every situation. You have relationships; you are responsible for putting all you can into them. You are responsible for your part in them, for making sure they are harmonious and they go well. The other person is responsible for her part in it. Hopefully, if all parts act responsibly it will be a great relationship and will fulfill the purpose for which it was created, giving all rewards, satisfaction and purpose.

This is valid for every area of your life: health, finances, spirituality, emotional well- being, your job, your house and so on. You have a part to play in all that. The thing is that most of the time people ignore the responsibility they have in an area or in many, and that is when the problem starts. I have portrayed the ideal relationship and what it needs for it to go well: all parts take their responsibility. I talk about relationships because all situations are relationships: couples, family, friends, work, home, circumstances. I include inanimate things like the house because you too have a relationship with things and circumstances. We know most relationships have many conflicts. That is because one or both sides do not fulfill their role, do not take responsibility and therefore renounce their power. When one part does that, power and responsibility inevitably fall on the other part, if the relationship is to continue. So there is an excess demand of power and responsibility on the other part. This is a conflictive situation most of the time, unless the part shedding responsibility is unable, due to past traumas or other reasons, to act as a fully responsibly agent in that situation. And the other part seeing this, supports that situation, taking the remaining responsibility until the other person is healed or able to act in full responsibility.

Unequal responsibility in any type of relationship, is very common. People have hang-ups and are not emotionally healed, most of the time. So they project their unsolved issues onto another person or people, resulting in a shift of responsibilities. This can happen consciously or unconsciously. But the balance must be redressed at some point, otherwise the situation does not embrace an evolutionary process for all involved thus sustaining dependency, and that as we know, is not a way to power.

As far as relationships with things and circumstances go, including work circumstances, you are responsible for providing in them what is needed, in as much as they depend on you. As a general rule you are responsible for everything that comes to your awareness, everything you notice. If you notice a bad political situation in your country for instance, you can intervene by praying, sending light, blessings and asking the Universe or God for a good outcome for the good of all. That is all you need to do unless you want to get involved more fully into politics or social activities that might be relevant. But turning your back on things, people and situations because they do not happen in your house or outside your front door is a mistake that most people make. This is our world, and people are our brothers and sisters, and a loving gesture, a generous action, or a simple prayer is something which is always within our reach. We are all responsible for the good of this world and the support of all life.

There are no rules as to how that full responsibility has to manifest. This is something you will have to find out each time, as you are connected with your heart and soul and your power, sustaining a consciousness of full responsibility. There are only guidelines of which these can be part, but you are the one who has to walk the path of full power and full responsibility and find the wisdom inside to walk it. Essentially, you are responsible for recovering your power and exercising it responsibly for your good and the good of all. Also, for your spiritual evolution which is what life and existence are about. In a nut shell:

You are responsible for making this life the best evolutionary event for you and for others.

If you don't increase your responsibility, there will be no growth. Without responsibility there is no expansion because you are not given more. With spiritual realities you are not given more consciousness if you don't increase your responsibility. Thus you need to take full responsibility for yourself if you want to ascend.

Responsibility and Attention Awareness

Your level of responsibility defines your level of attention awareness. If you are not responsible for something, your attention won't be on it. Why should it? It's not something that depends on you. But if you decided that was your responsibility, your attention awareness will be right on it. If things depend on you, you will be alert to them. The fact is that everything in your life depends on you. When you realize that your attention awareness is complete and total and is *on* all the time. The average person is *on* for the things he has decided have to do with him and depend on him, but he is *off* to the rest of the world around him. So the lack of attention awareness to many things around means people are half asleep most of the time.

That relates not only to things outside, but mainly to the things inside: to their inner universe. Body, mind, heart and spirit are the areas of the inner universe and are the responsibility of their owner. Responsibility for the body's health is often given to the doctor, be it a traditional doctor or alternative practitioner. They are both good at what they do well but they are a support, not the responsible agents for your health and wellness. Emotional responsibility is given to others especially the partner, who is often seen as the one who should makes one emotionally happy and keep him there. Mental responsibility is given to mass consciousness, others or the state of affairs as the reference on how to think. And it also happens to one's attitudes and beliefs, which are mostly set from outside. Spiritual responsibility is given to the church, priest, guru, or spiritual path one might be following, or to no one because one has decided that this area of consciousness doesn't exist.

If everything depends on you, the state of those areas depends on you, including what you do with them and to them. So as you sow, so shall you reap; and therefore as you treat your body, heart, spirit they will be. Ultimately there is no one other than you responsible for what you are, what you look like, how you feel and your spiritual evolution. You should of course, seek the help of the doctor when you need him and a spiritual master to guide you to spirit, but without giving the responsibility to them. Another way of looking at it: there is no one other than you responsible for the things in your life, the state of your life and everything in it. That is because consciously or unconsciously, you created everything. To most people this is not clear yet. It wasn't to me until I realized this fact. Now you can see the connection between power and responsibility: the more you have of one, the more you have of the other. And it is not fun to live a life without power, and it is not fun not to have full responsibility, because otherwise someone else has it. And you know what? That person or situation that owns the responsibility for that area of your life also owns the power. Thus, that person controls or rules your life.

Fun starts when we become fully responsible for everything. That requires us to take hold of all our power, and that is when we can create; that is fun. Nothing else is fun. If you don't own your power yet, you are not having fun because you cannot create, and if you cannot create it means a terrible thing: you cannot create what you want. That is why without power and responsibility, you will never be happy. Problem solved. We have unveiled the way to happiness. Now, do it. There is a difference between knowing and doing, thinking and living. And until you do it, this will not be true for you and hence it won't work its magic. With your attention awareness *on* all the time as a result of this, you will be present and therefore will enjoy life in the present. Also you will realize in what moment your power is moving away from you. As you focus on truth, truth will respond to you with its blessings and gifts. You have to do your part.

Awaken attention awareness and become fully responsible. To jump from one level of attention awareness to the other requires effort. To awaken the mind to a new level of alertness, effort is necessary to jump to it. Then to keep it that way is effort also, as the mind will have a tendency to fall unconscious again and go back to its previous level of attention awareness – where it does not require effort to function.

This will happen until the passion for life and creation is awakened enough in this process and it sets the mind free from the inertia and its slippery tendencies to go down — until you have a mind which is focused, present and powerful. You must desire your power, feel you deserve it and accept it. Then you will open the door to it. Otherwise it won't happen. At the end, the result of the taking on of responsibility is giving: you become a human being who is not looking at taking, but a human being that is naturally giving all the time as a way of life. To give fully, attention awareness must be *on* all the time. This is important since in ascension you are required to take on all responsibility that is yours. Get prepared, untrained consciousness rejects that which it is not prepared to take on. You cannot take on something you don't feel you are responsible for.

Take on what is yours. Spiritual ascension is your own responsibility. So start having attention awareness *on* all the time. Ascension is already happening.

Things to Consider...

- To meditate is to go to the source of love to acquire the state of love. Inside is where there is the love power. You can find it through meditation.

- With power things take less effort and are more potent. With it, everything is in harmony and flows without effort.

- Addictions are an act of not taking responsibility. Addicted behavior is powerless.

- Smile; fill your heart chakra with love and send that smile and love to a person or a situation to better it. Send it to the world.

- Be true to your heart's truth and do not worry about a thing. God is in you.

Love: The Greatest Power

"There is no love without power;
there is no power without love."

As you gain power you will find your expression of love takes many forms. Love is infinite; the expressions of love are infinite. We in society tend to see love as that which is soft, tender, but often fail to recognize the more power-driven expressions of love. Those ones in which love expresses more strength, authority and intensity. That is because humanity's power is sleeping and it cannot recognize power as part of love. True love has power, stamina, higher resolution, ability to act. It is not soft and weak. True softness and tenderness come from true power. Otherwise they cannot be there in a real way.

To let go is a great act of power and, often of love. To be able to say good-bye to something that does not fit anymore in our lives is a powerful act of love. This is true giving. Persons that we do not relate to any more, and we are able to recognize that, are situations in which we need to exercise our power. And then see that the only way from there is to let go. This naturally happens as you ascend. You have to come to terms with that. That requires an increment of power.

Power happens when you have cleared your channels of everything else that is not power. The issue is the amount of divine power you can hold; the amount of "channeling" God you can do, as opposed to channeling ego. Channeling ego is not giving your best. There is giving, but ego comes out to take. We are always bringing something out; it is a matter of choosing the right thing: that which works. This is the amount of the divine experience you are going to have. When you are with God, everything you do is giving. You have to decrystallize yourself to access greater love power. As everything that is not power in you is liberated, then you can hold greater amounts of love.

God has no structure, but has all the power. He is not crystallized. His cohesion is so strong that He doesn't disappear due to not having structure. That cohesion is love power. Otherwise without structure, He would just dissolve. This means God has no structure, but in order to exist He needs infinite cohesion. That is love. You need to increase your love to increase your cohesion; and you need to increase your cohesion to increase your power. So as you increase your love, power manifests. It is love that produces cohesion. It works both ways:

"More power; more love.
More love; more power."

Most people now, even many who are working spiritually, cannot fully hold the states of divine power. They lose them like sand through their hands. They don't have enough cohesion. So they are not so effective at holding the light for the Earth. They are not powerhouses: their energy leaks out. But with the right training they could be. Through the right spiritual work and concentration — and making sure that spiritual advance anchor to them — they can become more cohesive, loving and powerful. Then their giving would increase. This is important. The Earth needs all those who are in the light to be strong and to be able to hold the new energies, the new light. Humanity needs true givers with power, those who can radiate intense light because they have anchored the new frequencies in their body and aura.

The stronger a wire is, the more electricity it can conduct. That strength is in its section; the wider it is, the better. The same goes for people. As they work spiritually their energy channels become wider and stronger, and their aura does too, so they can hold the intensity of the experience of love and power that is coming in now. The stronger the wire, the more it can conduct; the stronger you are, the more you can transmit spiritual power, the more you can give. Your energy system is the same: strong physical, emotional, mental and spiritual bodies. They are the ones where the new energy and light has to be anchored; it has to go through them into your life and into the world.

The greatest power is love. Love as the creative and sustaining force in the Universe. Love is unknowable. Love is the cause of itself; it is the only independent thing there is. It cannot be known. You can feel it, be it, realize it, but it is a mystery. Love is the greatest mystery there is. It is amazing how it exists and creates everything. It is sheer power, total giving; it is beyond us and everything.

A structure needs cohesion to keep its form and be what it is, like a tree or a church. What keeps them like that is the inner cohesion of love. It is not science in the classical way; science has believed for too long that there is a physical force or magnetism inside particles of matter that creates things. But they haven't discovered fully yet that physical creation, the physical universe, has a spiritual cause. In a way what they say is true; that magnetism is called *love*.

God has no fixed form, has no structure. He can take any form: He is infinite possibilities. So to keep His integrity He needs infinite cohesion as we have seen. This is love. Humanity is moving towards this state on the ascension journey.

•

"We are caused by love.
When your love has no
cause, then you are truly
loving. That is real power."

Power Supports Love

In all respects, all that you do out of fear is an act of no power; all that you do out of love is an act of power. When you are in fear, you are placing yourself in a position of belief in your lack of power. This is with reference to yourself, but also relating to a situation, person, or event in your life. You see yourself as being smaller in the situation, smaller in power: you feel less power than the one you are facing. This is a belief you are holding, unless you are facing a lion and are in his territory. But most situations in life are not like that: the lions are a product of our imagination. Conquering fear is mainly about stop imagining… and start believing.

Acting in love requires freedom. There is an energy around someone who acts in love; there is an aura of confidence and self-belief, a relaxed attitude due to faith and confidence and a power supporting

154

all that. There is expansion, not contraction as is the case with fear. All that is the face of power. To exercise love requires power. True love is an act of power, and the nature and the burning of your love depends on the power you have been able to awaken and harness in yourself. Passionless love is a product of no power.

We are moving to a state of greater love in humanity. But it is necessary to understand that this will only happen if we increase our inner power. The new energies are bringing this alchemy in humans — the inner awakening of power. So humanity can finally move to those levels of love that have always been mentioned by the true masters and have been there waiting; but most people haven't had access to them. Stargate energies are breaking the vicious cycle in which humanity has been for a long time, in which it has been unable to move beyond the ordinary human love — with the mediocre results this has produced. Breaking that vicious cycle means catapulting human consciousness to higher experiences of power and therefore, of love. Finally the door is open for all.

You Are the Power in Your Life

When you increasingly assume you are all the power in your life, you realize that everything happens from you, there are no outside forces manipulating your life: it is you or your unconscious creations. Of course that power, as we have seen in another part of the book, comes from God. But you are the acting power, the one influencing your life with it.

Most people talk about life as if there were elements acting in their life that they do not control, unknown forces which nobody knows what their outcomes will be. They shed power away without even noticing it, instead of rooting themselves in their powerful centers and driving their lives with conviction. True is that the Universe plays a great part in things, but the Universe is our ally if we are our allies. If we take power the Universe will respond to that; if we don't the response will be what we expect: no power, less influence. The Universe returns to us the creations we put out through thoughts, words, feelings, and actions. What happens is that most people are not aware most of the time what they are doing with their minds, words, feelings and actions and the repercussions those have. And they get back the crop they have sown a long time ago without realizing it; that is what they are experiencing. But if we sow the seeds of consciousness and power we will experience the results in our lives, and our creations will be aligned with our greatest conscious vision. Eventually you reach the consciousness of, "I can create everything with God." We are alchemists; we can turn everything into goodness with the magic of love and light. God is our best ally in that, and that is the legend you can live if that is your choice; it is available. God gives you what you need.

If you are the power of your life, it means nobody does anything to you. This is true, although most people very often do not live as such. Human beings spend a great amount of time dwelling on what they think someone did or is doing to them. Listen to this: no one does anything to you. It is your psyche that "does" to you. But you project its unconscious elements onto others thinking they "do" things to you. Since those projections attracted those events to your life, you are the one creating them. As we gain our power back we know this is true. While we don't have power we only see people and a world that is doing things to us. This is a victim's attitude. This attitude is precisely one of no power. Acquiring your power changes the reality and the perception of the person. You might not understand that from your present place of relative power, but try to believe it. When you do, you will see for yourself. Realizing you are the power in your life is essential to move to the next level.

- Power makes you relaxed. When you are relaxed you have power. Tension is contraction; you are conceding power. The more power you have, the less importance you give to mundane things. The less importance objects and possessions have for you, the less things affect you.

You decide…

- The life you want to live
- What you do in your life
- How you do it
- How you feel
- What you think
- What you believe in

If you are not doing these things yourself, find out
and recognize who is doing them for you.

Owning Your Power

"I am absolute power."
"I am strong" – See yourself strong.
"It doesn't affect me" – Unwanted influences.
"Nothing affects me."
"Nobody affects me."
"I have faith in what I am."
"My value is on the divine."

"I do not feel guilty for doing what I want."
"For saying what I want and feel."
"I do not feel guilty for my decisions."
"I do not feel guilty for having or exercising my power."
"I have faith that I am well and that everything is well."
"I have all the power of God in my disposition."
"I have total conviction in myself."
"I am – with God Source – the only power in my mind"
"I only do that which I want to do."
"Nothing and no one has power over me."
"I am not afraid of being powerful and influential."

These statements can be very challenging to the mind and ego. They don't negotiate with half-truths. But as you become more spiritually independent and power-conscious, you will free yourself and your power-holding ties, and you will live these truths without flinching. Just take into account that at that time, you will see for yourself that they are the truth.

Of course, remember the golden rule when applying those statements into action and in your interaction with others: power and freedom are yours if always in exercising them you respect others fully — their power and freedom. Otherwise you are not exercising divine power, but ego. Divine power always sees all sides, not only one selfish side of the equation. If you do not observe good will and the use of power for good, you will fall so hard karma is going to remind you for a long time your mistake. So be very careful. I am giving you a great key to freedom and goodness; use it in the opposite direction, that of self-interest and stepping over others and your karma will make you lose so much power that you will have less than when you started. Power is about respecting others, the power and rights of others and all life. Otherwise it is not power, it is a dictatorship, a way to accumulate bad karma.

But realize that you have the right to your power and the right to your independence, that is: to be and feel what you want. And if you want to feel power, God supports you because He is there for that and created you with power. Help people as much as you can, as far as that is what your heart tells you. There are many ways to help. Sometimes not intervening is the best way you can help. It is not your responsibility how people feel; it is your responsibility to act in the best way. You might be losing your peace if you make yours the responsibility of how others feel. Then manipulation starts.

Find the reality that you do not depend on anything, that there is no outside force making you dependent. You are free to act in love. There are laws of love; those are the ones you must make yours. Invoke more light from God so that all this is so for you. God is always there liberating. You take it when you want it, when you open yourself. Own your power now and heaven, just there waiting, will welcome you very soon.

- *Visualize yourself as an angelical being of light, with Divine Power and power to bless everyone in every moment of life. See light coming out of you, out of your eyes.*

The Universe Works for You

To embody the consciousness of the Stargate we need to understand better the options the Universe gives us from an enlightened perspective. This is different from the third- dimensional conception humanity has had of the Universe until now. The Universe is on your side; the Universe works for you. You just have to understand that and know how that happens. But if you ignore this is the case, you won't understand many of the things that are going on, not only in your life but in the world at large. You must only accept the good. Do not feel at the mercy of; feel you dictate in your life the things you want to happen in it. So nothing else can affect you or manifest other things than the ones you want, because you are the one who has the power. Just make sure you own it. Feel a limitless power capable of influencing your life and the Universe for the good.

You are in life to use all the resources that are available to you to create the greatest creation you can. Use them. To do that you have to start by owning the power God has made available to you, so you create the life you want. Would it make sense if God gave you free will to create what you want but wouldn't give you the power to do it? That would be nonsense. We have free will, so we must have power with it too. You are in the midst of a Universe that responds to your wishes. With love you can create in it what you want. Dare to do it; that is all you need. It might take some true work, facing

159

your obsolete beliefs, those that limit you to this reality. It might be a huge task, but you must do it if you want to grow as a more enlightened person. Before flying high the ties to the ground must be loosened and freed. Take-off is not granted just because you want it. In our human condition sometimes limits have been created with a lot of care and over a long time. Change can happen, and it just takes a second. To manifest its full implications might take a bit longer. But to undo the things that we have done wrong for a long time, takes a while. And it is the wrong direction to have built a life full of chains to support the fears you have chosen to believe in. Think about it…

Power is not somewhere to be found; it is here. And a lot of people sit passively, waiting for things to happen or for the chains to disappear. You created them; you remove them. You had the power to create a life of slavery; aren't you going to have the power to undo that and create a life of freedom? Of course you are. But people often don't believe that. They surrounded themselves with limiting conditions and then decided to have amnesia as to who did that. A major awakening has to happen. This is absolutely necessary to realize in order to be able to go to the realms of light available through ascension.

The more power you use for good, the more it arrives. Feel that magic happening inside you because you have that divine power. Your cells regenerate, your life moves ahead, good things happen because you are there. You become full of light and power; everything is perfection in you. You have the power to influence life for your good and the good of others. Feel it. Don't allow your emotional body content of self-pity, or other low frequency feelings sabotage you. Dialogue with it, instruct it, take it to your domain of power and change those low frequency feelings for feelings of power. It is important that all areas of yourself, thoughts, feelings, beliefs, emotions, attitudes are joined in consensus: they unite with that objective. That will move you forward. The Universe works for you, you are the boss, you are not a subordinate; you are the cause. This is the truth. Most of humanity doesn't live it; most probably you don't either. But this is the way to go and the truth waiting to be manifested for you and all in these times.

- Have the consciousness:

"The Universe works for me. All that I want that is good happens. My cells are illuminated with love, power, magnetism, vision. I put love to something and it grows. I love and I attract."

The Universe: An Open Equation

"Belief is the seed; it is your crop.
Everything starts by believing.
What you believe, happens…"

The Universe is a quantum equation. This means that depends… on what? On you. We have seen this. We can go one step deeper into the workings of the Universe; it is the correct relationship with it for beings in the process of ascension. The Universe is not closed; it is open to manifesting possibilities. It answers calls, to manifest them. Those come from creative consciousness. This consciousness is in you and me. That creative consciousness is belief. Belief ordains the Universe and configures your reality on the screen of your life. Thus with your belief you manifest your reality. The Universe is a sensitive field that responds to your creation, through your belief. It is not a static and defined field; it is a live field of possibilities that defines itself constantly according to belief. That is your creative power.

What do you want to believe?

The Universe is not defined; you define it with your confidence and faith. The only thing that is lacking in any situation is your confidence... and you were waiting for it to be perfect... What is lacking is your decision, that you take your power. I often see people waiting for things to be perfect before they engage in a situation. They fear that it might not work because the situation is not ready yet, so they experience a kind of insecurity about the whole thing. They fail to realize that what is missing is their confidence, and that no situation will ever be perfect or ready unless they are, unless they place their confidence in it. As a result they never get involved with anything.

The equation of the Universe is open and therefore, everything is possible in it. A belief is a zoom on the field of all possibilities, and it considers just one of those. It does a "take" on the field of all possibilities and takes out that one possibility as real. That is the reality then; but it excludes all others that might be incompatible with it. So with belief systems one forms his own reality by picking out what each belief believes, and creates his personal reality. That take is what is considered "real." That is what manifests. That belief was the power to manifest it.

Power is to be invested; you are not meant to have it and that is it. It is to be used, to be invested in creativity, in good actions that generate goodness. We must never forget: power is God's power. We administrate it in our lives and get the benefits of that. His power is so creative we receive the spontaneous creations it generates, and those creations are there so we can enjoy the good they bring. You can believe in the best for you. New energies are supporting that for you. Do you want it? You command. So, "What is it you want to believe... now? Today?" This is your reference for life. You create it from there.

**The only thing that is missing in any situation
is that you decide to take your power.**

Old Belief Systems Are Over

If you think you have to have difficulties, you will have them. There are no truths, only self-made truths. The sayings that for so long have haunted mankind as pretensions of truth are just that: pretensions. People live through the eyes of a belief system humanity inherited over thousands of years... of distorted reality and absence of true knowledge. That has created a belief system that has been the reference book of humanity. "Things are difficult." "Life is hard." "You cannot do everything." "You shouldn't do that." "Death is the end." They are all statements of no power. As if we were at the mercy of life and we were hopeless victims that mean nothing and have no influence on how things are. This is a lie. You can move out of this system and live a complete different reality — on Earth — by changing the system inside you: your belief system. Change your awareness, recover your power and come join us in a dimension where life is lived in a different way, where there is no weakness, illness, death, hardship or difficulties. It is called: ascension.

Blessings of Universal Power:
A Question of Gratitude

There is a Universal force of all possibilities, as I mentioned before. Everything comes from it and is channeled for us in different ways through circumstances, people and events. Look at the blessings of that force in your life, then ask yourself how you feel about your life. Are you feeling miserable? Sad? Unhappy? This is because you are looking at what you are lacking. Look at what you have. Look at how you live, who you are, who is with you, what you do, what you can do... the manifestations of grace in your life. When you look at what you have, there are no reasons to be unhappy. There are no motives to complain, only to give thanks and continue to grow. Look at the blessings in your life. They all come from the benevolence

163

and abundance of the Universal Force. It is infinite power. We can continue opening up to the unlimited power of that force, welcoming more prosperity, blessings, love, power; we can surrender more to its goodness, love and possibilities: its infinite power of blessing. Or we can stop where we are. How much of it do you want?

Thanks to it, we can all live a life of true prosperity. If you don't, there is a need to review where and why that flow of universal blessings is being blocked for you. Undoubtedly, this is something you are doing, consciously or not. But once you remove that and understand you deserve all the prosperity there is available and see that you have not been cast away by that force — your guilt probably has — you will open the doors to communion with it. By opening more to it we can embrace and become one with the bounty and blessings coming in now.

Always see the positive: it is there. Infinite bounty is always there waiting to manifest through our open hearts into our lives; the bigger the space inside, the more we can be filled with it. Often what we most need to let go for this, is the idea of smallness and the contractions we have acquired through wrong beliefs that shed power off. Power is there; take it. His is the magnet that attracts everything to you. In my previous book, *The Violet Light: The Power That Changes Everything,* I said that love is what attracts everything to you. I haven't changed my mind; it's just that power is the other side of love. As I have mentioned, they go together: in love there is power; in true power there is love. And in that book I talk about the concept of *love power* as the essence of that mystical and great companion, the Violet Light, a great emanation of the power of God.

Let's find some quiet time and get involved with the high vibrations that a brief and powerful prayer will give us.

Prayer:

"We praise God from our enlightened hearts
in His light that fills us with joy, abundance
and love, in order to offer His gifts in us to others,
to life and to Him with all humility and gratitude."
- Amen.

Power declarations

"I am all the power."
"I am the power of God in me."
"I choose the divine freely."
"I choose love freely."
"I listen to my internal authority."
"Only I decide for me."

ELEMENTS OF POWER

Seeing Through the Eyes of Ascension

True Power: Detachment and Freedom

As you go on recovering your divine power and acting in the true sovereignty it gives you, you have to find a new detachment from the world. It means to accept a new freedom in the way you operate inside yourself, free from the pressure of the ways of the Matrix of the Dark. You need to make the matrix and its ways respect your freedom of action, which comes from the divine power and new consciousness in you. This can be tough. We have seen many aspects of this in the previous sections, but a new detachment has to be born in you.

You must find detachment from pressure, from what people think about you and your actions. You have the power in your life; you act according to that freedom and sovereignty it gives you. It is between you and God. It has always been this way. God does not object to your correct use of power. If others do, remember it is not between you and them. When you develop your wisdom and your power you use it for loving ways. Those ways might be original and new and always carry a teaching. It is inevitable, you act with true spiritual power in a world without it; you are always teaching a lesson in power and freedom. This is a lesson of love.

So when you act from your own enlightened power consciousness, you will be rearranging things and putting them and people in their place, if they aren't. In a world lacking the consciousness of true power, people will expect you to keep giving your power away so they can continue to function in their own ways of borrowing power, in the generalized unconsciousness and lack of love. Let everything pass without letting it stick to you. The more you awaken your true power with the new energies, the more you will move away from standard unconscious practices based on lack of power. This is necessary. As you ascend, you elevate the whole consciousness of humanity.

More power, more detachment.
More detachment, more power.

Power and Abundance:
The Cycle of Giving Starts with Belief

Nothing is ours. Power is made available to us from God, and the key is our openness to that. We have seen many of the aspects that rule this equation, as we are using the flow from the Source. Giving is the way of the Universe. For that to operate correctly you must have your power in place. Otherwise you will be seeking to take because you will feel a lack: a lack of power. This is also a lack of faith. Such lack hits everywhere and one wants to get. Giving maintains the cycle of God who gives to Himself through Creation benefiting all. Life creates life by giving and receiving. It means you cannot possess anything. The moment you want to possess something you become selfish and you stop the cycle: the flowing stops. Everything is the "goods" of God, and we administer them as we use them for good. This means to honor and respect; to love and be grateful. To give is ensuring that you receive. Thus it all starts by having faith and giving from there. If there is no faith you don't start the cycle, you just seek to get. Once you give you cannot stop it: you receive. By moving that provision you generate a vacuum ensuring the receiving: it will be filled with abundance. Sowing secures the harvest. God secures love and teaches the way to it. God makes sure you are a provider like Him.

**The more faith, the more you give, the more you receive.
The more power in you, the more you can give.**

So we know where it all starts. Through this process the Universe receives the message that you give, and the mechanism of receiving and expanding enters into action. You are a giver: you are positive, you have faith. If you are negative, you don't have faith, you don't give. If you believe, you help others believe through resonance. If you don't give, you invite others to not believe. If you give love, love will come back to you.

*"Faith is to give life the opportunity
to show you what it has for you."*

To have faith is to give life that opportunity. It is giving to it, and thus it gives you back. If you don't have faith you close the door on life. If you are giving it all, it gives you all: you open the door to it. Faith is to be with God. It is to be in the company of the Divine. Faith is giving life the opportunity to give you what it has to give you. The more faith, the more opportunities, the more it gives you. There is more real power in peace than in controlling; in letting go than in keeping. Again we find truth in Jesus' messages:

"You have been blessed, you that have believed."

God gives you everything as a result of your belief in it. What do you want? Start believing it. By believing it you have already given it to yourself, because you have created that possibility for you, for your reality. To obtain something you must first give. This is the way the Universe works. That first giving is your belief in it. When you give, give with the consciousness that in giving one gains, one receives; one doesn't lose. Know that it is by giving that you make it yours because it comes back to you. It is attracted to you and returns to you all the time. It makes its dwelling in you. If you don't give and you covet, you won't find love, peace, gratitude. And you ask, "Where is it for me?" If you haven't given, you haven't generated, you have not created – there isn't.

169

When you are filled with the presence of God, having renounced your ego identity, you want nothing. You are filled with the power of God. When you want nothing, you can only give. This is a state of fullness. This is where true service comes from: the realization that in God, we have all, and the only thing to do is to give of that abundance. Doing this now is the way to ascend: you are going to be filled with blessings from your true state of divine fullness. The high vibrations will pick up on that and will lift you. The less ego, the less density, the less weight, the more you can be ascended.

"Faith is the platform on which the gifts of God travel."

High and Low Power: Power Management

Higher power comes from Spirit. Higher power has wisdom, it takes everyone into account; it seeks the best outcome for all at once. Ego power is limited, it manipulates, it only seeks its own benefit. There is no doubt what the place to be now is.

An action is dealt with completely differently if you live it from higher power. Higher power is compassionate; lower power is cruel. You have to develop spiritually to have access to higher power. If you act from lower power you are undoubtedly immersed in ego consciousness. Spirit power allows you to act for love, service. Your consciousness must be transmuted to use power for the good of all, for compassion. With spirit power you use that power for the benefit of all, to help, to bless. You become an agent for good. You are an instrument of higher consciousness. You seek peace in situations, reconciliation harmony, unity. The other power seeks confrontation from the ego separation, opposition; definitely not peace. Confrontation that comes from higher power seeks resolution and to stir things up because they are too politically correct, too asphyxiating for higher consciousness to manifest and therefore, for love and peace to show. There, someone is always paying a price. And that price always means slavery: some are where they are because others are where they shouldn't be – under their tyranny. The equation is always the same with ego power: some gain, some lose.

In higher power, there is no price there is freedom: all gain.

So the more evolved and conscious you are the greater the use of power. Even if it is a small amount of power you access at any given time, your use of it is for good. In fact, the more evolved you are, the more true power you have.

Empowering Your Life:
Believing In Power — Not In Limits

"You have to make the most of what you have.
Be positive, don't think of the limit; dwell on
what you can do with what you have."

Often people dwell on what they are missing and in that they are missing one fact: the power they have. They have less power because they look for a power that is not there. Whereas if they focused on what they have, they could concentrate on the power there and use it all. That power is truly available; the other is not. Being positive in this issue of power is crucial. If we think of the limits, the things we cannot do, we are taking importance away from the things we can do. But seeing the things we can do with what we have opens a door to power. If we are not positive, we are missing opportunities. The same situation can be read in different ways. If you believe in yourself, you will see a mine of gold in your hands. If you are negative, you will undervalue your potential and your assets: inner and outer. As you undervalue those potentials, they do not become available to you because you do not believe they are there — you do not see them.

Faith opens your eyes to see possibilities that are otherwise hidden. That is the story of Avalon, a magical island hidden in the mists of a lake. Avalon could only be found by people who believed in it, people who believed it was there. Then it would appear. Avalon was beyond the mists, which would open themselves to those who believed.

Walk with faith ahead of you and doors will open miraculously. I was leaving a monastery with a friend and after joining the monks for their 6 a.m. service and sacred chants, we went back to the cottage to pick up our things. We didn't have the key, and the cottage was on the monastery grounds. As we approached it, my friend said, "The door is locked and we don't have the key." I continued walking regardless. That thought had not entered my mind and it wasn't going to do so then. To me, everything was perfect. I said, "Have faith." She said, "You are right. You always walk with faith in all you do." That comment made me aware of something I did spontaneously: to believe in the positive outcome of things, and always keep going ahead trusting everything would come out right. You can work at it and make it steady. That steadiness is all weatherproof; it will be there no matter what and it will develop to a point in which it is second nature. Then, no matter what the situation is, you still believe in the power of faith and in the perfect positive outcome. When we arrived at the cottage, I went for the door as if the only real possibility was that the door was open — and it was.

- *Doors open and thick mists reveal magical islands full of treasures. This happens by your conviction in possibilities. With the conviction faith in power gives you, you move away from limits and see possibilities that are otherwise hidden from sight. This is the right attitude to approach your ascension; all the mists will open for you and light will appear.*

172

Only One Power

The reality is that everything is God. God is the only source of power there is in the Universe. This is a fact. Any other seeming power borrows its power from Him. In the Universe everything is possible, also deceiving oneself. So one can believe one is the source of power, instead of God, and things have their own power independently of Him who created them. This is a world of disguises. God is hidden; this is part of the play. It is a play of consciousness, a way to become conscious and therefore, as God is. So in the structuring of this life things have been configured as if they have their own power. But God is behind them. God is all you see, disguised as what you see. But He doesn't end there. All you are, all your beauty is an offering of God to you. Your beauty and all else is the power of God. He makes you beautiful, His light does. Everything you do is because He gives you the energy and the power to do it. So do what you want with it, make a good creation of beauty and love and power for yourself and your life and offer it all to Him. This is your gratitude. In recognizing Him as the cause of your gifts and light you secure some things:

- Unity with Him – getting close
- Not falling into vanity – in ego
- Growing
- Receiving more
- Giving more – generosity
- Being more abundant

God wants the best for you, but if you believe in ego and its power, He knows you are deceiving yourself and that as a result, you will suffer. So it is better to believe in God and His power.

"Ego power comes up short. God's power is unlimited."

With each breath, in each moment, in each feeling, in each action, what you see is the Self; what acts is the Self, but you might not recognize it. Meditate; get to know your inner Divine Self. Let the joy in your heart invade your body, yourself. Rise to the crown of your head – top chakra – and be expanded to God. Put the other — the one before you — first, her needs, her feelings. Be yielding. Sow and you will reap. In giving, you receive.

The power of God works this way.

•

It is God's power active in each one
what is needed for global ascension.

The Power of Compassion

It is all about compassion. With it you see things you cannot see without it. The power of compassion is immense. You understand things with it you otherwise wouldn't understand. You act and care for life in a way that is only possible with compassion. In seeking the good of all, you are exercising the greatest power. This is the power of compassion. Teach your children about compassion and you will change the world. In compassion awareness you are not thinking about yourself but about being an agent for good — for the good of all.

"Ascension is about compassion."

Love with Power is Freedom

Many people think that because they love, they have rights over others. Then they impose their agenda and their needs on them: ties, chains and restrictions. Of course, that is not love, at least not truthful love. It is a love that has been distorted by the ego contents, and although the love is genuine and born in the heart, the ego has taken possession of it and is making its own case: using love for its purposes. That is why it is so important now, as it has always been, to clear the negative content of unresolved issues in the emotional body. That unresolved negativity will attach itself to light — in this case love coming from the heart — to feed from its energy and be resolved: it wants you to become conscious of it. That is why love often brings out what is not love, because it pushes out what might be impeding and interfering with its full and pure expression.

Those chains imposed on others — who are as confused as the doer because of the general lack of power on Earth's humanity — imply that a person object of love is accountable to the one who loves. It should be the other way around; he who loves is in a position of responsibility: loves and sets free. No one is to tie a chain around the persons he loves. In true love there is a feeling of gratitude for that act of loving.

True love is freedom. This love has power and doesn't need to own anyone. You love and set free. It is not that you love and create chains around your loved ones. This is a love that lacks power. It is the effect of love when people have not recovered their power. Most human beings work this way. That is not love; it is possession, the opposite of freedom. There is a great power in creating freedom, the quality of true love. A love that pretends to take freedom away is not love but fear. Love is the thing to do. The response of some people might be to not return love. But love is foremost a space that allows life to be. And allows people to be what they want, and at the same time it might want to provide the means for their goodness and evolution, and support that which they want to become.

The world is a place structured in the wrong way. Structures are based on an absence of God — absence of love and true power — due to a disconnection with Him. The world has therefore developed to compensate for that lack with a clinging to things, especially the physical form: fear at the base. It couldn't be any other way, a disconnection with the Creator and power source of life inevitably has to bring fear, a very basic fear; a great feeling of being without support at the mercy of whatever in the Universe. Thus creating attachment, control, manipulation, suffering, dependence, producing fear and angry reactions when what is, is being challenged. But what is, is basically a set of assumptions to hold onto a false case of security and safety: a game created by the ego mind to deceive itself as to how things really are in that major disconnection.

All that shows dependency due to a lack of true independence, born of holding power back. That is why the response of humans to love is often a neurotic one that tries to hold on to things to find a sense of belonging through it — and an unhealthy way to find a reference, reference that can never be substituted by the true one. And it will never be the same as that one. This is why unless there is a true return to contact with the source — where true power is — human beings will be in an unending search for something that will give them a sense of worth, belonging and safety; but as this can never be found away from the source, it is a process that is never fulfilled. This makes people consumers of everything: things, ideas and relationships. True love from a healed consciousness is the only thing that will give it.

"Independent love through power recovery is the passport to the new age."

Power Sustains No Excuses

There are no excuses to not do what you want — to act the truth of your heart. He who doesn't do what he wants is because he doesn't want. He doesn't want to feel rejected, doesn't want to be pointed out, doesn't want to be exposed, doesn't want to be criticized, doesn't want the risk it presupposes, doesn't want the responsibility …he doesn't want. This is the denial of self power.

The excuse is that: an excuse. An excuse to not doing, to not facing. An excuse to not taking power and acting on it. And it works as a deviation in consciousness: wanting to believe that there is a force or a reason that impedes it. It is a way to hide the true reason: that one doesn't want. Sometimes one doesn't want to be free to do what he wants because that implies facing situations that are challenging and issues that require attention and consciousness that need to be resolved before being able to do what one wants. And that is what one doesn't want to recognize and resolve. To advance to a place worth being, you'll have to come out of this deceit and enter the realm of no excuses. When you have no excuses to do what you must, to accomplish your life plan, to evolve as you are supposed to, then you are free. If you want to ascend, there are no excuses.

**"You have excuses or
you have power."**

Declaration of Independence

*"Dominance is dependent.
True power is in freedom."*

A lot of people expect others not to betray their "truth," so their ego is not broken. The only way to function in sanity in life is to be truly independent from this situation.

This is a declaration of personal independence and freedom that summarizes it. A very valid and useful one in these times:

"Don't ask me keep your ego alive by not owning my power and serving your purposes of keeping you in illusion. Propose what you wish, suggest to me, if you feel that way, but leave it up to me to decide what is for me. Don't ask me to follow your expectations, to

177

do what is valid for you, that I act as you believe I should act. Don't ask me to give support to your ideas, belief systems, your vision of the world if they don't support your own power and freedom, Recognize that what you see is not what I see; what you want is not what I need; what you expect doesn't give me joy. I respect all that in you, but it would be inconsiderate to want to impose it on me. Thus you also have to accept and respect my vision, my feeling, my action — my way."

This is a declaration of independent self-power before others, not above others but in their presence and interactions with them. In a world that sells power in exchange for easy comfort and unconsciousness, people expect others to do the same so no one confronts them with that lack of power. This is to want to remain asleep. The price is too high. Again we see more of that declaration of power:

"Don't ask me to be your servant to keep you asleep; to be slave of your slavery. I cannot and will not support manipulation, lies, acting as you want me to, to keep you sleeping. Maybe you don't like me waking you up, but beside me, you cannot be asleep. To keep you asleep, I would have to deceive myself and pretend to be something I am not. That, I will not do. I know what I have to do from myself, to what I have to and want to be loyal to: God, His light, His truth. If you come close to me, you will have to awaken. If you don't want to awaken, don't come close."

"You can ask me to be myself because it is the only thing I can give you. Ask this of me honestly without it being colored by your expectations, by your lacks, by your needs, by your script, by what you believe of life, by what you want me to be for you, thus renouncing everything that is not love, not loving or not respectful to me. You will be free and will find peace next to me because you will allow me to be myself and be free, and that will generate all the love you need, and that you are looking for and don't find in other ways. Ask me to be myself; otherwise you are asking me to be you, and that is impossible; it is selfish and there, you feel very lonely. Ask me to

be myself to be able to accompany you in love. Don't judge me for bringing you light. If you open up and receive it, it will bless you."

Self-Faithfulness

"Be faithful to yourself..."

...is the first law of life and conscious evolution.

You cannot be faithful to another's will and be happy. Unless this is the Will of God. But then His Will only seeks your happiness.

The Power of Freedom:
The Aboriginal Connection

Aborigines are a manifestation of power and freedom. We can learn from their ways. We need their freshness and wisdom for our path. And to become more like them to get closer to the fifth dimension. Read about them in this writing I did years ago. I was looking at a tapestry with aborigines. This is what I wrote:

The aborigines

"Aborigines are great masters. They go almost naked... vulnerable — they are exposed and therefore in touch. Since they are in touch they have knowledge and wisdom and feeling. With feeling they are present and in reality. In being exposed, they lack rigid structures and therefore they have movement. Movement takes them to dance — inner and outer cosmic dance — this takes them to joy. In dancing they are light, let all go and become free. In being free they are at peace and that way, they know God. Since they don't have structures they are free to move and flow; this way they adapt, avoid conflict and evolve while they stay young. Movement takes them to rite and ceremony to celebrate the sacred. The dance-ceremony of war symbolizes the conquest of themselves, since the enemy is only inside. This makes them wise. They have a great deal of power because they don't have the crystallized and limiting structures of civilization. Thus, they are in contact with the heart, soul, Earth and cosmos."

"Barefoot in contact with the Earth, they live in the natural cycles, and in this way they maintain balance. The lack of structures also makes them simple, uncomplicated, happy. In being exposed, they are sincere without additives; they have nothing to hide. That is why they don't play roles; they are themselves. They cannot pretend being something else. There is no deceit, they are in touch: they know who they are; one sees what they are."

"They are aborigines... free beings. Being aboriginal, means being authentic. For as long as they have movement, they will be alive and free from rigidity, dogma and fear... they will always be able to enter into the cosmic dance. Free, they become living spirits in the cosmic dance of the Universe. Dance takes them to rhythm, and rhythm to life. Dance takes them to raise their vibration and that, to the mystical experience."

Keys for These Moments

Don't accept limiting habits. Open your heart's vision and break all limits.

"God is with me in this moment." Have this consciousness.
"God is supporting me in this moment." Live this truth.

What effort are you making to break the inertia of your habits? The thought patterns, the inertia you have created year after year that takes you to the same things, to the same thoughts, same actions, same results.

Pain closes the heart. Love comes and opens the heart. First thing it finds is pain, and it closes again. We have to keep opening our hearts until we are purified from their pain and reach love in them.

So you need to consider this:

- Check the pain in your heart.
- Clean it with violet light
- Forgive
- Enter into love
- Enter into peace
- Keep your vibration high

Understand who you are serving. Decide who you want to serve. If you are on the path of retaking your power and liberation to gain your freedom, you will serve compassion and love. If you lack compassion, you lack true power. This is a fact. We have seen it in depth here. And in the light of the new energies on the planet, you will either break the structures that limit you or they will be broken for you. Initiating ways are those that open your consciousness through an induction of divine light and place you in the consciousness of divine planes of awareness. This is what is taking place on Earth: there is a global initiation, a global opening of consciousness.

When suffering comes, there is the tendency of evasion. A part inside does not want to face it. As man escapes those events, life takes him there for him to see his own shadow, his own suffering — the dark side. That is why there are adverse circumstances, karma and in astrology, the role of Pluto facing us with the way we live. Integration is the name of the game with shadow dynamics. And that is what these mentioned forces do and what they bring for human beings: triggers for those areas not enlightened within. For the man who has done his work inside, planets and karma influences act as an enhancement of his spiritual achievements and don't bring such intense and dramatic events, but rather more harmonious and light circumstances. Karma, Pluto are not there to make you suffer. They act so you grow because that returns your power to you, since you only have power if you integrate your shadow side. Pluto helps you with that. And using Pluto as a symbol, you become the highest, the eagle: you fly... because you are free. There is great power in being able to fly; if something holds you down, you cannot soar.

It happened with Jesus... He descended to hell for three days, then he resurrected. Do you get the message? Do you want to go to the highest? Recognize the difficult in you, accept it. Integrate your suffering; integrate your shadow.

- ***"When someone is in peace, he generates peace.
  When someone is not in peace, he creates suffering."***

Things to Remember

- Don't negotiate with your power.
- Your power is only yours.
- Do not give it away in exchange for something else.
- Your power is your greatest possession. If you exchange it for something else, you will always come out loosing.
- Nothing is greater than it, so keep it.
- There is no good or bad.
- You are either full or empty.
- If you are empty, you are in love.
- If you are full, you are in ego.
- It doesn't mean it is necessarily a message from God.
- Otherwise, you are giving power to things, giving your power away.
- Things mean what you want them to mean.
- You are bigger than the power you associate those things with.

ELEMENTS OF CHANGE

Stepping Towards the Light

The Truth About Change

"If the fire of change is not there for transformation, for alchemy, where are you going? That fire is passion."

The awakening of truth and power is deep business. Personality and ego don't want to be awakened. Afterwards, they will be thankful. What ego or personality is going to say to the light, "Come for me, I am ready to die." One percent of all humanity maybe, if it is that much, has that understanding and is at the point of change to welcome a metamorphosis. The rest would do it reluctantly. Many believe it, but when something touches their most profound beliefs, they rebel. They want to change but there is so much fear that they don't let go. Then there is no advancement; they keep going in circles. They want to change but think it is a simple change when their entire system has to be redone. Yes, there is going to be a lot of suffering when most people see what the change implies; it is already happening. But letting go and accepting it reduces that to a great extent making a huge difference. When they see the implications of the process, most want to maintain the same reality they have constructed — even if it makes them suffer. They are not ready to let go.

Change for people is often seen like taking the programs off of a computer. They go on thinking they are the programs, until someone sees that what she is, is the computer — the God part — not the programs running on it. Now it is time to realize this and change the programs: install those that generate love until they are ready, and when ready they will boot up with a new reality. But things come to a peak and then dissolve; otherwise there is no resolution for many things. Then they become transmuted in that intensity. When things are that crystallized, they are not easy to move. They are either dissolved or shattered by the energies available. The light coming in is like a dissolvent or a laser beam. It has to do the work, and it will do it. We cannot stop the liberation of the planet now.

Spirit is coming with greater force every time and it is not waiting any more; it is another wave and another thrust, and more structures are dissolved and shattered. The vacuum left has to be filled with light and love: Spirit. Old habits have a tendency to repeat themselves, but light will be more intense until inertia is gone and the step to anchor the new realities in each one is taken in consciousness. Then consciousness will start to be there in real time. We are still far from that globally, but the new energies are working intensely so that everyone has the opportunity to do just that: know true freedom.

The Mind and Its World

The mind is the world of duality. In it, there is no peace. Thoughts come and go; whims appear and dissolve. There is nothing stable, nothing real. It is a good tool to be used to function in life but, as the general state of humanity shows, it is not a good place to live. The mind does not conceive of unity. It lives in separation, and if all you know is your mind your life will be equally divided.

The mind is a tricky place, full of deceit, traps and delusion. One has to go through it to come out free from it and its illusory world. The way to do it is exposed in the next section. The mind is an unhappy place. There is restlessness, avidity, greed. That is the path to hell. There is no peace in it. There is never true satisfaction. And this mind has taken man where he is: confusion and hell. Man has created a world configured on the premises of the mind: lack, insecurity, dissatisfaction. From it humanity has created a false sense of security making this world a false home, and has supported it through the creation of weapons, physical, mental and emotional. This is a world of lies lived in a pleasure-seeking way that always brings dissatisfaction. Obviously such a system is very weak and susceptible to being altered and shaken any time, while this false home has its end at death. Such a world needs to be defended because it cannot survive by itself. Therefore the obsessive way of life of humanity based on preserving this illusion, this illusory way of life based on separation, defense and turning a blind eye on the inevitable end of it. Thus, living as if that sure end wasn't there. Such a system can never bring happiness. That is why a serious alternative is necessary.

Let's look at it.

Meditation and Reality

Meditation is the best way to get out of the mind. Meditation is the supreme way to enlightenment and the path spiritual masters have walked to become spiritual masters. This made them enlightened individuals. Meditation is communion with God inside. It is opening up to merge with the presence and energy of the god that dwells in you, which is your individualized God spark that makes you divine. That spark can be ignored or known. Ignoring it is what most of humanity has done to a large extent over thousands of years. Thus, the world we have. It doesn't matter what you do, providing it takes you to that encounter. Otherwise, your life is mostly empty. And although it might be full of wonderful things, those are ephemeral, and sooner or later they will leave your life and you will have to find joy somewhere else. The permanent joy and freedom lie in that divine part. But if it is not known, it is as if it wasn't there.

Meditation is the way of moving out of the world of the mind and ascend to the higher part of oneself. Then stepping into the worlds of light of ascension is far easier. Meditation is a path to ascension and to the reality behind this world of illusion. If you want true peace, you have to move beyond the mind to the realms of unity; that is where light is. Truth is a permanent state of peace, unity and love that is not conditioned and dependent on what one has or what happens. Light is truth. And thus through meditation you can go beyond the mind to the worlds of light that await you beyond it. The truth is that you are light, a divine expression of love and ecstasy. And if you are not experiencing this reality of yourself, you are missing out in the best thing in life.

Since the mind is a tricky place, one needs a guide to go to the light. With him, you can reach the highest realms of light — something highly recommended. But what he does is to show you the way there. A spiritual master said to me once in India: "The spiritual master is there to show you the way to the source inside. Once you find the source, you go there to drink." In this beautiful teaching, he was saying that a spiritual teacher has a function but he is not substitute of your own Self or the aim of the meditation. He is there to take you to your Self: the divine in you. Once there you don't need a spiritual master because your own divine self has become so.

Unless you know what is beyond your mind you know nothing real. Believe me, if you will, this world is illusory, although it might seem so real, dramatic or wonderful. It is just a reflection of great worlds of light, bliss and love, and as a reflection of them, it does not have its own light, the true light. The fun is in knowing the place where this world comes from. It is like being in amazement at night because there is full moon and that is greater than the nights without a moon. It seems so fantastic… one thinks it is wonderful to have that light. But the light of the moon is just a reflection of the light of the sun; the moon doesn't have its own light. What is great is to know the light of the sun. Likewise this world dimly reflects the light of those higher worlds of light, which like the sun, have and generate their own light. You can live an amazing experience of life by knowing the worlds of self-generated light. They are there; I experience them constantly, and also do those who have walked the inner path with enough intensity and commitment.

Another spiritual teacher I knew said from his state of spiritual achievement, "There is nothing greater in life than to conquer the Self." At the time, I was a beginner. Now I can fully confirm the truth of his teaching. To conquer the Self, it is necessary to go through the mind, face all its tricks and reach the realms beyond it. Meditation is the path there. When the mind has been touched by meditation, it is transformed. Those realities inside encountered in meditation start to enter the mind, and alchemy takes place; it starts transforming it into an enlightened mind: one capable of being at peace. Such a mind serves the light; it is at the service of unity. The mind is supposed to be the means to perform certain tasks, but it is not supposed to be the ruler of life. It is also not the place to live in. The Higher Self is the place we must dwell in; there is the vision, the power and the light to lead our lives. Living there is what makes sense. And therefore we need to find the consciousness in us that has what it takes to be a master: the Inner Self. Then we have to put things right. We have to put on the throne the real king and the servant in his correct place.

All this is relevant in this work because the Stargate event gives us an unparalleled opportunity to make that move: going beyond the mind to the spheres of light inside, to know what lies beyond. In this journey man has the opportunity to know what is immortal in him, and through this enter into a revolutionary change in consciousness that will completely transform humanity and the way it lives. It is a jump from slavery to freedom; from being a slave of a conditioned world and mind, to being sovereign in the worlds of freedom and light.

More and more, the Stargate's high energies will bring the possibility of experiences close to those of the higher worlds found in meditation, moving all from the mind to Spirit. And bringing humanity out of the crazy world of the mind to enter the peaceful realms of Spirit. But to enter fully into that experience one has to take a step. Meditation is the best way to know and anchor those higher energies of the Stargate in ourselves. And the way to infuse our beings so much with them, that we truly reach the frequencies of the fifth dimension so we can ascend, leaving this obsolete world behind. This is the plan Stargate has behind its coming.

Stargate's energies bring the opportunity to know the eternal with its true satisfaction, and put an end to this human experience and world full of suffering, mediocrity and that has death as its end. In this way humanity can rise to the realms of divinity where another world is awaiting it, where all will know true unity and peace.

"Contemplate reality from stillness. You can't see anything from anywhere else."
                                                            - Jesus

Flowing

Flowing is essential at this time. We are entering into a new way of moving forward, and we have to develop an awareness of being in a process that moves ahead like never before. In the past we could be somewhat static and delay our progression or our changes sometimes indefinitely. Now the dynamism of the energies doesn't allow that; we have to keep up with them. There is no other way now. The pull of the energy current is very strong, and it is of such a nature that the static ways we knew before just cannot take place any more. We have to keep in a moving awareness and learn to flow with everything and every situation that comes to us. That means we cannot hold onto things, especially the things that are being changed as a result of our change of consciousness. The rhythm is fast and we have to keep going to keep up with it. Of course, we can be still and have our time for relaxation, but it has more to do with the inward attitude, an attitude of openness and readiness to see things move in our minds and emotions. The movie inside will be changing and rearranging itself as people's levels of consciousness — globally quite asleep until now — are awakened and brought into the picture. If you are very crystallized, the energy will move you more and the flow of water that the melting process will generate for you, will be greater. That is only a sign that you have not dealt with your past — pending issues. You basically have not worked on yourself, in developing your consciousness, at least not in a deep way that would take care of those key spots. We have to be like a river: rather than living in static ways, learn to live in a process that is constantly moving, constantly changing. Like the Tai Chi sequence that moves continuously without stopping, but that also carries a stillness inside the movement. The wind blows and we bend with it in a dance that allows us to be part of it, part of all.

The power and love of the present energy moves rigidity there, where it finds it. Something — the energy — is doing it. Before this moment if you did not move it, hardly ever something else did. Now a current of high vibration energy — light — is moving everything, whether you do it or not, so all things and beings are being progressed forward and there is no chance to ignore those crystallizations. The energy is forcing everyone to evolve, and as the crystallizations are hit by the energy they move, they open up to reveal the mysteries they hold and show all the areas were growth was stunted. Then people are loaded with the contents of those packages so they deal with them, resolve the issues that are pending in them and acquire, by doing it, a higher vibration, as they get rid of karma and enter into love. This has to be done. Sooner or later, everyone has to do it, in this or another lifetime. Now, due to the cosmic time in which we are that requires a radical growth in consciousness for the planet and all beings in it, this process has been brought to the present. And we have to flow with it.

If you resist, you will break, as I mentioned at the beginning of the book. Like the dry tree that is not flexible and not able to bend with the force of the wind; it cannot flow with it. Flowing like a river that takes you upwards towards a higher and better reality, is fundamental to reach a good destiny. To dare to let go is crucial to reach it, and to have a good process along the way. Like the story at the beginning of Richard Bach's book, *Illusions,* in which the creature that lived holding on to the bottom of a river bank had the courage and vision to let go, searching for a new existence, and found that the current lifted it up and freed it from the limited existence it had. The current took it on a journey of discovery, but especially freedom. Other creatures living in that same way farther down the river were in awe at such a "high being," which could fly past and above them expressing such freedom. We must, for the sake of our sanity, let go of the old ways of life we have been holding onto for so long, and find a new freedom like in Richard Bach's story. That is available in joining the ascending current of energy now present on the planet.

Life is Different Now

Life is different now. I am sure you have noticed. Things and people are behaving differently. You are too. Personality is being altered; new things are awakening inside each one making people act in new ways. You do things, and they don't seem to have the same effects as before. Feelings that were there have to be lived, they cannot be denied anymore. You see your relationships differently; your job doesn't have the same appeal… A great change is going on and nothing seems the same. What is happening? The high energy of Stargate is activating new things inside everyone and altering the consciousness of everybody. The vibration inside people is stronger; that affects their consciousness and perception. This vibration is changing the perception one has of oneself and life. Because one is different, one sees everything differently. And all people and things on Earth are being changed by this new vibration. So all you see and everyone you see seem different because they are.

Rules have changed. There are a number of things you can do before that, starting with asking yourself a series of deep, relevant and meaningful questions. The main one is, Who do you want to be? And the other one, How do you want to live your life? There are other important ones...

What more could you be doing now? Think for a moment, about your life... What else could you be doing to improve your condition in the light of what you know now? What could you do to fully embrace a quantum change? How could you move in the direction you truly want to go? What changes could you introduce in your life for that? What things or ways of living could you let go, so that the new visions and new energy could come more fully into your life? What could you do now, knowing that what you are doing now is the sowing of your future? Excellent questions...

What you do now is your future; now you are creating it since now you are sowing its seeds. You need to move now in the direction you want to go. How are you using your time? Your energy? What thoughts, feelings and visions are you having now? All that will create the future you will live. Answering all these questions and acting on the answers will bring the power back to you. This clarity inside is a requirement for ascending.

Own your rights

On the other hand, you have to live like there is no future. This is to live in the present. In doing this, new doors will be opened in the present, which you don't see now — you don't have access to them. In living the real present we recover all the power and all the love; the present is the place of power, the place of love. To live in the present is to do what you want to do now, from consciousness, not from fear. Fear takes you to do what you don't want, because in fear you have given your power away and therefore your rights; rights to be and to create a deserved better life, future and reality. As you own your rights to be what you deserve and what you want, you stop conceding those rights to something or someone else that will say what you have to do and how you have to live, which is what happens when you entertain the consciousness of fear. In this new paradigm you own the responsibility in your life in a new complete way: you own your rights. How many decisions are made out of fear? Little decisions of the daily life that amount to big creations over time. Creations of a life and circumstances that often are not what you truly want from the depth of your heart.

To be in the present is to channel the light into action, into the world, into your life. This is true service. Light brings higher consciousness: that which works. To be in contact with the light within is to own your rights.

"If you want to ascend,
you have to own your rights."

New Inner Changes

One of the important changes that are taking place inside is the activation of the inner codes of the DNA. Inside the DNA there are light codes that are dormant and contain information and consciousness. The connection of those codes with our consciousness has been inactive for a long time. The DNA has filaments of light that are connected to the aura and the structure of consciousness in every being — to the light body. Those connections have been unplugged from the inner system, and the full Christ Consciousness has not been able to manifest in people for a very long time. The Stargate alignment brings a connection and activation of these filaments of light of the DNA.

In increasing the light within through meditation the connections of DNA are activated and awakened activating the light body. This body of light is the natural and crystalline state of the Self. The DNA codes bring information and messages of consciousness that are fundamental for our life and evolution. Those messages are not necessarily worded messages, but come in terms of vibrational frequencies, intuitive feelings and visions about ourselves. We do not have to do anything; they are incorporated as vibration and new energies in us. We only need to allow the process to happen naturally, and once a vision or a clarity of feeling comes along, we must act on it. By being aware of this process, we help it. By meditating we increase it dramatically. The codes also hold memory, past life impressions, life mission codes, talents... and power. While they are asleep or deactivated the experience of life is limited. When they become activated, life changes and moves towards the recovery of a full consciousness. That is our reality, our normal state. This also brings more light to the physical body which as we saw, becomes less dense, lighter and traps less the consciousness in its dense form, which is like a prison to it.

This is ascension, the rise in vibration that progressively converts everything to the light. This makes the Divine Self manifest more, and along with it all its consciousness potential. The body, the mental and emotional fields become unstructured and they turn more fluid, agile and faster in vibration; ideas do not trap us as much; neither do concepts and especially beliefs. The belief systems start to collapse since they are made up of solidifications that now, with the high vibration melt and free the consciousness trapped in them to give a perception of reality that is different, more real and according to the truth. We start seeing reality, not illusion.

In the section *Practices for Ascension*, there is a specific practice for DNA activation.

- *Faith is possibilities. In a substratum of high vibrational energy like it is the case with the Earth now, those possibilities of good and light are manifold; they multiply exponentially. This high vibrational energy present on Earth now is a door to create all possibilities — if they are for the good. We must take this opportunity to manifest the greatest things, our greatest visions.*

193

Actualize Yourself in the Present

It is fundamental that we actualize ourselves in the present and stop carrying the past. This is the only way to move forward now and to have power acting in us. We must close the past, solve it, release it. The changes in the present now cancel all agreements, decisions or plans from before. A second ago is past. With this new perspective we can really move ahead. Even if what happened last hour wasn't good or wasn't what we wanted, we are in present at this moment and can create a new reality now, leaving all that in the past. The Stargate energies favor this process and this way of living now. We must team with them and avoid carrying the burdens of what is not light from the past, even from the last minute. We can chose power, light, freedom, prosperity, positive action every moment in present. And we don't have to look back to the past for reference if it is not what we wanted.

"We redeem ourselves in the present every moment."

Things must be lived in full consciousness

Things that come up should be lived fully and be consumed or resolved. These are times to be very aware and go through processes fully conscious, not halfhearted. We have to be very aware what it is we are doing. A lot of things are going on at once, and we can become easily confused. Things will come up due to the effect of the high energies, and we will have to face them and process them. Many times we will have to deal with situations or emotions from the past. Closing is the name of the game. We must be closing everything. This is why we want to be very aware in present, so we do not keep alive things that need to be closed and left. If we are not fully aware of them, they will keep coming back until they are fully processed and completely closed. We cannot ignore processes or things that come up for us because those are the things that are pending: the things that we didn't resolve in the past.

We can only enter ascension free from pending issues.

The experience of the moment

Everything is an experience and therefore it has an end. It doesn't matter the experience, what matters is to enjoy, learn and love in it. Enjoy, while the experience lasts. This is also being in the moment. And do not to grab the experience wanting it to be permanent. It is important to accept that is has a limited lifespan. We have already seen the only things that don't have a date of caducity.

Sacred time

Each moment is sacred; honor God.
There are no special moment; all
are moments of God. Thus they
are all sacred moments.

❖

"I am in love in the present, and from there I cast a response of love in the present." This is an act of consciousness. Moving away from unconsciousness is making a positive decision, here and now to serve the present.

Reality Check

It is important to be sure you are touching reality now more than ever. In order to do this, there are some points you should observe in the questions that follow.

I. How do you understand reality?
What is reality?
What is your reality?
See how both interact: do they relate?
Do you ignore reality? Do you ignore your reality?
Is there a relationship between both?
The idea is that they are the same or very close.
This rarely happens.

II. How do you react to that mix?
Do you play the victim?
Do you assume the role of superman or superwoman?
Is there acceptance of reality? Understanding?
What contradictions are there?
Where do you place responsibility?
Who or what controls your life?
Where is your power?

III. How is your engagement with reality?
How do you create your reality?
Do you take an active part in it?
Do you just let things happen?
Are you a leader or a follower?
Why?
Are you willing to take charge of your life fully?
Is your reality a compassionate reality?
Is there love in it?

IV. How do you live joy?
Where is your joy?
Where does it come from?
Do you let it fill your body, mind, heart?
Do you express it? Share it?

Guidelines

- Reality is how things are. Your reality is your own world: how you perceive that reality, the way you feel about it and your interaction with it. It is completely subjective.

- Your power should be in you. If it is in someone else, you need to take action and recover it.

- Responsibility must be in you, in the issues that are yours. Responsibility which is not yours must not be with you.

- Your reality must be a compassionate one, and there must be love in it. Otherwise you are way off the mark, and you will never be happy with how things are now. You need to introduce the elements of magic: love and compassion. They make everything happen.

- You should be creating the reality you want for yourself. This will force you to take full responsibility for you and for your life. You do this by being clear about what you want, visualizing that image for those situations, working in that direction and having faith in it. In a word: owning your power.

- Your joy comes from you and the healthy and conscious interactions with God, others and the world. If they are so they will be creative and will produce joy for you and others. Joy must come from the creation of a loving, peaceful, prosperous and free reality which is useful and beneficial for all involved. You will then experience joy in the creation and in the enjoyment of that creation. Joy must also come from your connection with your own Self. This is the most important aspect of life and the most genuine and everlasting joy. If this is lacking, everything else is secondary. A priority is to access this experience: everything comes from it.

- *"Be finished with falseness and hidden issues. If you are one with what you love, there is no space and time between you and that. You attract it to your life immediately."*

Reality points

- Any reality that is not coming from God is not *the* reality.
- Any reality that is not love and wisdom is not real.
- You receive the amount of love that your fear allows.
- Fear is the portal keeper.
- Free of fear, love and bounty will be yours without limits.
- Never fear responsibility for abundance, for your good fortune.
- What is reality? "Reality is my faith."
- If you have no faith you can do nothing.
- So you can do everything if you believe.
- Faith is the key ingredient, and the first.
- Free your mind from doubt, fear and disbelief.
- Logic of compassion, not of judgment, rules.
- As long as there is shadow, there will always be fear.
- Because there is a part of you that you don't see.
- From the small ego you will always see the same: that you are small.
- When you release fear a great love will be born in you.

"The only thing you have to do is love and everything will come to you."
— *Saint Germain*

PRACTICES FOR ASCENSION

The Way to a New Reality

Keys for Ascension

This section contains some of the greatest keys for ascension. They touch the key areas that need to be activated individually and collectively for ascension. They are all related to the elevation of vibration and the activation of the light inside. This light activation presupposes moving from the physical body consciousness to the light body consciousness. This transformation is what is going on, on the planet behind the scenes. The practices are focused on the need to anchor this transformation and produce the manifestation of the new reality of light for all. It is a main step, not the end of it. But it brings a total increment in the light of a person and the activation of the light body. Since the light body is the vehicle for ascension and the reality of people's higher consciousness, all the practices here are related to it.

These practices are to be taken as a step-by-step process and not something that has to be done all at once. So work with them as you feel, without pressure. Take your time and find your own rhythm to do them. If you decide to do them all together, leave at least four days between each one. The effects go on after each of the activations. Once you have done them all, you can do them again at a later time with more intensity. These activations have been done in my live courses and meditations for ascension for many years, and they are very powerful.

Liberation of the Heart

Before entering the meditation, free fears in the third chakra — solar plexus area — with violet light, white light and pink light. Visualize them for a few minutes each. Then you can proceed with this meditation. As usual, stay a few moments with each instruction.

Breathe deeply and relax...

♥ Surround yourself with violet light.
See violet light entering your heart.
Dissolve the armor of the heart with violet light.
See it dissolving, melting.
Enter into the heart with the violet light to accelerate its vibration and free it completely.
Feel the armor totally dissolved; the heart becomes purified.
Fears are disintegrating, along with the pain and old feelings kept there.
Unexpressed love is liberated. You can feel it.
The heart is becoming clean.
Emotions, feelings that come up, allow yourself to feel them.
Stay for a while in this connection.

♥ Now, the heart being purified, the golden light manifests inside it. First, it is like a small sphere of light; then it becomes bigger.
It goes on radiating brighter and with more intensity.
It fills your body, mind, chakras, aura, soul...
It envelops you.
You start to feel a profound peace.

♥ This light expands beyond yourself,
to your brothers and sisters of humanity, to their hearts ...
It fills them with light and peace.
It expands to humanity... the planet... the Universe.

♥ The violet light surrounds you now.
Blue light comes out of the violet light.
It surrounds you, your body.
It fills your crown chakra.
It circles your aura, closing a circle of blue light around you.
It fills your aura.

♥ The heart chakra and top chakra on the head,
become united with blue and violet light.

When ready, breathe deeply and slowly come out of the meditation.
Give thanks.

Activation of the DNA

Inside the DNA there are codes of light. These have been mostly deactivated over a long time on Earth, and all life here has not been able to anchor the light of its Higher Self —the divine consciousness or light body — due to this. It is necessary to activate those codes of light back to move in the new direction of full consciousness and divine awareness. With this process we can activate the cell memory and the cosmic consciousness in the DNA codes. This is necessary for ascension.

Allow yourself to go into each instruction for a few moments.
Use at least thirty minutes for the whole activation process.

- Bring your mind to quietness.
- Concentrate on the breathing.
- Breathing happens; life happens on its own beyond your will.
- Focus on the space between inspiration and expiration.
- Breathe towards the crown of the head – top chakra.

- Feel the bliss of this connection.
- Become surrounded by violet light.
- The violet light goes into your cells.
- It penetrates into the cellular field.
- The filaments of DNA become activated.
- Your cell memory of light becomes activated.
- You see your cells emanating light.
- Feel you are light.

Affirm inwardly, slowly:

"My light body becomes manifested."
"My cell memory of light becomes activated."
"My stellar codes become activated."
"My light codes are activated."
"My stellar consciousness is activated."
"My cosmic consciousness is activated."
"My light body is activated."
"I Am the light of the Self."
"I Am liberated from the limits of the planetary matrix."
"I move beyond the limits of planetary consciousness."
"I Am cosmic consciousness."
"I Am light consciousness."

Feel the chakra on the top of your head and the heart chakra – center of the chest – united with light. Feel also that the third eye – center of forehead – and the chakra on the crown are united. Feel that your consciousness is cosmic.

Get ready to come out:

- Stay in silence for few minutes.
- Breathe deeply three times.
- Slowly bring your consciousness to the here and now.
- Feel the mind, body, spirit connection in the present.

- Become conscious of the physical body.
- Give thanks.
- Open your eyes.
- Come out of the meditation.

Do this any time you feel you need to activate your cosmic consciousness or want to intensify your connection with your light body, your Christ Consciousness. Do it no more than once a month. You can also do it only once and leave it there.

Activation of the Light Body

This practice is for doing the light body activation fully. This activation is deeply related to the activation of the DNA codes. DNA contains codes of light that are part of the light body.

Take some time each day to clean out old feelings, to purify and resolve them. Sit down quietly, observe your feelings, breathe deeply and let them come out before you, so you understand what they are and liberate them with love, forgiveness and surrounding them with violet light. Bring clarity and harmonization to yourself by connecting with the natural rhythm of your breathing and by focusing on your inner peace. The light body will anchor itself more fully on you as you clear unresolved issues. If necessary seek professional help for this.

Live an impeccable life. Be honest with yourself and God at all times and do not deceive yourself with false motives. Make sure you see that all your motivations for acting are loving, beneficial and seek the best for everyone. Do leave aside any thoughts or impulses to act looking only at your benefit, especially if this is in detriment of the good of others. All this will attract the light body into manifestation.

Activation

- Enter into your inner peace and silence.
- See a ray of violet light coming down on you from heaven.
- Enter into this powerful, loving vibration.
- Connect consciously with your light body, seeing surrounding you, an image of yourself made of light.
- Invoke the manifestation of your Christ Self; feel it manifesting.
- This is the wisest and most divine part of you, not a force outside.
- Feel you are in presence of this wise, luminous being.
- Feel his love, wisdom and peace.
- Give the command of your life to your light body – Christ Self.
- Feel the inner clarity of your Christ Self.
- Feel a body of light surrounding you by visualizing a field of bright white light around you.
- Feel its powerful vibration…. the peace and joy it brings you.
- Become one with your light body. Merge with its love.
- Stay there for a few minutes.
- When you are ready, come out breathing deeply a few times.
- Become progressively conscious of your physical body.
- Give thanks.
- Connect fully with your physical body and the here and now.

Let's open our hearts to our "I Am Presence" of our Christ Selves so that it bathes us and heals us with the balm of its presence. The more it manifests, the more ego disappears and its neurosis vanishes. This way we find the peace of the light within.

Activation of the Chakras

The chakras hold some of the key connections of our consciousness. They need to be open and working properly to process the energy to the relevant areas of consciousness they represent and support. This is important for a good ascension. This practice gives them a great opening and balance for our ascension work.

- Visualize a golden rain of light entering you through the Sahasrara – top chakra.
- Go to the base chakra at the base of the spine with the golden light.
- Visualize the gold light in each chakra for one minute, from the first one at the base of the column to the top chakra, the Sahasrara, at the crown of the head.
- When reaching the Sahasrara and becoming activated in the light, a cone of golden light appears, going up from the crown of the head, like a pagoda top.
- Feel the divine power in each chakra.
- Feel the consciousness of divine power being activated in each chakra.

Breathe deeply and come out when you are ready.

Activation of Faith

- Breathe deeply three times.
- Contact with your heart and see it full of violet light as faith.
- Invoke the masters of light and ask for faith: Jesus, Buddha, Mother Mary, any master you trust.
- Let fears go – faith increases.
- See the blue light coming to you from heaven.

- The blue light fills you completely with its vibration of divine power and faith.
- Take the vibration of faith to your physical body, to your cells.
- Take it to your emotional body, mental body, causal body, spiritual body.
- All the particles of your being are full of faith.
- Feel the power of faith within you.
- Ask the power of faith to fill you with faith.
- Invoke Archangel Michael to fill you with faith.
- Think of him. Feel him and his Divine Power of faith with you.
- Receive his radiation of faith, his grace, and his power of faith.
- Go to your chakras, from the base of the column to the top of the head.
- Establish in them the blue light as faith.
- From the top chakra, top of your head, connect with the Divine Father in faith.
- Your connection with God is the source of your faith.
- Connect with your physical body.
- Breathe deeply, become aware of the here and now.
- Give thanks.
- Slowly come out.
- Open your eyes.

Power Activation of the Organs

This meditation activates the base energy and specific quality of each organ. It also activates the Stargate energy in every organ, as well as its power.

Enter into a quiet time by breathing deeply a few times
and quieting your mind and feelings.

- Visualize a rain of gold light, very soft, like drops of light falling on your top chakra at the top of your head.
- This rain enters into the top of your head.
- A golden ray is formed.
- It goes to the organs: heart, stomach, lungs, kidneys, liver. See that happening.
- The energy of every organ harmonizes itself with the light activating its energy: inspiration and elevation for the lungs; joy and love in the heart; will, power and determination in the kidneys; sympathy and support in the stomach; flexibility and compassion in the liver.
- The negative quality in each organ becomes transmuted: fear in the kidneys; lack of joy in the heart; anger in the liver; sadness in the lungs; disconnection and insecurity in the stomach.
- Each organ is activated in its energy color: red in the heart; deep blue in the kidneys; white in the lungs; yellow in the stomach; green in the liver.
- A blue ray of light enters and activates the organs with Divine Power.
- The entire body becomes activated with Divine Power.

Breathe deeply three times… Slowly come out of the meditation. Give thanks to God and the energy.

Contact with Your Stellar Origins

This reality is obvious and becoming more present on the planet these days. Most people have stellar origins. By recovering contact with them, an important part of your consciousness and light is recovered, as well as your cosmic memory. This is relevant since recovering the memory of who you are and your origin means being aware of a greater part of yourself. This also helps you go beyond planetary consciousness to widen the perspective to cosmic consciousness, which is far more real than planetary-bound consciousness. Also in this expansion, one can access more divine and universal attributes, qualities and abilities which can be of great help in life and ascension. You may dedicate half an hour to an hour for this connection.

Connection

- Enter into silence and inner contact with your Self.
- Connect with your Higher Self seeing the light of your crown chakra.
- Invoke the energies of your Higher Self so he locates your stellar contact —that is, the stellar system, planet or star from which you come in your origins.
- Once contacted, invoke its light.
- Invoke the recovery of your stellar consciousness of those origins.
- If you have located the stellar system, invoke it also saying, "I am the light of Orion," if that is the system, or mentioning the system you have located for yourself.
- If you have not located it that clearly simply say, "I am the cosmic light of my stellar system."
- Experience the joy of this connection, feel this light. Be part of it.
- Come out when you are ready.
- Give thanks.
- Breathe deeply.
- Connect with your physical body and reality here and now.

You can expand this connection and meditation as you feel appropriate for you under the guidance of your Higher Self.

Contemplating Ascension

- The heart has the power to heal you and transform you. Feel its light and love-power; expand it to your body, mind and emotions, spirit, cells. Feel how it transforms everything.

- The power of forgiveness, of wisdom is there.

- Archangel Michael said to us the final battle of consciousness, of light starts here: the final battle of light within oneself and without. This is about eradicating darkness on the entire planet, as well as for individuals, families, and society; it is recognizing darkness, integrating it, illuminating it, and thus dissolving it.

- What is darkness? It is the twisted goodness inside everyone that has turned bitter and evil as a result of not being able to be expressed.

- We are guilty of or susceptible to such behaviors because of having a non-illuminated ego.

- When you can, forgive because you also have things that need to be forgiven.

- Every situation has a hidden treasure in it. We do not see it at first, and we judge things as bad. But good always comes from what appears "bad" because life and God have other plans: to enlighten you. And sometimes difficult things happen because at the time, it is the only way you are going to be able to do the work of light on you.

- I personally have come to realize that I have to live in a way in which no aggression is projected from me to others. In a way that all aggressive energy is not directed to anyone but released in a healthy, harmless way, like activities and sports. I dream of a world in which every individual does not attack and harm their brothers or sisters in any way. It is as

209

simple as basic.

- It is time for humanity to grow enough to behave in a loving, non-destructive or harmful way to itself, others or life.

- All the hassle that we create in our lives is not the fault of others; it is what we create in our lives.

THE JEWELS OF STARGATE

Living the Life of Ascension Now

The following are the two most precious sections of this work. The first one *How to live the changes of the Stargate* is a comprehensive list of advice that shows in detail, the stepping stones that will carry you every day to the consciousness of Stargate in living life. The second, *Initiation on Divine Power* by Archangel Michael is one of the most powerful activations we have experienced in our live courses. Given many times to the audience of a Stargate live course, it has dramatically changed the vibration of everyone present and has shaken the Earth with its incommensurable power and the powerful presence of Archangel Michael. If you concentrate on a specific part of the book, this should be it.

How to Live the Changes of the Stargate

This is one of the most important aspects brought to us by the Stargate consciousness; it is a new way of life, a map to a great treasure, a path to freedom. Stargate energies bring a lot of change. These are the keys for this process of planetary ascension. These keys point the way to go, in the present manifestation of energies that are changing the rules of how things work. This is your guide for everyday life, because this is the way to go.

- Meditate as much as possible in your inner higher self.

- Have the awareness that "I am the light of my life."
  You are the light you are looking for, the light you are invoking. Be aware that the light comes from you. Ascension is a kind of graduation. And this implies a level of mastery. You cannot be a master if light is not in you. A master's light comes from his Higher Self.

- Keep alert – avoid being "asleep." Look at things from the sixth chakra, not from the third chakra.

- Have clarity within and without — harmonization. This way the light body becomes integrated.

- Bathe and impregnate yourself with the violet light: body, mind, emotions, chakras, aura, spirit; letting all go — the past.

- Listen to yourself deeply. What is your Self asking of you? Your feelings, what do they want? Your body? Do it, but only if this is not harmful to another. Remember, you do not want to create more negative karma. You want to create good karma with good actions, those that benefit you and others. If you have purified yourself enough, those feelings will be for the good. What you have to learn here is that those good feelings have to be lived; you can no longer repress that which you desire, that which is your dream, that which you know will make you thrill, that which ultimately is the dream or the mission of your life. You should know, you won't feel realized or happy if you do not live it. Cherish your dream and put it into action. Do it. Live it.

- If your body says, "do such thing," that is the way. "Do yoga," you might hear inside; then do it. That is the way. If it says, "Need to sleep," then sleep. You might have been going with little sleep for a while or need to sleep more to integrate the new energies. "Relax." "Play sports." "Sing." "Dance." "Laugh." "Cry." The messages might be of a different nature.

- Impeccability. Live in this way.

- Follow your intuition. Seek guidance in you, not outside. You are God, remember?

- What should you do with your life now, in every moment or situation? First, get connected. Feel the inner impulse — your inner voice — it is your Divine Self, which speaks to you through the heart. Follow it. Don't question it with your mind. Do it, give yourself to it. Check, first, if this is good for you and others. Otherwise, it is not a true message from your heart.

- We are in the times of change from the logic of the mind to the logic of the heart. Mental logic is obsolete; it no longer fits a changing reality, a reality that does not work with parameters and fixed ideas. Learn to truly swim, and improvise like a jazz musician.

  You can start saying to yourself:
  "What is the logic of the heart here?"

- Break all limits to your expression. Check that it is appropriate and respectful. Then you should express yourself freely. Being disrespectful is not being free since you are infringing on the freedom of others. Be yourself and allow others to be themselves.

- Contact your inner child — spontaneous and wise — who has no limits to his expression.

- Clean, purify, resolve feelings.

- Do not hold on, let go of what goes and, with love say good-bye to it and smile. You are liberating yourself.

- *Flow, flow, flow;* do not block yourself. Fly. Do not look for maps, roads. We are no longer moving on the earth; we are moving through the air.

- Do not insist on things being as you are used to, because they are not going to be.

- Remember that what the worm calls the end of the world is what you call *a butterfly.*

- Support yourself – find relationships with friends on the spiritual path. Learn from each other the *new rules*, the new ways of functioning. Discover them together.

- Visualize, affirm and manifest what you want, but make sure you always say: *"Thy will be done."*

- Ask for blessings and good for all beings.

- Support and help in what you can; act but do not worry about anyone, each one is being taken care of and has what is his.

- Have faith and total confidence in God.

- Ask your Christ Self to manifest fully. Ask that he take charge.

- Ask for divine grace for you and for all.

- Mother Earth has given us this message: *"Ask for light for all, ask for the ascension of all; forgive, let go and love; carry the golden light within your heart."*

- Have forgiveness and mercy — without conditions.

- The violet light, being the highest frequency available and the energy of transmutation and liberation, is crucial at this time. It takes you to ascension. It is very important to use and meditate on the violet light. Find out all about it in my other book: *The Violet Light: The Power That Changes Everything.*

- At any moment, in any situation, be calm and use the violet light. Relax, take a distance, be detached; remember the teachings here, and remember that everything is taking you and all to ascension.

- Invoke Archangel Michael. Ask for his protection for you, for all.

-

"Being true to yourself is being faithful to God in you."

Activation of Your Inner Power

Initiation on the Sword of Power of Archangel Michael

This is the most powerful part of the book. The moment in which we go beyond words, beyond the book, to touch the essence of it, in a spiritual experience. Get ready. This is the opening of the door, a powerful connection with your inner power. This is the most potent tool to free you from the Matrix of the Dark inside you and influence the collapsing of it in the world.

This sword is very powerful, it is the sword of power and freedom of Archangel Michael. This is one of the most sacred and beautiful moments of my live courses. The divine light, the love and the power are so present and intense, we don't want to leave this moment. Archangel Michael has always been there with his melting love and power. This initiation frees you from many things that are chaining you; it removes chains of slavery and activates your inner power at the conscious and energy level of your soul.

Read and feel this invocation to get connected with the purpose of the divine power of Archangel Michael, and to open up the doors of grace to receive his precious gift of Divine Power through his sword of light.

•

Set the right atmosphere for you. You might want to lower the lights, switch off phones and perhaps light a candle and seek some solitude.

Take your time to quiet down. Breathe deeply... relax.

When you have been in silence and serenity for about ten minutes, you may start.

•

Invocation

"Beloved Michael Archangel of Divine Will and Power we are here reunited your brothers and sisters of the family of light, in the name of the Father, His Will, His Light and Freedom; grant us the Grace of your Divine Power and allow us to receive your sword of Blue Light of that Divine Will that you represent, so that with it we can serve our liberation and the instauration of the Divine Will in us, others and around us, cutting and annihilating all that which is not the Divine Will in us, to recover our power completely. So be it in the Will of the Father. Thank you."
- Amen.

See the presence of Archangel Michael with you and in His presence receive the sword of blue light coming from him. Floating in the air, it reaches you. You take it with decision and feel the Divine Power with which it invests you, which emanates from it. It bathes you and fills you completely. Receive this energy. Stay in it for a while.

Now, see with clarity how the sword of blue light touches your chains of fear, limitation and attachment, and due to its extremely high vibration makes them explode... the chains in your heart, mind, body, spirit, the chains of fear...and you are set free. This is happening now also, for every human being, liberating all of humanity.

Stay there for as long as you feel.

When you are ready, connect with your body, the present, the here and now.
Breathe deeply a few times. Very slowly, come out of the meditation.
Stay in this state of high energy.
Breathe deeply.
Give thanks.
Open your eyes.

Give thanks to the Divine Power, to Archangel Michael, to the Grace and Will of God. Stay there quietly and observe how you feel the energy in and around you. Stay in the consciousness of that state.

After receiving the sword of power of Archangel Michael, cut fear and guilt with the sword, and cut dependency inside yourself. Use it any time it is necessary.

FINAL REVELATIONS

The Consciousness of a New Humanity

Living the Changes

This is what an ascended humanity looks like. These sections here represent the main guidelines of consciousness and attitudes of the Stargate once it has gone through the changes presented here. These are the attitudes that the humanity of the Age of Aquarius would have — the ascended humanity.

This section masterfully complements the issue of ascension. The chapters here are all developed from the Stargate revelations brought about by its energy. All these are necessary for ascension. They are some of the gems we must master and become one with. We need to understand life as human beings, from a different perspective: a more enlightened one. And this can only come from above. This wisdom and messages are not from this level. They are pure light from the ascended dimensions. Words are distilled from that light essence and make these messages have a deep resonance in our souls.

The importance to know and understand the new rules so we flow in the new ways is essential at this moment, if we want to expand to a new dimension of life. Old ways don't work anymore. As we advance we discover what works and what doesn't, and here the guidelines for this have no price. As we look for everything inside and go beyond what we thought was the planetary reality, we can discover a new way of looking at things that will give us true freedom, a place from where we can create a new reality. We need to come to terms with understanding what our reality is and what our role is in creating it. Also, we need to have a deep vision of one of the most important aspects in the ascension process: faith, its magic and its relationship with power. And we need to look at all that from a completely new and eye-opening perspective. We also have to learn the relevance of passion and, contrary to many beliefs, we will discover that it is developed as we grow spiritually and that it is the only true way of living.

Things are not what they seem. They have never been. But as our eyes are opened by the Stargate power, we can finally become initiated in this mystery and truth. Some important prayers are also essential elements of this section. So let's get into some deep and fun journey of communion and discovery of ourselves, God and some of the most amazing secrets of the Universe. It is all worth more than gold on the way to ascension.

Love: The State of Ascension

What we want is to be able to issue a response of love to whatever happens, avoiding a response of fear. Such a response is defensive. It comes from ego, from smallness — contraction. It does not contain joy. The grace of God is the best help we can have for that aim. It is in it that we can reconnect with our true source of power and recover our grace-filled state, and from there emanate love. This allows us to see innocence, to avoid judgment, to understand. This has the power to transform our hearts and our minds, cleaning them so we can respond to life with love.

- *"We need to dismantle this world and ourselves
  to become structured again with light, love and faith.
  Then we will have a New World; one that makes sense."*

What Matters is What You Feel

Live this truth; it is the only way. This is your truth as an ascended being, and sooner or later you will have to come to it. This is the way to exercise your power; there is no other. Living what you feel is coming from power. Enter your heart and find what is there. Living what you feel is what will make you happy because there lies truth and joy.

Whenever what you feel is painful and is not a joyful experience, enter that feeling and give it your conscious attention. This will release it, and when that process of living the encounter with your pain is over, you will experience the bliss of liberation that is your natural state. When you find you feel sadness express it, cry and release the feeling. When you feel you have resentment, talk to the person you feel that towards and express your feelings with that person. This is the only way to have freedom. You will make sure you do not create more damage to yourself or others by doing this; you won't harm them. You will seek the expression in an appropriate way. If you need to hit a mattress you will do it, and release that frustration physically, but you will not be attacking someone. That will not heal you; it will only make things worse. And again, if you need help, seek the support and counsel of a wise friend or a professional, who will help you release and come to terms with your hurtful feelings.

As you recognize, accept and process the feelings and express them, you will release the heart and make the necessary space for love to manifest. This will be shown as reconciliation with someone, a reencounter with yourself and your truth in life, a liberation that will allow you to be honest with yourself and choose the path which is right for you: that which truly makes you happy. But your truth inside, in your heart must be faced and recognized, then you will be free to be yourself. This is the path to happiness and power, because this is empowering yourself, the way of the ascended being.

The New Relationships

"... are those of sharing from each one's recovered power."

In these new times relationships are changing a great deal. No relationship based on lies or that hides the truth will survive. This is why there are so many divorces and separations at this time. Also, friends and work relationships are going through a lot of changes. Many friends no longer find a common ground to stay together. Vibration changes in everyone are creating separations and new encounters: those that are vibrationally alike.

The parts of a relationship have to be aligned for it to work. If their motivations come from the Self they create encounter, peace and love: light. If they come from ego, they create opinion, separation and no encounter. And that is not allowed in theses times; vibrationally, the price is too high. If they want a higher relationship, they will have to go to the highest cause, that which works from and seeks, in the other, the divinity. They will seek to serve a higher purpose. It will be a relationship that creates light and brings it to the world. They both need to come from their High Self for this. From the Self any opposition of wills is dissolved. From the Self the cause is common and there is no opposition, because it is one. If you are in the ego, you are not interested in truth; you care about defending your ego.

With the entering of the new energies of Stargate, power has been awakened in everyone, and relationships are evolving to become true vessels of that power. This is supported by the individuals within it, empowered by the ascensional energies of high consciousness coming to the Earth to create a new awareness in humanity. We are moving towards spiritual independence. This also means independence in worldly matters. This retaking of inner power will make all more detached and therefore independent from others, emotionally, financially, and spiritually. Then relationships will be truthful ones because they will not seek to take power from others or become a deceitful power struggle, which is what happens when you have not recovered your own power. Truthful relationships are based on the common and mutual respect of the other's power and freedom. You have power and share from it. You give of what you have and the other does the same. Such encounters are creative instead of destructive and generate joy. Sharing joy and evolving together is their purpose.

The new relationships are being created as individuals own their power more than ever, and will be formed in the recognition of one's own power and the other's power. All the parties in the relationship will see, accept and support the other's own sovereignty. Powers will add, becoming relationships of united power. Increased power will be for the objectives of the relationship; no one will be less than another. The result of this will create a space of power, freedom and love for creating the best for the benefit of all.

The true union comes from two complete and free beings that unite to share from their plenitude and strength. Therefore *free* here means not dependent on the other. That independent strength and plenitude of each one is the guarantee of independence, and of the fact that they come into it from a state of independent power, necessary to avoid the relationship becoming a power struggle.

In the intimate aspect, intimacy between a man and woman is the encounter of offered mutual joy: the gifts that each one has to offer the other. To give joy to the other is one's own joy. This is the consciousness of the new age: seeking the wellness of all. Happiness comes from seeing others happy and doing, in love, what one is able to do to accomplish that. Shared joy is the vision of new age relationships, whether intimate relationships or otherwise. And that joy comes from inner power and light being awakened, and it seeks to serve The Light. That offering of joy to the other in close relationships is a free event, where joy is not demanded for oneself; space, both physical and psychological, is respected as is the will of free giving of each self to the other. Both meet without eclipsing the other, without possessing each other, becoming one but respecting each other. These are relationships with light, from the light and for the light. This is what will create a new age.

●

*"With new relationships, it is possible
to create a new society of divine beings,
an ascended society with conscious and
light-serving relationships."*

Supporting Power Awakening

Never lose contact with the fact that there is a great need for power awakening on this Earth and that with your good actions you are supporting that. And be prepared to make some mistakes in the way of miscalculations sometimes, as you learn to trust your awakened power, while you gain greater confidence in being a vehicle for awakening power. All this requires a move from being concerned about what happens with power outside to bringing your attention totally to God, inside.

> *"I take power from my ego and give it to God,
> the God part in me."*

This means taking power from ego, the one we have given it. We retake the power given to the ego and stop giving more power to it. The same with the truth we have been developing here: "I take my power I have given to people and give it God." The importance is with God.

Prayer

*"Father take away all that
which is not holy in us."*
- Amen

Death Consciousness: Life Enhancement

This might sound scary at first, but it is not so at all. In the indigenous traditions of most of Mexico death is seen with joy and the dead, as in many cultures, are revered. This tradition has survived to this day and is present in the culture of modern Mexico. They celebrate the dead and death at a specific time of the year, and it is a happy, sweet celebration. It is also because they make sweets and sweet bread related to the tradition, which can be found at any food shop. It is a celebration of light and of projection to the beyond, as attitudes and consciousness try to reach that realm beyond the known life. It is a realm that means the moving away from this world of limited consciousness and reference. There is power in seeing beyond limitations, and that includes the limited and obscure idea of death. Experiences of what is beyond this known life can be lived in meditation, and that is a way to have a good impression and knowledge of the worlds of light beyond this one. It is also a way to experience the expanded consciousness and freedom that is there. I have had very powerful experiences in my many years of meditation related to this: the encounter with the light inside, travelling beyond this level of perception and awareness through levels and dimensions of consciousness full of love, wisdom and ecstasy. A place you would really want to know.

I also recommend the works of Doctor Raymond Moody about the realities beyond this life. He had direct near death experiences, and then explored those of others over the years and concluded amazing facts, which are contained in some of his books. What most impacted me about his work is that common essence in the experiences related to going beyond this life. They all essentially went through the stages of leaving the body and seeing it consciously from outside and above, entering a tunnel, which had light at the end. At that end entering a world of light and meeting loved ones who had parted, and finally, having an encounter with a being of light, which most people associated with God or Jesus. This common essence of the experiences beyond death has a great similarity with some deep meditation experiences. In those, you go through a tunnel, you see light, can meet beings of light and you merge into worlds of light to experience a higher expanded state of consciousness. In both ways, there is light and joy, immense bliss and freedom, and also infinite love. Doesn't that say something crucial to us? It is talking about the dimension beyond this life. I would call meditation a *beyond life experience.* When meditating, you come back because you are projecting yourself to the realm of Spirit from a living state and from conscious intent. At death it just happens; this is what happens.

Those experiences can be accessed in those two ways, ways that are able to take us beyond and show us what the realm of Spirit is like, to show us that it is there; that there is something a million times better and happier than what is known here. But if we are here, there must be a good reason for it: spiritual growth. So when we go beyond we can reach higher levels of that light and expansion, because we have earned them. So it is good to use the time here to know those levels of existence and light, and not waiting to know they exist when parting from this earth. If you know these levels of light death is a completely different experience than if you don't know them. Living with that experience and knowledge makes life completely different and the joys of it are unimaginable; also when you know the experience of the light and part from this world you go to those levels of light you have earned.

The indigenous Mexican people say, "Have death as an advisor." There is such tremendous wisdom in the indigenous traditions and so much power in them. The idea they present about death is to live life while having death as advisor. In that way we aim at having the idea of death present with us constantly, and that inevitably has an impacting effect on the way we live life. If we do not forget about death, we will be placed in the awareness that every moment is worth all, and that it is the opportunity to live and act in the best way and most loving way. Because that is the only moment there is. We don't know when death can happen, so we focus mainly on life living each moment as if it was the last, not living half dead or asleep, but being fully awake. We focus on the present moment which is the only one there is; we are dramatically brought back to the present and can know the present is the place of power. We can only exercise power in the present. If you want to influence your life, direct it in the direction of greatness; there is only now. You can only act with power in the present; there is no other time in which you can exercise power. So life gains a new dimension, and we realize we need to exercise our power in the present. Always remember that truth:

"The present is the moment of power."

Now is a moment of gold to experience the best, if you chose the best, and that is in your hands if you exercise your power. Do not leave all merits for later, do them now. Living life with the consciousness of death you focus on doing the best, in performing actions with merit, because the present moment becomes a moment of gold, you open your heart to God, to others, to life, you transmute your karmas, love your brother, you unite with life. In a word: you seek to live as high a life as possible. In this way you make death a friend.

You can make every day and every moment, a moment of preparation for death in which you live attending everything and everyone, and don't leave things for another day or year. Sometimes it is not possible to do this fully, but it can be done as much as possible. The idea is that you live up to date with all and everyone. It is not good to reach the end of this life with pending issues, to say, "I wish I had done this; I wish I had said this to that person and enjoyed things." It will be too late. You had better live it now. Thus being up to date with everything and have everything solved. And this will give you a greater sense of meaning and will develop in you a lighter and more joyful attitude to life. I invite you to try it.

Also, you see your physical vulnerability and develop, discover, and unite with your spiritual invulnerability. You focus on the truthful, the real; you give importance to the real, you stop deceiving yourself. You situate yourself and your awareness here and now, become more conscious. You want to enjoy, not suffer, so you seek more intensely to create joyful realities. You undoubtedly concentrate more on the eternal aspects of life and of yourself and give less attention to the ephemeral. As Jesus said to me once:

"He who seeks the union with God is safe and sound."

Forgiving is Seeing the Truth

"It is important not to leave aside tenderness, sweetness and forgiveness; to realize that only God is necessary."

Forgive yourself truly. This is necessary in order to set things right inside yourself, so you don't have hold-ups and ties that block your movement forward towards your true freedom. You must forgive all in the light that those that wanted you to be limited and dependent, were full of fear as a result of their lack of light, and in their weakness, they tried to get power and therefore, confidence from other human beings, amongst whom there was you. This might have been coming from the system — the Matrix of the Dark — its servants, people in positions of global power or in positions of power in your job, family, or the people around you.

You must understand that when they embrace the light, they will be fully empowered and will not need to use those dark ways to get power, because they will be getting it from the right place. In that awakening they will start to leave those old negative habits, which only served the purpose of enslaving many and benefiting a few "clever ones," who thought they had worked out a way to get ahead, selfishly, and because they thought were smarter than the rest, they thought they could do it and get away with it. Of course, you and I know they won't. So we can forgive them for their error and be thankful we did not fall for that foolish way of being; and if we did, we no longer contemplate those ways as a valid ways of acting.

So forgive yourself and use mercy and forgiveness with others. Have mercy for all. Bring liberation in that forgiveness. Liberate yourself. This is the right place to be now.

The Power of Giving

When you give, you have power. When you truly give, that is an act of love. So love is an act of power. When you give, you are the king. When you give, you have the Universe at your feet. Truly giving is done without expecting something back. When you truly give you emanate a freedom that is picked up by others, and they are attracted to you, to that space of love. It is like a magnet. When you give, you don't get stuck because you are radiating; you don't pick up negative energy. To truly give you must be in a state of power. If not, you are not truly giving because your giving will be tainted by your lack of power, and that giving will look for power as its motive for being. In giving in a true way you empty yourself and the Universe fills you up. This becomes a current of abundance in which you are constantly giving and the Universe is constantly filling you up. In such giving there is no thought for you; it is all going out of you. There is emptiness of self-thought. This giving is love in action. Thought is substituted by flowing in the present. You hold back nothing.

Look after, take care of, be responsible for, support life. This is what you do in true giving: you support the process of life wherever you are. Take into account that the opposite of this giving is contraction. Contraction is not giving; contraction is fear. Fear is not giving. You are either giving or taking. Nothing has detrimental influence over you because you are in possession of the greatest power — when you are in communion with God. This is the state of awareness everyone is moving towards.

Drawing the Line

"I don't care what others think of me."
"I only care about what God thinks of me."
"And what God thinks of me is my truth."

"Only I decide how I feel."
"Only I have power over how I feel."
"I am all the power — ALL — in my life"

"Nothing takes me out of my serenity."
"Nothing outside me affects me."
"I don't give the power to affect me
 to anything or anybody."
"Nobody does anything to me."
"I do not take what doesn't belong to me."

Having the correct relationship with God and with His power-full reality is a must in these times. Here in these statements of truth, the essence of this is reflected. They place power where it should be and in the relationship which should hold it: the one between you and God. This is the quality relationship to be entertained. All other correct relationships will come from this one. But if this one is not right, other relationships won't be fine. Those are the relationships of the world we are leaving behind: power games.

You have to realize the context for these statements. Obviously we do not refer here to good things or the positive ways in which close and loved ones will affect us. We are referring to the negative expressions of power due to a lack of it, or because of putting it in the wrong place. Also they refer to the world at large, to people or situations, close or far, that due to unconsciousness might act in harmful or detrimental ways, and of course we do not want to be caught in that. We want to exercise our freedom in the choice of things that we want to be part of. With that consciousness in mind now, you might read again and incorporate these power statements into your way of living.

Regarding the last sentence of the list above, it refers mainly to the things people take from a situation or from another, attitudes, guilt, responsibility, blame that does not belong to them, but due to bad power management one is walking away with a load that is not his own. We must be particularly aware of those events in which that happens, because they happen too often. We need to draw the line. This is a healthy and conscious act of power on the way to a new consciousness.

A New Intelligence: Teach How to Fish

In the true and clear exercise of power we have gained, there is an awareness that tells us exactly what is ours and what is not. When people with a less than clear awareness of power don't take what is theirs consciously, they will push things towards another person. That is so with consciousness: it will seek completion and light — the light of conscious recognition. So when an unconscious motivation or attitude is not made conscious by its owner, it will pick up on the consciousness of the person nearby. In other words, if a person is not aware of something in her, someone else will. If that is you, make sure you know if you are taking something that doesn't belong to you. You can help, but everyone has to become wholesome and responsible for all areas of their consciousness — or unconsciousness. This is fundamental in order to make the right steps to sustain the liberation of ascension. We must act with a new intelligence in power management. So that help will be correctly applied if it directs the person towards the conscious recognition of her issues, rather than helping by taking responsibility for a weight that is not yours, and thus keeping the person in unconsciousness. Otherwise there is the risk of supporting irresponsibility and taking on a burden indefinitely. Remember Jesus' words:

> *"If you give fish to a man, he will eat that day; but*
> *if you teach him how to fish, he will eat every day."*

You can give fish to a man while you teach him how to fish, but eventually he will have to be responsible for his own fishing. This is the only way to sanity and a healthy communion between humans: not to be burdens to others. And of course, a totally different thing is to take charge of people who due to their karmic situation are unable to provide for themselves. But don't allow self-appointed beggars around you. Show others, gently but firmly the way to their ascension.

Responsibility & Magic

In taking full responsibility we become true co-creators with God. It is then that He can use us to unveil His power and make it available to us; it is then we are good partners to Him. He feels the joy of creation with us, because we have said to Him: "We will be true partners. I won't be a zero in the Universe, I will assume my responsibility in the scheme of things." And then the flow of life, power and magic truly begin for you. Until then, you are not able to do anything because your power is fragmented into many pieces given to wrong beliefs, people, circumstances, and you are not capable to pull anything together that is worthwhile. If you are creating true goodness in your life, you are doing well: you are owning your power there. You can only work magic when you own your responsibility.

Most of the people who go for psychotherapy are people who have not owned their power, and the lack of responsibility has put them in a situation that, over time, has created deep trouble for them, and they cannot figure out how to get out of it. They need help in undoing what they've been doing wrong for so long. They did it for a long time, and now their creation doesn't work anymore. They have lost magic and they need to recover it. Troubles start when magic is lost, out of bad habits and not supporting life and its flow in the appropriate ways.

Magic and a magical life happen when we take responsibility for everything in our lives. Then being open to the Universe and having recovered power from the shadows, we can influence life in great ways because it all depends on us. This means a total recovery of power and responsibility; otherwise there is no chance to have that influence. Magical outcomes come from freedom: the space where things can happen. And freedom is based on power and responsibility.

We give responsibility to the doctor or someone in that role, for our well-being, to spiritual coaches for our spiritual advancement, to others for our emotional well-being. This way the power of magic is lost and with it, the power of creation: one is not at the center of things and losses the ability to influence them. People have been creating idols and giving responsibility to them and thinking they are great, that they have a great life with so many wonderful allies. They have been fooling themselves: unless things are in their hands they won't truly move forward, and that is mainly in the direction of freedom, the space for magic. When we become dependent on those figures, they are not allies; they are self-created enemies: we give the power to them. If someone owns your power, he is either leading you to be ready to own your power, or he is your worst enemy. People are giving responsibility away and feel they do not have to think about that issue anymore. Like with the doctor, they go to see him, and if there is nothing wrong they don't think about their health any longer; they carry on with their life normally until the next time they feel unwell. Feel sinful? Go to the church, speak to the priest, have confession, and after praying the absolution all is well and you don't think about the issue any longer. Where is responsibility? When you take full responsibility, health is maintained looking after it in the right way, every day. Being spiritually engaged means constantly having a connection with the right ways and God within, and being aware of the state of the heart, where the right actions are performed from; there will hardly ever be a need to go to the priest or the doctor. Magic is alive inside.

New age *means a direct connection with things and God, without intermediaries.*

It is crucial for a change of consciousness to take full responsibility for ourselves. The ascension energies of the Stargate are demanding that we take charge. They are powerful and they can set all our power free, providing the best ground for a magical life. They can bring the recovery of the power given away and the liberation of dependencies created as a result of that and maintained over eons of time. They can cut all their ties and, freeing them, send power back to whom it belong: us. Then we have to sort out what is out of place and assume that which is only ours: power. Because that is the natural state of things and how God created us. We are not gaining anything new; we are recovering what we are. We are moving to the zero point. This is where everything starts. We cannot invest money and do any projects if we are in the red. This is the same. What is happening now is that debt has the real possibility of being cancelled. Humanity has lived below zero for a long time. People have been in debt and thought this was normal. It is not; it is madness, because it means you have to borrow, and what people have been borrowing is power. This has been very dangerous: it has created the world we have had. Such is the dramatic importance of owning the power that is ours; if we don't people will keep fighting with each other in the name of some wonderful cause that has at the depth of it, a fight for power. Because it is an asset that everybody has lacked and everybody has been after. And where are you going to get it from if you don't go to the source of it? Others: your brother or sister, "thy neighbor." You can think of anything… slavery, not the one tied with chains. There are many subtle chains that don't squeak when you move… and are far more dangerous. They all have sought to control people's power. And that is always illicit. All people are full of those chains until they emancipate from a disastrous situation of lack of power. The presence of chains means the freedom of magic is gone.

The energies available on the planet now are full of gifts. The main one is that they allow things to go back to their original state: the magical state. So they are supporting your resolution, as your awareness awakens to divinity inside to take command of your life fully. Then and only then, can you work magic. This happens by taking full responsibility, taking your power back from where it was sent by you, and being fully responsible: co-creating the world you want for you and others. When responsibility is given away, you have no power to work magic in your life. You are not a powerful being when you refuse to have responsibility. The more responsibility you own the more magical you can be; the Universe takes you seriously and works with your greater vision and inspiration. Finally, as people are liberated and hold all their true divine consciousness, their responsibility will have no limits; this is what God is like. This means people will be able to influence everything for the good and create the magic this needs. This is the God-realized state that everyone must comprehend.

A friend of mine said: "As long as you are not a problem for the Universe, that means a lot." You might not do anything to help the world moving ahead, or might not want to contribute to it; but at least if you are not a nuisance to it, you won't be in the way of its evolution. If you don't impede magic happening and developing in life and the world, your life will be better and magic will keep flowing in your life. Magic allows you to live without limits in freedom and joy.

"To live without limits. This is the vision
of the magician: everything is possible."

The True Temple:
Power and God Are Inside

I have often seen people going to a sanctuary to worship Mother Mary or another spiritual embodiment of God, while on the way they step on others people's ways, infringing on their rights and

235

freedom; the very ones they pretend to be exercising. God is inside; the temple is inside. Going to worship to a holy place is wonderful and many times necessary, but there is a great myopia in that the people who go to those places and don't respect others because that worship and the worshiped figure is "more important." God lives within every human being. They all, each one should be treated as a holy figure. One cannot push people aside because one wants to have an encounter with a divine presence as if the rest of living beings were less important and would not deserve the same kind of treatment. That is not very divine. Every living being has the right to the same reverence, and that shouldn't be eclipsed in the presence of holy figures, of when someone else exercises his rights. This should be the vision of an ascended person.

God is inside; the temple of God is the heart. Insisting on seeing God only outside is one of the biggest and most terrible mistakes human beings have being performing. It is seeing that divine power is only outside. So there is a permanent dependency on holy places and holy figures. In this way there can never be peace. The beauty of accessing God and power — which is His for you — inside is that people become spiritually independent. And that is the greatest achievement of all.

Very often I have seen people with unhappy and tense expressions after visiting a temple. I understand most people are in great need. Many are suffering. But if the equation was reversed and they started to look for that power of redemption and healing inside, the communion with a holy place would be more complete and meaningful, and no doubt most would leave the sanctuaries with happy, smiling faces; the grace and the temple would still be there with them as they leave.

Society and wrong spiritual teachings have perpetuated over thousands of years the idea that there is no holiness in the human heart, because they have seen people as sinners. And that belief has been taking power away from them. And in the same blow they have made them permanently dependent on a system of redemption that has kept them forever tied to external power for their liberation and meaning.

It is time for the emancipation of any type of spiritual chain. It is time for the resurrection of the Truth, the one that says that every human being has the right to be recognized as divine because he is a son or daughter of God. And we don't need that to be proclaimed by spiritual institutions, whatever they might be; it is a claim we must make from within ourselves in reconciliation with God, as beings that acquire the consciousness of the New Age: feeling truly related to God. That is the only true claim and the only one that will work.

If power is within us, we have the power to connect directly to God. We just have to do it. Try it if you haven't, and the more you do it the more you will find He is there. He will recognize you immediately as a valid interlocutor, and you will find out that you do not need intermediaries to do that which only you can do so well. This is the way for the new times. It is part of the past attitude of irresponsibility — and I must add, a very convenient way of doing it — to pass on to an intermediary figure the responsibility for God connection and communion, and let him do the job so people don't have to worry about it. But you know... the job is not being done unless you do it. Because you have to find Him inside, and until that happens, something very crucial in your life will not be fulfilled. Going to any kind of spiritual service once a week is a great thing. I do it many times. But not to consider it as a substitute for the main, direct connection with the divine, which is your right, joy and responsibility.

No ceremony is a substitute for living in the inner divine temple and communing with God within, at any time, every moment of the day. Going once a week and then forgetting about it is a very comfortable way of dealing with the greatest truth in life. And such a superficial way of doing it, that the hidden infinite treasures and ecstasy of a direct and deep communion with the divine remain unknown. His spiritual patrimony is not shared with whom are His spiritual family. The one who loses out on this is you, and humanity as a whole.

Stepping ahead towards a responsible way of living spiritual realities is a must for these new times. This is the greatest exercise of power people can do. This is the natural state of the ascended beings.

Inner Self Contact

You may follow this guided meditation to have a deeper encounter with your divine Inner Self.

- In the heart there is the chalice of the Holy Grail, where, baptized with the Light of the divine Christ Self, we access all the abundance and Divine Grace.

- It is from there, where from now on we drink from the Divine Source where all the Love, Power and Wisdom are for our life in the New Age.

- It is from the Christ of the Holy Grail in the heart that we enter into communion with the Divine and with every brother and sister.

- From there, there is the unity with all. The divine point common to all.

- There is where the energy is, not in the personality or ego.

- There we find the connection with the feminine energy of love, tenderness, compassion that accesses the Christ, others and God.

- We have to spend more time in communion with the divine inside. It is the only thing that is really worth investing in.

Prayer for the World

You can all enter into daily prayer in the morning to ask God for peace in the world. Human beings alone are incapable of achieving it. United in prayer with God, we will attain it.

We can use these guidelines for praying:

- Let us ask for peace.
- For the victory of the light.
- For the submission of the dark.
- Let us ask Heaven to intervene.
- We can visualize the planet and humanity. surrounded by the divine violet light.
- Let us ask the Masters and the Saints to pour their light, grace and blessings upon the planet.

Let's pray:

"Beloved Father, we ask you for peace for the world.
Beloved Father intervene in the world for the good of all.
Father, take charge of this Earth and Humanity."

"We ask for Light for all, we ask for the Ascension of all.
We forgive, let go and love, and we carry the Golden Light
within our hearts.
- Amen.

This prayer was brought to us by Mother Mary.

- During the day you can repeat your own mantra, if you have one and send it to the world for peace. You may make a prayer of petition for peace every moment you can during the day, and do it while seeing the world surrounded and bathed by the divine Violet Light.

This extra effort is worthwhile. If we all do it, the difference will show. You can be a factor of unity. Wherever you are, whoever you are with in every moment and place, be a factor of unity. Manifest unity, reconciliation, peace. Promote unity amongst all. The way is reconciliation and union. Constant gratitude to God for His blessings is something we must always have.

It is crucial not to have fear. It is the great enemy. It is the problem of the ego; that is why it is so destructive. We must concentrate in working the light, in opening our hearts to the light. Let's remember that the life inside every being is the same. And the God they pray to is the same. We are all brothers, sisters, sons and daughters related to the same Divine Father-Mother.

Moving to Ascension:
The State of Joy

For years I have practiced deep meditation daily. I have found immense regions of joy and bliss inside. I have found inner peace, a peace that doesn't exist anywhere in the world; an experience of inner bliss and joy anyone would give anything to have. There is such a feeling of relief. Unless you have experienced it, you cannot imagine it. This has allowed me, and many others, to live in an ascended awareness in many ways.

As we explore the inner universe of our divine consciousness we find an incredible power inside. It is the power of joy. Its power lies in the fact that this joy does not depend on anything, and therefore it is permanent. If it was dependent on circumstances, it would be there sometimes and it wouldn't at other times. It is there without cause; it just happens inside. It is there waiting to be known.

As time has gone by this experience of divine ecstasy has become more present in me, until it has become permanent. And from then on, it has become even more exquisite. I don't claim merit from this, the merit is God's. What I have done is to go to find Him inside; that is my merit: the effort and attention I have put to that aim. But the reservoir of ecstasy was there. I always say that if people would put a tenth of the effort they put into achieving things in the outside world to go to that heaven inside, their lives would be wonderful... and the world would be a kind place full of goodness. Not only would they find true happiness with a tenth of the effort, they would hold that happiness. The Kingdom of Heaven is inside each one.

When you have that experience you are really powerful. You don't depend on anything to bring you happiness. You don't depend on anyone. That independence is true power because you are free. Power comes from you. If you ask yourself what do people want power for, the answer is to get satisfaction, influence, to feel important, to be the center of attention; it's about ego. There is so much seeking after power. People want to feel powerful; they think this is the way to happiness. But they seek that power outside, and if that is so, it will be through acquiring things; so this power will go away with those things. Nothing is permanent outside. It is a weak power the one people find outside. People need to feel powerful, fulfilled, big. Well, you get that and more by looking for it within.

Imagine a joy that doesn't depend on the weather, on your job, friends, financial situation, emotional situation, whether you are alone or in company, that is independent from what you have and who you are, where you are and what you do. This is like a dream. Well, God has dreamt it for us and it is there. Isn't that joy powerful? Very powerful. It exists. It is there for you and everyone. People don't know what they have inside. It is amazing. The treasure that is worth more than all the treasures they seek everyday is waiting inside each one to be discovered. The power of joy. The Stargate opening is taking everyone in that direction, it is showing everyone that the power outside is meaningless. And it is opening the eyes of everyone to see the beauty of what is waiting within. An inner ascension is necessary to access that powerful state of joy.

Imagine there is a thick forest, immense and deep. In the middle of it there is a garden of beauty, peace, warmth, with a lake that emanates a magical energy of sweet ecstasy that draws everyone near it. Imagine it is full of peace so deep you never want to leave that place. You feel absolutely bewitched by the enchantment of such beauty full of serenity, colors, flowers, trees, light. No needs, no time, no rush, no conflict... just peace, joy... just love. Well it is something like that inside, but better. That place exists; you just have to get into the forest and find it. It takes hard work, it takes facing your dark side; it takes wanting to do it. But those who have done it know there is nothing more worthwhile. And only those know of the bliss that is there. That forest is inside you; that sanctuary is inside you. Unless you go in that direction you won't find it. Believe that: there is nothing like the joy inside; it is beyond your wildest dreams of happiness and ecstasy. My words don't even come anywhere near it, and I am not exaggerating. Don't look for joy outside; you are wasting your time. True joy only exists inside, so this is a place you will have to go sooner or later. I recommend you do it sooner. Now is the perfect time: all the help is being put to that aim.

It will be very difficult to ascend if the processes presented in this work are not fulfilled. In fact, it will be impossible. When you enter realms of high vibration and you haven't brought your dark side to the light, it will be set off. And all its dark contents will be brought to the surface very intensely. This is unbearable. It is something very difficult to handle. The pain, agitation, unrest, unloving thoughts, all those dark contents coming into the conscious mind and physical body, the sensations of those energies not processed; it is a real shake-up. All this work and this time on Earth are to prepare people to have a new vibration so they can enter finer realms of light: dimensions of pure joy. If they are not purified from pain and unhappiness, wrong habits that don't create light, they cannot hold in their systems so much light and joy. It is like two magnets that repel each other.

All this is a preparation for ascension. To merge with something, you have to be like it. A drop of water can become part of the ocean; but sand will just fall to the bottom and stay there. To be part of the light and joy of the fifth dimension, you have to have light and joy inside. This is very important.

Questions of Power

The question is: What am I doing to create this situation?
What do I do to change my internal alchemy?
Not, how do I make something different happen outside…?
But, how can I be different, generate an internal alchemical change?

High Vibration: Blessings for All Life

As you raise your vibration your responsibility expands. This essentially means that your reach out is bigger. As vibration expands in you also does your energy, and you touch more the reality beyond yourself. In low vibration there is low consciousness, and the main concern of that person is with himself. The increment in vibration takes the person outside himself to encompass others and life at large, until there is a connection and a feeling of relating with the Universe as a whole.

As you become bigger and encompass a greater perspective, you seek more to flow and to harmonize. So you are less and less an obstacle and increasingly more an agent for goodness. If you are not a problem for the Universe that is a lot. What you can do is make sure everything that comes out of you is a blessing for life. This is achieved by being in a high vibration. Make sure your actions and words are a blessing for others, for the Universe at large. You may feel: "I am the light of God. I bless; God blesses in me." This is "through me." My words, actions, feelings, all in me only blesses. Each breath is offered to God.

Spiritual Charisma

Charisma is a gift, a way of being and of dealing with life. It is something indefinable in the ways of a person that shines through her eyes and that has a magnetism that is irresistible. True charisma comes from the inner light that has a spark, impregnating everything about that person and her actions.

There is a certain absence of ego in this radiation and a genuine flair that moves hearts. It is the art of being out of the way, an absence of useless control, a free flow of energy and purity. Truly powerful people have spiritual charisma. I mean powerful in the sense of having recovered their inner power, far from what the world calls "powerful people" in a material sense.

You too can develop spiritual charisma as you ascend. As you recover your power and stop worrying — they go hand in hand — you will open new paths to flow in interesting and magical ways, since magic will be available to you from your unity with the source of power. This source acting through you, will empower you, and as you are out of the way — free from manipulative control for results — it will impregnate you and everyone else through you. That generates a magnetism like a field of energy that attracts goodness... and everyone's attention. Such magnetism is charged with beauty, positivism and good will. It just happens; it develops naturally as power is recovered. It is a state of grace — a very desirable one. You cannot go out to get it: the moment you want it, it's gone. Because ego comes in and then you are not out of the way but in the way, and charisma doesn't happen there. It will instead happen as you seek the highest and the best, and as you give it to others and to life. It will happen as a byproduct of your honest devotion to the light. This is the state and the aim of an ascended person.

You should want to have spiritual charisma, not because of the attention it naturally gets, but because of higher motives. You will be immersed in a state of peacefulness, absence of worry and lightness, which will provide a fantastic ground for good things to manifest. The absence of worry is mainly an absence of self-concern; that moves the energy outwards and towards people and life. That can be felt. There is space inside, and that attracts. Something full doesn't attract because there is no space in it. The creativity of the Universe goes past it. People who cannot access that, often have an agenda and they are worried about it. It is the ego's agenda. And that is always something very uptight. When there is no agenda you flow with the present, with what happens and you give the best response to it.

> *"The space inside you is sought by the Universe*
> *to create goodness."*

With spiritual charisma you are not looking for something specific, you are just in the present experiencing your connection with divinity and living from there. This is the way to live as an ascended human being: no recipes; everything comes from the high connection and manifests in the appropriate way from it. Nothing else matters because whatever happens is divine. The power that is making it happen comes from God, you just allow Him to do it. And you trust the result is okay. To get to that, you must have had a deep realization that those ego realities and actions are not interesting because ego has no real power, and at some point you stopped being interested in it. You then surrendered to higher power and saw that what it brought was worthwhile, so you made a commitment to using it and to giving up your small will for a greater will. This is clearly related to the attitude of the spiritual warrior.

All that doesn't mean you stopped acting; it means you act but looking for higher motives and higher outcomes: those that benefit all. The steadfastness in that is what creates a field of charisma in

245

you that is always present, and is powerful enough to be noticed... by the Universe. You are its ally. Spiritually charismatic people are the ones who can serve its purposes and will do it — those that are for the good of everyone. This is what the Universe is really concerned about. Another word for this function of the Universe is compassion.

Spiritual charisma is a sign of a powerful presence as we have seen, acquired by a spiritual revelation inside about how things and real power work. Furthermore, spiritual charisma is something that shines through a person who is really concerned and absorbed in service. True service is an attitude of giving, facilitating the process of life unfolding before oneself in the best possible way. That best possible way will be a non-ego driven energy, but will be visionary: able to see what is really best for all. That vision is acquired after a great spiritual development, the only one capable of tuning the eyes to discerning vision: spiritual vision which is not fooled by the delusion of ego, often disguised as "wonderful projects" but that only seek the ego's benefit.

Spiritual charisma is a sign of power, spiritual power and a connection with divine will. It is the sign of someone who has recovered his freedom and feels the consciousness of being a child of God. Such an individual is an instrument of the power of God and therefore of His love. As we ascend we move closer to spiritual charisma.

"Spiritual charisma is a God-filled state."

Service in the New Times

There is only one way to go towards ascension: service. The less ego, the more service. The less personal conflicts you have, the freer you are to serve. As there is emptiness of personal karma, one can act in real time. That acting is for service. When consciousness has been cleared, the channel is clear to serve. This is the interest that arises in a consciousness free of personal karma. One moves from karma to service, from ego to serving in love. This is a process of inner ascension. In such emptiness from personal conflict you are taken to real time: you do that which is needed at the time; there is no delay, no time. There is the speed of the present, immediacy: you are there in the required moment — synchronicity. That is service in the new times.

"I don't want to serve; I am service.
We must be available in service, we
must be a space for it."

Passion: The State of Truth
Living Your Highest Possibility

"When your inner fire burns
intensely your power is alive."

A lack of power needs an infusion of Spirit. You feel Spirit around you, clarity comes... you act. That act is love in action. When Spirit is in you, there is feeling, action, service, creation: passion. All these reach out to people and the world with beneficial outcomes. If you don't have passion, fire doesn't come out and things don't get done. Issues are pending. Life is not lived, and evolution doesn't happen. You are not living. When you act with passion the Universe responds and creation happens. This is the play of Power: life is lived in love. Love is a creative force. Be aware of the message the Universe is sending you. Then you will know how you are doing. Essentially, you need passion to have an engaging and fulfilling life; you need passion for change to move towards your highest possibility. You need passion for your ascension.

"In passion you are infused with Spirit"

How much do you want God? What is the strength of your passion? You bet twenty percent, the Universe equals the bet. Wanting God is wanting what He is and what He has; it is wanting Him happening in your life. This means a number of things: knowing who you are, becoming free, being free from suffering and accessing all power. With that, everything is possible: knowing true love, accessing true unlimited bounty, enjoying complete peace, living in joy and bliss. Most people when asked would say they want that. But their bet is very low. In fact, they do hardly anything to make these a reality for themselves, although they "really want it." It doesn't work that way. Passion has to be there. Wanting is not enough. This is the difference between wanting and passion: passion gets you there. You must want something one hundred per cent, with fire in the soul to manifest it in your life, to see it there. More so with God and all He brings. God doesn't do everything: asking God and that is it. It is asking God and you doing your part. The greatest part you have is to make the space for Him. How much space do you want to make for God in you? What things fill up that space? What is it you would not let go? Then, how much do you want that happiness? Read that line again: "Wanting God means a number of things." But it requires letting go of all that which opposes it, that doesn't let Him enter. Your passion will make the space necessary for Him to settle in your heart with the kingdom of joy He brings.

God does not negotiate. You either have passion for Him and His gifts or He would not enter into competition: He would let you have other things. This makes sense: you have to be clear on what you want. If you want the toys of the ego and suffering, that is what you will have. He gave you free will, remember?

Passion is the state of an awakened heart.
An awakened heart comes from love, not from fear.

Passion for being, knowing, living and serving God... This is what will carry you through illusion and towards a permanent state of

248

bliss and truth. For me, passion is exemplified in that comment from God to Jeremiah, 29:13:

> *"You will search for me and you will find me*
> *when you search for me with all thy heart."*

If you don't find God within no doubt your passion is somewhere else, and as such it will not bring the desired rewards: encounter with perfection and happiness, the products of encounter with God. He brings the love beyond imagination. It is true, as He says to Jeremiah, and as anyone wanting to find Him has experienced: you will want Him and His experience as a priority; otherwise He will let you be with whatever is your priority. That is because only God is necessary. As we search for Him in the wrong places and search for power in the wrong forms — idols — He will not show up.

> *Do not give your power to any idol, image, figure, symbol,*
> *situation, person or circumstances, other than God.*

Undoubtedly, you will be let down. Humanity has been deceiving itself for too long, placing hope in corruptible idols and then experiencing let-downs and being disappointed. It has chosen badly. How can you not suffer when you have placed your illusions in a god of sand? How can you then, when it collapses, cry as if something failed you? Isn't that crazy? Then why do people do it all the time? God is not the dialogue of priests because people have to become religious; it is because it is what makes sense. There is not true joy anywhere else. It is about becoming realistic, becoming practical and intelligent.

Passion for the good, passion for joy, passion for creating the best; this is passion for God... In the acknowledgment that God is where all that is. God is who sustains it. This is God's passion. No one ever has that passion for love and goodness. "I am busy being happy. I am happy serving goodness." This is what I can do as a human being: find my joy and express it through my life. This is the highest passion I can have. This is what I can do with my life and it is an offering to God. He gave me the power to do what I want with my life; in this way I am serving Him, because this is the vision He allows me to have for myself and manifest it. This simply means, honoring, acknowledging the power that gave me life to develop my life project. It means serving God in whatever way it takes. I might be a musician. I do it with passion, I love it; I make of that my service to God. These can be anyone's feelings. Serving God is not what priests do; it is what we all do when we live passionately. Because that passion of burning love for that thing we love doing is an offering to God for giving us the power, and with it the opportunity to do that which we most love. That is our self-realization, then we experience divinity in it. This is serving God, exercising our passion. When you are busy with your passion you have no time to waste on silly things. You have no time to not be happy. Unhappy people are not passionate; they have not found passion in their lives.

As we get rid of the past and karma and we move towards ascension, we will find our true passion and mission in life. Other meaningless things will move out of the way and we will find a new aim for our existence. When you find your passion and develop it you will be serving others. Because a true passion is truly fulfilling, and it is always something that touches others in some deep way.

You are happy when you give all. This is power. You give all that is in you. This is passion. Then you are full, abundant. If you do not give all that is in you, you are unhappy, you think you have a lot because you keep, you retain and you are tied to what you retain. And your energy is occupied in retaining it. That is a state of no power, no passion. When you give everything, you are constantly being filled by the bounty of the Universe. This is what makes you happy: giving all and receiving more to keep giving.

"Passion is God giving to Himself; in that He creates life."

Everyone is God within. The drive of everyone to give, to create life, to interact is the drive of God seeking to experience Himself, in every possible way through every possible style. It is God showing

His passion. All parts of life giving to all others: they are all serving each other. This is what generates life and creation; this is love. This is the passion of God for life. This is the way we must be to be powerful and happy. When two lovers come together they offer themselves to the other to manifest the complement of the other, and become complete. A passionate union of opposites seeking to experience completion.

"If you have enough passion, everything is possible. Passion generates light. Light generates passion."

Passion is expansive. Expansion is unity, and becoming bigger expands power. Contraction is becoming smaller and therefore losing, minimizing power. Love expands itself, fear contracts itself. It is clear the way to go if we want to walk the path of passion. Ego fears the expansion and eventually the union with God, infinity, because there are no limits there. Ego lives in fear, which is a life of limits; ego has no passion. Passion is going beyond personal limits. In this way ego has a sense of control. But he controls nothing. He cannot control God so he fears Him. To control something you must be bigger. The biggest state is God. And from there, there is no need to control. Passion is a state of truth and fearlessness, a total state of living.

It is not by contracting but by letting go, embracing a superior reality that one becomes expanded into power. All those who have been great have done it uniting themselves with something greater than them. They were experiencing passion in that. They lost themselves in the ecstasy of unity with something great through their passion.

"You set your ego on fire
in your passion for God.
And you are reborn from
the ashes to your higher
Divine Self."

❖ *When your fire doesn't burn your power is low; passion is lacking. When Spirit hits you, you act on it. This awakens your passion.*

Faith & Ascension

Faith is power. Faith is essential for a happy, prosperous and evolutional life. It is necessary for things to go well. Faith is a necessary state in these times of change, and once inner shadows are integrated, faith will be a natural state of being. So with shadow integration on the path to ascension, faith is an essential element that will be incorporated.

Stargate realities are going to show everyone the state of their faith. They will show you where in you there is a lack of faith, and will inspire you to see why and seek the solution. Faith must be active in everyone for ascension. Let's look at some of the aspects that are most relevant to the subject of faith; some of its greatest enemies and its best allies.

"Faith moves the Universe synchronically."

Faith is power

Faith is a synonym of power. It is the way in which power works. Faith moves things and brings them to manifestation; it is sheer power. Wherever you are going, it is faith that takes you there. Faith is the law; with it everything is on your side. Everything opens for you; nothing, no other force can interfere. Faith creates the path and takes you there. Faith is your creative power. As we have all heard, faith moves mountains. If you want something, have faith in that; have faith that it is so, and it is so.

Everything is possible with all the strength, with all the faith. It is like the fire of the forge, it forges you like trained muscles that can bend a rod of steel. The challenges of life are to develop our muscle of faith – and of love. And to open our heart more. And with more faith, to make it all possible, to make love possible. It is so comforting to have faith, to be certain things will develop and happen in the perfect way because God is there doing it.

If God doesn't give you what you ask Him for, most probably you haven't done your part. More faith is needed, more passion, you have not opened up to Him – to His power. If you ask God, "Give me one hundred thousand gallons of water for the swimming pool," He will say, "Where is the space?" Get working, and when you have dug out the hole and it is ready He will give it to you. When you make the space in yourself, He will fill it up. Faith is what makes the space.

"A faithful heart makes wishes come true."

Faith or doubt

Most people who doubt on this planet, believe that their doubt is the reality. They believe that there is something to doubt in the manifestations of life and think this is real. They don't realize that doubt only exists in their minds. They believe that doubting protects them, that it protects their vulnerability. What they do is condemn themselves. Doubting makes them vulnerable. They are afraid of ending up deceived, but they don't fear living in doubt, which is hell itself.

An infinite force of love and creation is there before everyone's eyes all the time. It is whatever we want to call it. But doubt can blind anyone to see it. The ego is afraid to be let down by something it cannot control. In fact, the ego is afraid of a power that is beyond itself. People who don't doubt have certainty in things because they believe in the goodness of the Universe; they believe in the positive. One must ask himself:

"Why do you choose the path of doubt?"

You can believe or doubt. One way is creative, the other destructive. People who doubt as a way of living do so because they don't have certainty in themselves; they doubt because they don't have power within. People with power don't doubt. They are firm, confident, compelling, dynamic. Maybe the Universe behaves one way with some and another way with others? ...Or maybe the Universe behaves for the favor of some, and those who don't have its favor need to doubt it?

Essentially doubt is a terrible obsession because it short-circuits your power. Doubt makes power leak out. Doubt is what can sabotage your ascension.

"There is no option; the only way is to believe.
It is the only sane option and the footwear
necessary to walk towards ascension."

Note:
Due to the high energy coming to Earth at these times and to the divine plan prevailing now, before other – individual – plans, faith will mainly work when it seeks to serve the light, and that service is for the benefit of all and it helps in the evolution of all. This is an important angle and needs to be taken into account. The general teaching of faith is still valid and should be applied; just take into account that what you desire and ask for must be in line with the condition mentioned, to have the best chances of manifesting.

- *Everything is going to have more strength and more power if it serves the light, brings the Divine Plan and is in the service of love for all.*

The Magic of Faith

"In fear you cannot love because
you are worried about yourself.
Love means having not a care
in the world."

Leave worry, eradicate it from you. Dissolve it completely. This is fundamental since keeping worry alive short circuits your faith and your power. You stop the magic of faith. And without them, as you know by now, there is no ascension. Worry itself is a statement of not trusting; it shows a lack of faith in the area of the worry.

Be carefree, detached, fearless.
This is the ascended attitude.

People with worry are tense, have contracted energy; you don't want to be with them: they have no magic. People without worry are relaxed, their energy soothes, expands; magical things happen around them. You want to be with them, they are light. Aim to not have a care in the world. Do not be mistaken: this is faith, not carelessness – you are invoking magic. What's the difference between a child and an adult? Children don't worry; that's why they are so nice. Don't we all see and feel there is something magical about children? It is their carefree nature, their absence of worry. It is not that because you are an adult now you have to worry, and kids don't worry because they are kids. No. This is what most adults would have everyone believe, because they worry. The thing is that worry starts the moment power is lost. And that happens as the child grows up and enters progressively into the conditioning of adults, and becomes an active member of the Matrix of the Dark.

Conditioning comes in; power goes out.
Then magic is lost.

So most people worry about health, self-image, self-importance, love, the future, the present and the past! They worry about money, sex, being happy, work, relationships ... everything. The equation must be changed:

"Worry not; care."

So we take care of everything, just the same as we do with worry, but without worrying. We are so afraid about what can happen to us that we worry. "What will they think of us?" "What will they say to me?" "Will they love me?" "Will we have what we need?" At the end everything is a cause for worry, and we have made worry a way of life.

When you worry, you are giving your power away.

We must leave worry aside and not give power away. If you are not afraid of anything happening to you, it will be so. Faith is magical; it makes things happen in the way you believe. Worry attracts that which it worries about. Then the ego mind says, "You see, you have to worry." This is a crazy vicious cycle. Once you stop it, you will be free from it; you will start living a new life. If you try it, you will be amazed. Years ago I was worrying a lot about certain things. I learned:

"The less you worry the better it goes."

I noticed that when I stopped worrying, things went very well. Many of you know that. But many are still worrying. You need to break out of that; then you will be happy. Leave everything to God. Care about nothing. Do your part, get involved, take part in life but leave the results to God. Be free. This is why detachment is such a high teaching: it is essential for a sane life. It has been taught for thousands of years in the spiritual teachings of India. If you are detached, you don't worry. It is what is missing in the balance of the equation of life: care but be detached. It is not true you are going to be careless or cold. That's nonsense. You are going to be free, more loving and happier than before. Then you will be more effective and do things better. Try it.

Let God take care of you and everything; act, but trust.
The ascended man is a worriless man, a man of faith.
You cannot ascend with worry.

Change worrying for being with God.
Think in God and not in the worry.
Thus, you will resolve it.

Children Live in the Present: The Time of Magic

It is good to study the master of being carefree and magic: the child. Children are so wise; they don't have nonsense in them. According to their vision of the world and life, everything they do makes sense. Can we say the same of ourselves? We must learn from children. They are not concerned about all the nonsense adults worry about. Adults worry about nonsense most of the time. There is too much attachment to the unimportant and not enough concern for the real, the valuable key things in life. Believe; God will provide.

Children play, live life and are careless. They are not worrying about things or outcomes. They live in the moment; they are being themselves. The present moment is the place of magic. We must learn to be like that in these times; we might find that everybody loves us... and things go better. It is a challenge for all to dare to try it. It is a key issue to identify your worries, tackle them, understand them, release the cause, release them — let them go. Most often, you worry because you are afraid of losing control. Most of those things you don't control anyway. So why worry. Isn't it true that most people worry about not getting what they want? They need trust.

We do what we have to do to get what we want. Then we let it go. This is trust. If it happens, it is meant for you. If it doesn't, it wasn't for you... at that time. There is something better coming. It is necessary to have a more sporting attitude towards life: to believe in the good. Fear of people not taking you seriously stops you from smiling and being carefree. Power is in us, in our divine part. God takes us seriously. Place your confidence in the power of God and you will have plenty. We need to break habits of thinking and doing, break rules of how to be. Worrying is not going to change a situation. Trust is. Having confidence, seeking a solution; these will change things. You can care, be careful people without worrying. The key is restructuring to be like children, to open the heart; there are no excuses not to love. Children are loving naturally. They have open hearts, they are not structured. The choice is to love or to suffer. In fact, there is only one choice since love is the only real thing. To move to this carefree nature and trust in the present is the place to be, to join the full power of the impulse of the new energies.

Living Without Problems

One of the keys for this new age of new energy is learning to live without problems. This is not something that will happen just like that; it is an attitude. If you have the attitude of, "I don't have problems," you are sending a powerful message to the Universe and that will manifest in your life. If you keep thinking, "I have this problem," you are making it so. You are keeping the problem alive. By not giving energy to them, problems tend to diminish and disappear. Problems, like everything else, feed on energy. Focused attention and energy; this is the gasoline that keeps things going. The moment you take no notice of the problem in a situation, it stops being a problem and it doesn't have energy to stay alive. Then the situation is there but it is not a problem anymore. The situation might still be there but you have changed your attitude. You stop declaring there is a problem in it and you are free to seek the solution. Most probably, you will see that in doing this, the situation changes or the solution manifests itself spontaneously. The essential attitude is, before any problem situation to say:

"I have not a care in the world. I trust God in this."

And you say it with a matter-of-fact attitude and with serenity. Understand that you create your life. When you worry, you have reasons to worry. When you don't, you don't have them. The less you worry the better it goes, because this is a call to faith and shows your trust in God. By doing that, you are out of the way and God can take care of everything. This is why it works. This is the magic of faith. If you master all that, you are becoming very well prepared for ascension.

●

**"Doubt is the path of ego to nothingness.
Faith is the way of God to infinity."**

❖

You can get out of your house every morning
with these thoughts:

*"I don't care what happens;
I will be caring and happy."*
"I care about doing the right thing."
"I don't care who I meet.

259

I will be happy."
"I am free and worriless."
"Everything is an illusion."
"Nothing is forever."
"Nothing outside matters."
"What matters is inside:
attitude, love, giving, faith."
"God takes care of everything."

Perception & Relativity

"Thoughts are not reality.
Everything is perception.
Change your perception
and you will change your
life."

Reality is subjective, unless one is enlightened. There is no reality as such; there are only thoughts and belief systems that are projected, and seeing them, we think we see reality. Everything is perception. Change your perception and you will change your life. Perception comes from your projection, and projection comes from your beliefs. In other words, you believe something, you project it out into the world and that is what you perceive, because what you believe, that will be the truth to you. That will be your experience. So you don't see the reality; you see your own beliefs. A person believes the world is great, and will project that reality and then will perceive everybody is great. He will experience it and attract that reality to him. And it is just a belief. You choose the reality you want to experience. You create that reality: you choose your own movie. So you experience what you believe. That is why it is so important to acquire power; it changes your experience of life. You can see possibilities with power. Then you create without conditionings, the life you want.

Things mean what we want them to mean. In the book, *A Course in Miracles* which is a classic in the spiritual literature and has been out for more than twenty-five years, it is said that things for themselves don't have a meaning; we give the meaning to them, and because of our faulty perception, we suffer; that meaning is a hurtful one. As *A Course in Miracles* says, not much is needed:

**"The small change in mentality by which
crucifixion is transformed in resurrection."**

As you gain power your wrong, limiting beliefs fall — those that do not hold or support your power. As they fall you will be closer to experiencing the reality, not the projections of your belief system. As they fall, your power will increase. Most belief systems are based on fear and limitation, and that is what people will see and how they will live: according to that supposed limiting reality. Just look at the world to notice this. What power sees is infinity. A person with her own power sees all possibilities, doesn't see limits. Everything is possible for her, and she lives that way. She is always breaking down belief systems and breaking through the illusion of the limited reality of this world. This is a being that moves from the cross to freedom. This is an ascended person.

Limited power = limited reality
Unlimited power = endless possibilities
Power = prosperity – no limits

It makes sense. You define limits according to the power you embody. With little power, few things are possible for you. With great power; many things are possible. Your power colors your perception. When you have none, perception sees little. When power has been realized, perception goes beyond all frontiers, and so does reality. Change your perception and you will change your life. Love is the only perception common to all, because it is not perception; it is the reality. To perceive love, power must have been recovered fully. Then there is the freedom to perceive love. You are free when you choose freedom. To do that, you must perceive freedom and must have acquired your power. Freedom is a sign of power.

As you increase your vibration because of the Stargate frequencies, you will see further through the illusion of this relative world and go beyond thoughts; then you will start to have a glimpse of reality: it was always there hidden behind the screen of thoughts and deceiving belief systems. This is a sign of ascension.

Relativity

This is the essence of detachment. Detachment makes everything relative. This expands on the subject of being carefree and worriless. It is important to escape the realm of the mind through meditation. This gives people inner peace because it pulls them out of the sphere from where they normally work: the worrying mind. As you meditate, you understand how to exist in worry-free realms and states of mind. The peace you will find will keep you going with this, and will show you the relativity of the world around you. The ordinary mind is full of things and worries; if you are in it, you will see its contents and experience them. You have to move to the higher or universal mind in you; there lies peace, bliss, love, understanding — relativity. You need to introduce that perspective into your life. We all do, if we haven't. By escaping the ordinary realm of the mind you know truth, see truth, contemplate truth: you are free.

This detachment from the mind and its lower mundane contents is a revelation. It gives you the relativity that is necessary to lead a happy, sensible and truly productive life. You become the observer, that higher part of you that doesn't get involved: it is just watching everything. It is always there. You will understand and feel its wisdom and love. Life is always relative. You either know it or you don't. If you get involved in a situation and believe it's real, it will be real. If you think you can die, you will experience death. But if you don't believe it, you won't experience it. It is the magic of faith. It works this way. People experience what they believe. It is just that they think they are experiencing reality. It is just their beliefs and they associate them with reality. People who believe differently from the consensus, those who have broken free from the Matrix of the Dark experience a different life, but they don't come out in the news. So it seems they don't exist. Yes, we do. There are many other ways of living other than the ones we assume and have been taught. They are just not interesting to the powers controlling things on Earth; they are not so juicy in commercial terms.

Serenity comes from meditation as it takes you to the higher realms of yourself, your divine aspect, your I-God. This is the place of relativity. As you explore those realms you can bring the peace there to your daily life. Eventually, nothing will take you out of your serenity; your relativity will be so awakened that you will be free from the phenomenal world: it was an illusion anyway. From that serenity you understand that everything is an illusion. You will live, since you are here, for your personal mission of evolution and for helping others, but from a different perspective. As this process advances, you will live in the serenity and the real understanding of this fact. You will pierce reality and the daily life with serenity. You will be a blessing for others and the Earth. In fact, there is no one reason to lose your inner peace. Resistance is what takes you out of serenity. As you enter into the awareness of relativity, you will be loosening the ties of this reality and ascension will be happening naturally in serenity.

Prayer

"Beloved Father, in the name of all give us your infinite mercy to become free from the mind and return to our natural state of supreme peace beyond thought, beyond limits, beyond ignorance, beyond the slavery of the mind, so that we all know the supreme joy of your being in us. So we know supreme peace, infinite peace — your love. Thank you, Father."
- Amen.

The Truth About Life

We all know what we have to do with our lives. Deep down, we know. The important, the essential. And the essential is not how much more money I want to earn, how many titles to please my ego... new car, bigger house. It is not in the whims of the ego or the mind. The essential is: what you must really do. Who must you forgive? Who must you love? Who do you have to help, and how? ...It's about love, and loving takes many forms. Here, that *must* is not compulsory; it is the direction in which things go and work in the Universe. It is consciousness; it is opening the eyes and taking care of the life which is before you and those in it. It is about how you use your free will and what you create with it... with the power God has given you to use.

Most souls come to this world to evolve in the specific ways they need to, and love is always the path and the goal. Then they find this world so appealing that they want as many things for themselves as possible. And they start the race of acquiring things as they get further away from the point. The spiritual point. The love point. This is what life is about, not polarizing riches. This is the reason for poverty in this world. If love was the reason, riches would be used for the benefit of all.

**We don't need political systems; we need a spiritual system.
And that is based on love and caring.**

Life is about opening the heart and loving. This life has a purpose. A human life is given and received with some objectives: it is not given randomly. You have lessons to learn, some evolutional steps to take. Examine your conscience. You know if you are doing it or not. Be honest with yourself... this is a golden opportunity.

People renounce the greatest joy for some powerless toys that make them unconscious. The greatest joy lies in the greatest power, in the source of it: God. Most people haven't understood what this life is about. Some toys will give them momentary satisfaction; God gives it forever, and it is infinitely more satisfactory and blissful. Some people want to trade the light of the sun for the light of a match. Isn't that strange? We shouldn't ignore the purpose of our lives. You must recover the memory of why you are here, if you haven't, and act in the correct way. This is a golden opportunity to evolve. Take it intensely, take it completely.

❖ *The purpose of life is not to have material success, to have a great image, or to gain great material possessions; the purpose of life is evolutional. It is that you live in a way that allows you the greatest evolution, the greatest spiritual growth.*

Wise Advice

What is the way to live life in these moments with the greatest wisdom and effectiveness? The answer I got from a master can succinctly bring light to that. I asked Jesus at one time what to do in conflict situations. He said:

"Detachment, innocence, compassion."

Detachment
"When faced with unwelcoming situations, do not get involved. Stay aloof. Don't let it touch you, that which comes from there – it is not personal. Why do you care? Make no judgment."

Innocence
"See people's innocence – their ignorance. See distance over the event. It is a son of God, might be confused, not awakened. Make no judgment. Maintain the vision of innocence. Apply forgiveness."

Compassion

"Say what you have to say. Say your truth, with love, and put sweetness in it; detachment and innocence will allow you to. Smile. Make no judgment."

He also said: *"To everything, put sweetness; love and take judgment away. And it will come out perfect — whatever has to come out."*

- **"Surrender to what your heart says, before plans, doubts, musts. Choose what it says without guilt or judgment – with trust. And don't worry."**

God the Best Ally:
Personal Power or Divine Power

"Only God is watching your life. There is no more audience; you act for Him. He expects you to do what is best for you with His gifts, His power. If you act for other audiences you are giving your power away. He expects you to be faithful to yourself, to your joy. It doesn't matter what others expect from you."

Power is in the Will of God. It is almost saying that the Will of God is the power of God. And in His Will we will find power. The Will of God is always going to be manifesting abundance: love, power, wisdom and peace for all. His Will is always the higher cause, so other causes or motives will recede before it. This happens when one wants to leave aside his small will and give the Will of God the space and opportunity to manifest. Then one invokes it and allows that to happen: it gives God the freedom to express Himself in one's life. If in a situation those aspects of love and power are not going to be a product of it, His Will, will take us to the circumstances by which it will be done.

If we offer everything to the Will of God, we will have to listen to it, feel it, go to the heart and see what vibrates there. We will have to align ourselves with it. God is not going to impose His Will. We have to unite ourselves with it and then it will manifest. His Will is going to melt our hearts with His love. It is there when we are one with it: His Will is love and loving. We are one with it when there are no obstacles to love in our hearts. We do this by giving everything to the purposes of the Holy Spirit: doing things with the clarity of the objective — with the clarity that it is for the objective of God. Then whatever comes, it's from Him. The difference between the master and the aspirant is that the master always makes God his objective. That, to which you have surrendered is your objective; that is your power. When this is an idol in whatever mundane and unrecognizable form it might take, that is where your power is placed. That is away from the Will of God.

As a person, I can only accept and work in the Will of God when I have cast away my personal ghosts. It is then when I recover my will. Otherwise they have it. If I have recovered my will, then I can move freely and put my small will aside to welcome the Will of God in me. Otherwise, if I don't control my will because of my inner ghosts, I cannot offer my will to the will of God; I cannot say, "Thy will be done," because the ghosts will, will something else: their agenda. To be possessed by goodness, I must have expelled evil from myself by returning it to the light. To be possessed by God in this way, I have to have cleared every other possession in me. This is the direction in which mankind is going: clearing lower possessions to embrace the greatest light.

When one has ghosts in the closet, one is afraid of them. So one is without power because he doesn't dare to go to them to get his power back, because he is afraid of them. It takes decision, desire to be free to become fearless and do the job by going to the closet and facing them; then one becomes free. One overcomes fear by doing that which one is afraid of. That is growth; that empowers you. That sets you free.

High vibration ends all possessing. As the fire that enters into a log and takes it, making of all its particles light, crystal: "Christ." This happens because the high vibration is a greater blessing. High vibration is a superior blessing, and it imposes itself. The only way in which you will be at peace is by taking all your power from your inner demons and from their external projections in people, circumstances and places. It is in surrendering that there is power. Surrendering can only be done to a mighty power of good. Other surrendering to other entities are attempts of the ego to keep going: that is not true surrender. It is just the opposite; it is deceit.

If you have not entered into all the depths of the abyss you cannot have all the light, because you have not illuminated all the obscurity, and there will always be some shadow that will surprise you. This is the path to make the Will of God enter you: everything else has been cleared. Ascended beings work in the Will of God.

> *"I can be well without the need of anything or anyone, because I need God and I have Him."*

God's Will and Detachment

Learn to leave it all as it is, without being controlling. Accept things without wanting them to be different. Do this as a practice of detachment now and again. The day we leave, everything will remain as it is. So... detachment. The possibility of things being a specific way is not better than another, in many cases. It is only a search to please our minds. We must discern when that is so and when it is not, so we can influence people, things, and situations that will truly be better with that influence; if not, we must learn to leave them alone. In any case, people and things have their divine order and process. The plan of God is inevitable. That means the right divine outcome for all things and beings, and this will manifest sooner or later. We are just not very good at recognizing it, and we are easily fooled by appearances that often displease us, but in the eyes of God, His work is being done. A greater way of being is to align oneself with the compassionate Creator and seek to discover when and how we can be true instruments of His peace and plan. This is detachment: you do act but leave the results to God.

Joining the Will of God

"I want nothing; I want what God wants — what God in me wants." This is your higher will, not a will different than you; it is the will of your Spirit Self, different from your ego will.

The only difference between the master and the disciple is that the master has surrendered to God, to service, to serving Him. While the disciple is still trying to keep his ego alive. The master then becomes graced and enlightened. He is free; he is free to serve the highest.

"Put God first and don't worry about anything."

•

"The disciple believes power is his.
The master knows all power is God's.
Ascending is becoming a master."

Guidance From God

I asked God how to live my life, how to serve Him, in a recent time of my life in which nothing seemed to be happening. This is what He said:

*"Take care of the present,
what needs to be done now;
the people, the things in your life,
the small details, the small actions
of every day. As you serve in the
present you will see the path to follow."*

I was doing it, but if I hadn't He would surely have also said also:
"Take care of your spiritual development."

Let's never forget...
*"Work on your capacity to send
love. Start with yourself."*

Creating a New World

*"There is a great responsibility
in doing the right thing."*

If you do the right thing, this will send a message to all consciousness on the planet that this is the thing to do. This will create a resonance in everyone that will move them to take the correct action in that situation. Maybe it doesn't matter to tell a little lie now and again, and nobody knows. But if you come out in the open and are simply honest, you will move people's consciousness towards doing that same thing. You will be supporting honesty and giving it energy, and probably most of the time people will be honest with you. It is a wave of energy and consciousness that you send out into the world: it is picked up.

So it is not a matter of you doing wrong things nobody knows about; it is a matter of what you are going to give your support. You might think that with those small things nothing happens. Those things do count. Thoughts, intentions and actions create reality and thus create the world, for you and all. Those things have an influence in the world at large. If you do the right thing in the small daily actions, somebody else will be doing the same thing through resonance. If nobody wanted wars, there wouldn't be any. Things happen because there are enough people wanting them. Sure, Costa Rica will never be in a war; they don't have an army. Through that resonance, more and more people will be doing the right things. And eventually things will start to change and take a new direction.

Too many people support things that are evil or bad for life and others. And those things are perpetuated. Things won't happen until enough people want a change. This is the concept of critical mass. When enough people want and support peace, the planet will shift. With the Stargate energies the resonance for peace and good things is increasing exponentially: people's hearts are being opened. And the Stargate energies themselves are wiping out evil and lower vibrational energies by dissolving them and transmuting them into light. But we must do our part. This is for us. Stargate has come for us, for humanity to be free and evolve; for the planet to have peace. It is for all of humanity and Earth and the Universe. Earth is part of a cosmic system that needs things to be okay here.

"If you want a new world,
start creating it."

Ascension: Commitment to the Light

"With a closed heart you interpret life.
With an open heart you live it."

First and foremost, there has to be commitment in each one for his ascension. Evolution is personal and optional, but only to a point. The drive to become what one is in essence is inevitable, and sooner or later it will awaken. But one can individually choose not to evolve for eons of time. Also, that drive will move any being to seek greater states of love and power and light, essentially awareness. This is where fun is. Staying in a non-evolved state is suffering. So the situation is self-evident. God gives free will and one chooses how to walk his existence. Nonetheless, there is a compelling force inside everyone to strive to attain the highest. This is because God dwells within, as the essence of each being. So a sensible commitment to evolve will be oriented towards recovering that inner consciousness. It is, after all what makes sense and the only place where there is unlimited love and power. So free will away from that God essence will always be temporary, although it may last millions of years. But eventually all beings will want their kingdom of light back.

This is one of those times in which most beings around are wanting something else other than what has been going on, on this planet and in their incarnations for a long while. And what they want is essentially their power back, and the life it will create for them. And this is individually and as a whole. But commitment to the right energies and the right path – ascension – is necessary in order to get there. So far, the greatest commitment is still to low energies and the world of ego. Commitment is there, and it is very strong. It needs to shift to Spirit, the spirit part in each one. As commitment moves from ego to Spirit, the ascension energies enter increasingly into the person to establish themselves there and do their work. Commitment to the divine creates commitment from the divine. You have essentially said: "Yes, I want it."

For ascension, there needs to be a commitment to the highest inside you. In that commitment you will channel your highest possibility. The commitment to the highest will reveal that in you. Then you will manifest its expressions instead of ego, because of your commitment. And you will have been transformed in an alchemical process through your commitment to the highest. So those things will be expressed naturally in you. If there is no commitment to advancement there will be a standstill — passivity. There won't be life force. One of the important things to be achieved is peace; peace through commitment. This is a sign of inner power. Life is commitment; creation is commitment. People believe it is fun to not live a committed life. They don't realize they are dead inside without it. If you cannot commit to the highest in you, to goodness, to love, what is there inside? Life is commitment. Just look at the Universe. A seed is committed to give life to a tree; a planet to stay in an orbit. What if Earth did a different orbit every year?

"Love is commitment. Commitment is love."

The commitment of nature is an expression of its love. Love that brings peace is commitment. To live outside commitment is to live in a sort of hell because there is no peace. There is no creation.

We are ascending; we are going to heaven. The opportunity is here. *We* includes the Earth, because Earth itself as a live being, is ascending. The planetary system is going up because it is time for these new and higher energies to be here and take all up. But one is free to resist and to not be part of this. I don't recommend it. But there will be other options for those beings that do not want to live this ascension to higher realms of consciousness. A lot of people resist being taken out of hell.

It is in the commitment to the highest that the ego has no option; when you have given yourself to God in you. You have said *yes* to your god part and *no* to the ego. Only in this way you become a master in spiritual martial arts: every time the ego comes up you dismantle it. It is from there that you see it: you unmask it all the

273

time. That commitment will make you strong before the forces of ego that still live inside you.

> ***"The ego always wants to find reasons
> to question the things of the spirit."***

But for a soul committed to the light and thus to ascension, there is nothing that can stand in the way.

❖ Prayer

*"Help us Divine Father, help us to serve you.
We are ready to receive you and to anchor the
light on the planet. Anchor the Age of Aquarius,
the Age of Freedom. We want to be the eyes,
the hands, the arms, the heart of the Age of
Aquarius."*
- Amen

SUPPORT SECTION

Support for Ascension and Power

Completing the Connection

This section includes some of the practices related to many of the things spoken about in the book. These aspects are a great help for ascension when integrated and made conscious. They need to be looked at in some way or another; here in a brief focused way, you have some effective elements of support. The one about breathing light helps to assimilate light into body and aura, to help the light body integration. The last one, *Guidelines for Consciousness Focus*, is a sharp list of the places where your consciousness should dwell to maximize your development and use of energy in living a life towards ascension.

Ascension Essentials

- Vibrate high
- Use violet light at its highest potency – intensity
- Increase love
- Die literally to the ego = Christ Self is born
- Work to develop your light body
- Be free from fear
- Meditate as much as possible
- Liberate blockages and ego in third chakra
- Have compassion and humility.
- Forgive and let go
- Be in the Christ Self

Contact with the Inner Child

- Breathe deeply three times
- Go inside
- Connect with him/her
- See it
- Feel it
- Love it
- What does it say to you?
- Listen to his/her needs
- Integrate them

Keys to Make Your Life Work

- Put God first – your divine part
- Increase your faith
- Recover your power
- Keep serenity
- Make others well, happy
- Serve them – without losing your power
- Serve God
- Stay in high vibration
- Love

When You See the Dark in Others
...as your own dark side projected

- Welcome your shadow side
- Forgive that dark side you see in them
- Forgive it also in you
- Thus you forgive yourself

- Use violet light to transmute it
- Love
- Integrate your own dark side
- Don't reject your own darkness
- See it, welcome it, illuminate it

Breathing Light

- Breath consciously in your natural rhythm
- Have the awareness you are breathing light
- Hold the air for some seconds before releasing it
- Fix, with your intention, the light in yourself
- Fix the energies of ascension:
- in body, cells, aura, soul and new codes of light
- Do it by intending to do it
- Do it every day for five minutes, for a while

Power Status Check

With these guidelines you will be able to check the status of your power in your life. By checking your power status frequently you will be able to develop an awareness of where to focus to spot power leaks and important cessions of power. Eventually, your training will take you to function in a way in which you immediately recognize if you are giving power away, and act immediately to not give power away.

Ask yourself where it comes from
Whatever you are going to do, any changes, ask yourself:
- What is your motivation?
- What is your vision?
- Why are you going to act like that?

Are there any strings attached?
- Which ones are there?
- Is there pressure from someone?
- Are you acting on it?
- Are you pressuring yourself?
- Why?

Don't act from fear or guilt
- Make sure your action is free from fear or guilt
- Reject any acting coming from fear or guilt
- Anything that you do out of fear or guilt must be out of your life, or do it from love
- Make an agreement with yourself:
    Face fear and guilt every time they come up
    See what is behind them
- Have the acceptance that feeling uncomfortable is not wrong.
- Every time you face negative habits, you will feel discomfort.
- Every time you try to change them, you will feel guilt or fear.
- Accept that and confront them
- Don't give value to the feeling of discomfort from facing fear or guilt.
- What your ego wants is to not break habits and to not feel discomfort.

Question your habits
- Question all your habits
- See what things you do from habit
- Don't do anything out of habit, not even talking
- Decide what it is you want to continue doing and what not
- Even the important things in life, including being married from habit.
- Remember: habit = unconsciousness
- Unconsciousness = Karma = suffering and reincarnation

Recover your power
- Recover your power and freedom from habits
- Act free from habit – act from conscious decision
- Act freely, respecting your right, respecting others
- Make sure your motivation to act is free from fear and guilt
- Act free from pressure from others and the system, as much as possible.
- Trade negative habits for actions in consciousness
- Generate self-consciousness in everything you do
- Stay true to yourself no matter what, with all the consequences.

Where to dwell to come from power
- Be faithful to yourself
- Make no sacrifices
- Take your responsibilities
- Face your ghosts
- You deserve all the good
- Be impeccable
- Act from the truth of the heart
- Nothing happens to you without your intervention
- Power in your life is only yours
- Everything obeys to a higher purpose

Remember these

"I am the resurrection and the life of all my power"
"There is no power outside me to act in my life"
"Nothing relevant happens without my consent"
"I am the power in my life"
"I deserve all my power"
"I accept all my power"
"I have the right to all my power"
"I have the right to be who I want to be"
"The Will of God is that you are what you want to be"
"I am free because I have all my power"

Synthesis of the Process of True Compassion

This is a practice of higher compassion. You may do this when you feel ready to move to another level of compassion and when you are clear that this is a higher way to it.

- Transmute the need to intervene in the process of another.
- In not intervening, you respect his process and this takes him to his power, his resources.
- Intervening is an option.
- The other option, higher compassion, is seeing that everything has a purpose.
- This supports the other's process and helps without intervening.
- From neutrality you radiate love; you support from love.
- From love, you facilitate the awakening of love, consciousness and power.
- When you don't intervene, the person finds his own resources – finds God.
- He goes to God to find the solution; he turns to God.
- He acquires more faith and reestablishes the missing link with the Creator: the source of all power.
- Your power is limited. You offer him a greater power by helping the alchemy of the inner activation of his divine power.
- If you allow him to invoke you as his saving power he can become dependent.
- In taking him to invoke his divine power, he attracts God and His power and becomes independent.
- You have served him in the highest way.
- You will have to use your discernment to see what is best at any given time.
- So you might help, point the way, help someone out of a crisis but support his independence and lead others to find true power inside, in God.

- Don't allow others to become dependent on you. Don't allow yourself to become dependent on others.
- All this is also valid for yourself. You invoke your power inside instead of seeking the solution outside and the dependency on external powers.
- In doing it for you or with others, it can be done progressively while the consciousness of dependency is overcome and you all move to depend on your divine inner power; thus going further inside to base life on that inner power.

•

Now the energies are there to give people the option to move away from suffering and dependency, from dependent and codependent compassion, to the divine consciousness of communion with true power that makes people independent. This is true giving, true peace and true love.

Violet Light Connection

Having talked about this potent energy for ascension, I didn't want to leave out a contact with it, and although there is a whole book published about it, where I go into it in depth, I wanted to share with you two important aspects of this amazing light, which you can use to help your ascension. They are independent; you can use one or the other or both. It is important to have a contact with the violet light, after all, it is the energy of the New Age, and everything happening with Stargate is to open the way to it. For a deeper connection and all practices with the violet light for ascension, see my book on it: *The Violet Light: The Power That Changes Everything*. All details are at the back of this book.

Violet Light Invocation

"Beloved Violet Light of the Holy Spirit of God, I invoke your Sacred Presence so you are with me and transmute with your divine power and love any karma that might remain in me, and through you, all my fields physical, emotional, mental and spiritual become harmonized and all the blockages become liberated, those that might be there blocking the realization and manifestation of total success in my life and the development of all my divine potential in all areas of life.

I ask your Sacred Presence to be with all my dear ones, my friends and all the brothers and sisters of humanity, so they may become liberated from their karmas through you, and through you the Divine Essence, the Christ Self in each one, becomes manifested as the Divine Essence of Power Love and Wisdom of God, and they all enter into full freedom and peace according to Divine Will. Thank you." Amen.

Violet Light Meditation

Simple and powerful, this meditation will provide you with an initial connection with the violet light and its frequencies for ascension, as a first step. I recommend you spend at least twenty minutes in the morning and the same time in the evening in this meditation.

Many people have said to me over the years that they couldn't meditate and that with the violet light entered that state of meditation almost immediately. Others said that they meditated but with the violet light found it far easier to go within, and felt a deeper experience. Find out what it has for you.

Meditation

- Enter into meditation breathing deeply a few times, closing your eyes and relaxing.
- Become aware of your inner state, your vibration; body and mind relaxed
  in serenity.
- Focus your attention on your third eye, in the center of your forehead.
- Visualize a white light coming from heaven, surrounding you completely.
- Stay in this vision for about one or two minutes.
- See this light becoming a gold light.
- Stay with it about one or two minutes.
- See this light becoming a deep, bright violet light.
- See it surrounding you completely. It takes you very deep.
- Stay with it at least ten minutes.
- When ready, breathe deeply three times.
- Become conscious of your physical body.
- Become aware of your surroundings.
- Slowly come out.
- Give thanks.
- Open your eyes.

Guidelines for Your Consciousness Focus

Here is a list that is worth more than gold because it is a quick reference to be used at any moment, which will help you focus on the important at any time. It shows the key elements on which your consciousness should dwell. It is a very precisely designed list for these challenging times.

- Keep the consciousness of "I Am" all the time
- This is your high Self
- Keep vibration high – use violet light
- Contact with your Higher Self
- Have a sense of humor
- Simplify
- De-crystallize
- Keep alert
- Concentration
- Focused attention
- Inner clarity
- Listen to yourself
- Self-observation
- Impeccability
- Follow your intuition
- Keep connected with Spirit
- Quiet your mind
- Stay in the logic of the heart
- Improvise with wisdom
- Express without limits – with respect
- Contact your inner child.
- Detachment
- Flow
- Feel
- Transmutation
- Liberation
- Recover your power
- You are free
- Seek to contact cosmic, universal consciousness

- Devotion – passion – surrender
- Softness – tenderness
- Firmness
- Share
- Visualize – affirm your truths
- Ask for all
- Help, support with detachment
- Have faith in the divine.
- Have complete trust in God
- Act from the Christ Self
- Open up to the Grace of God
- Forgiveness – Mercy
- Focus on ascension
- Love
- Feel and contact the Ascended Masters of light
- Give yourself to the Divine Will
- …and enjoy the ride!

•

Let's remember that the only valid passport for our ascension, for the new age, is love and forgiveness: compassion.

Final Comments

As a final touch of this amazing journey I will leave the closing to Jesus in one of his most recent messages. He speaks of the dark side as the *sepulcher* and shows us the power is ours to leave the dark behind and embrace the light. No conditions, no restrictions: the kingdom of the light is ours.

Message from Jesus

In this message from Jesus in resurrection day 2007 we are motivated to take a final step in our moving towards the light which is freedom, by harnessing all our power and deciding to come out of our own darkness – come out of the sepulcher. Our darkness here means the past, confusions doubts, old destructive habits. In coming out of them we raise to heaven. There is often fear to come out of it. To come out of the sepulcher is the first act of power towards a life of freedom.

Time to leave the sepulcher

"Resurrection is to return to the estate of Truth.
In what state are you all in? Love?"

The cobwebs of fear occupy a space that belongs to love. You are afraid of removing fear because you fear the vacuum that will leave in you. Fear accompanies you, itself and its accessories which are many and you don't recognize them.

The state of Truth is peace and love without conditions. This presupposes a blinding glow that leaves nothing in obscurity. It is you who resists light. If not, then whom? And your creations forgotten in your consciousness and spirit, fruit of a path full of dread, and their instruments that have been filling your inner spaces, physical, mental, emotional. In those areas there is no peace; there is no light in them, they resonate in another frequency. You put all that there – you must throw the old furniture away if you want to redecorate the house. The great light of Resurrection shows you the things that are useless. Be its accomplice and throw away the useless. Ask for light to see. Ask for more light to discern.

Through resurrection, you recover your state of truth, but you must cast out what is useless. Resurrection to the light of Truth – to true life – since you are all half dead for having embraced darkness and death. All that must be released in order to resurrect and allow the light to ascend you to the truth. If you are not in greater love, light, peace it is because you are not releasing that which fills the spaces of love – you cannot resurrect by living in the past. With resurrection the past is dispelled; there is only life in the present.

What are the terms of resurrection?
Releasing, freeing, forgiving, closing, transforming, transmuting, advancing, courage, enlightening.

The light of resurrection is now with you. Hand everything over to the light and worry not; she takes care. If there is light, the rules are the rules of the light. Don't insist on lesser ways or forms, in doing it yourself; let it be done in its enlightened ways. God is there. Rules have changed; the way is upwards.

The sepulcher is where darkness lives. Come out of it – believe in eternal life. Give permission to your cobwebs of fear to dissolve in the light. They are only thoughts – this is not reality. Finally, you end up being frightened by your own thoughts.

I resurrect welcoming my truth: "I am the light."

The light: by you releasing it all, it elevates you. But you must let go. The secret, the key is: by you releasing it all light carries you, it elevates you. Shadows have you when you identify with them. Resurrecting means: you must leave death behind. Listen to this:

"I give myself permission to come out of the sepulcher."

Light opens the door to the sepulcher; but you must want to come out. God is waiting for you.

I Am Jesus the Christ in the Resurrection

❖

As you go within for the encounter with your inner self, the energies of the Stargate will be more fully available to you, and you will be able to absorb more deeply into your being, their frequencies of power and love for ascension.

We'll meet in ascension. Good journey to the light!

Kahan

"We raise to heaven the chalice
*of our hearts in gratitude to God
for Him to fill it up with His light."*
                    - Amen

Contact the Teachings

Kahan gives live courses and workshops on Stargate and the new energies for Earth. He also gives courses on the Violet Light, the energy of the planetary change. See the information below and visit our website.

Live Courses

Stargate: The Live Course
Stargate 2012: Recovering the Power for Ascension

This is the live course of the Stargate. It takes you to recover power in a very direct way. It unveils the essence of the ascension vision for the end of Earth time. It is the living experience of the teachings of Stargate. And it leaves you with a high vibration that emanates intense power and love. The teaching shows how to work with the new energies. By recovering power a new dimension of love is manifested: true compassion, the passport for ascension. Essential parts are the integration of the dark side and developing the awareness of true compassion by recovering the lost power hidden in the dark side. It includes the initiation of the divine power with Archangel Michael live, a experience of power beyond this world; something not to miss. You can ask us to bring this course to your area any time.

Other Courses

The Violet Light: The Power That Changes Everything
The New Energy of Earth

This is the main energy for the acceleration of spiritual evolution in these challenging times. It increases the vibration of the soul in such a definite way that it transforms people's experience of life completely. It burns karmas at a speed unknown until now, awakens or expands Christ/Buddha consciousness and manifests true prosperity. It is a powerful activation of the inner light; profoundly resulting in a greater mastery over yourself and life. The energy of grace here is very strong. See the website for full programs and details.

Knowing God

Teaching about the reality of God Seeing God beyond dogma, superstition and fear. Direct revelations about the truth of this universal force. Understanding how God works and how to relate to Him. It provides the impacting experience of a direct contact with God.

We Bring the Teachings to You

If you want Kahan to give the live courses in your area, please send an e-mail with the heading: "We want the teachings" explaining details. Take into account that there must be sufficient people for us to travel. Write to: violetpowerful@yahoo.com

Other Books by the Author

The Violet Light: The Power That Changes Everything

The Violet Light is the main emanation of light of the New Age. It is the ray of light of the Age of Aquarius. This light is the major energy activating ascension on the planet. This book is about knowing and connecting with the energy of the violet light and incorporating into people's lives this immense gift of Spirit. The book takes you all the way to the powerful connection with this energy. This has a profound impact on your spiritual evolution and daily life. This is the full story of the new spirituality and consciousness for humanity. It also includes powerful meditations and practices to transform your reality, create the life you want free of karma and full of inner peace, power and prosperity.

Flying Within – A challenging novel

This is the story of a high-profile executive that arrives at his office one day and unexpectedly leaves everything. He creates a new life and starts to trust the unpredictable as a guiding force in his life. He starts to challenge his ways of thinking and living, his assumptions of what is real and valid, and he discovers the astounding truth behind all that. New intriguing people appear in his life and unexpected realities develop as a result of the secrets they embody, taking him to a new consciousness beyond ordinary life. This leads him to the discovery of an amazing power and light inside. The story is based on the profound and transforming journeys within the spiritual dimensions explored by the author, which distill high principles applicable to anybody's life. This novel that challenges reality and people's assumptions. It unveils some of the best kept secrets of the inner journey.

Music & Concerts

High vibration music composed and performed by Kahan is available. This is cosmic music of high frequency and it emanates beautiful light. This means that it elevates the frequency of the person while listening to it. These themes are full of high vibrations and will increase the resonance of your aura and expand your light. It brings to you the vibration of the higher planes of light, and gives you access to the consciousness there. It is beautiful music that inspires and elevates. It has a very atmospheric quality that creates an ambiance of peace and love. CDs available. Visit the website for details. Live concerts performed by Kahan are also available for booking.

Support Material

Extra help on dark side work. For in-depth psychological work on the shadow, you can refer to a masterpiece in this field: *Fear No Evil, The Pathwork Method of Transforming the Lower Self.* Published by Pathwork Press, Madison, Virginia, USA. Also, by Debbie Ford: *Why Good People Do Bad Things.* Highly recommended.

Meditation Groups

You can create working and meditation groups for ascension based on the Stargate teachings. Visit our website for details. If you have created a meditation group or want to create one, let us know so we can support you. Send us an e-mail with the heading: "We have a meditation group."

Always go to the inner temple of light in your heart and trust the guidance of your luminous self.

Namaste.

E-mail: violetpowerful@yahoo.com
Website: www.violetplatinum.com

About the Author

Paco Alarcon-Kahan is a world authority on ascension. He has been involved in oriental and occidental spiritual currents for more than twenty five years. As a result of his deep implication he acquired a strong connection with spiritual energy, gaining access to great spiritual revelations. From them he developed a number of original teachings to bring spiritual energy and its power to people's lives. He created a wide range of courses to provide a new and deep understanding of the spiritual nature of man in an innovative way, making spiritual experiences very accessible. His teachings reveal all the potency and depth of the spiritual realities, bringing people closer to the real experience of God. He aims at uniting the power of Spirit with the day-to-day life. Kahan is also a composer, and amongst original Jazz, he composes high vibrational music. The concerts he gives have an impact on the consciousness of people expanding their light. He often gives interviews, conferences and courses in different countries. Kahan has written three books about the changes on Earth, the new energies and the preparation of people for ascension to a new vibration and consciousness.

Printed in the United Kingdom by
Lightning Source UK Ltd., Milton Keynes
140443UK00001B/76/P